a boundary 2 book

American Indian Persistence and Resurgence

Edited by Karl Kroeber

Duke University Press
Durham and London   1994

© Duke University Press
All rights reserved
Printed in the United States of America
on acid-free paper ∞
Except for the essay by Linda Ainsworth, "If Texts Are Prayers, What Do Wintu Want?"
the text of this book was originally published as volume 19, number 3 of *boundary 2: an
international journal of literature and culture*.
Library of Congress Cataloging-in-Publication Data
American Indian persistence and resurgence / edited by Karl Kroeber.
p.   cm.
"A Boundary 2 book."
All but one essay reprinted from Boundary 2, v. 19, no. 3.
Includes bibliographical references (p.) and index.
ISBN 0-8223-1459-2 (acid-free paper) : $34.95. — ISBN
0-8223-1487-8 (acid-free paper) : $13.95
1. Indians of North America—Ethnic identity.   2. Indians of North
America—Cultural assimilation.   I. Kroeber, Karl, 1926–.
E98.E85A48   1994
306'.08997—dc20   94-10679

338667

Contents

Native American Resistance and Renewal

Karl Kroeber

Official observances of the five-hundredth anniversary of Christopher Columbus's unexpected—and undesired—arrival in the New World were supposed to be described as part of a "jubilee." This rubric was devised in Washington to defuse the opposition of Native Americans to treating this quincentennial as a celebration. The compromise title is symptomatic of how the significance of "the view from the shore" is becoming recognized— albeit slowly and painfully—as a valuable perspective by both politicians and intellectuals.

More important than resistance to mindless festivities for an offtrack European explorer/exploiter is the astonishing increase in the Native American population during the past quarter century. The raw figures and percentages of growth compiled by the 1980 census (impressively surpassed by figures for 1990) soared well beyond biological probability. Increasing numbers of Americans desire to admit, or to claim, Native American ancestry. The implications of this cultural phenomenon dwarf those of the Indians' not inconsiderable demographic expansion, dramatizing a radical transformation in the attitude of Old World immigrants to native New Worlders.[1] Many of the first Europeans in North America came to regard the native inhabitants with respect, and even admiration. But an eagerness of immigrants to align themselves genetically with American Indians is nowhere to be found in North America—until our moment in history.[2] This volume seeks to illustrate something of the character of this moment, above all as it is reflected in our literary/intellectual culture. To this end, we have brought together a variety of diverse commentaries, including those of people making no claims to any kind of special *red* expertise. Thus, writer William Overstreet, through a review of James C. Faris's book, articulates central features of an intelligent "amateur's" responses both to the actual experience of persisting Indian ceremonialism and to the intellectual/ political controversies surrounding descriptions and assessments of these controversies by revisionary ethnologists. Jack Salzman's interview analogously offers a perspective on how Native American problems appear to the director of a major institute engaged in fostering interactivity between an Ivy League university and the many and highly divergent ethnic populations of New York City. This introduction, therefore, will do no more than sketch a few of the historical forces whose interactions have constituted the character of this particular moment to provide a contextual outline for the diversity of subjects and perspectives presented in the essays that follow.

The history of white-Indian relations may be divided Gallically, if crudely, into three phases. From about the middle of October 1492 to about the middle of the nineteenth century was a period predominantly of conquest and destruction of native peoples. The next century may be described as the ethnological period, for in it there were significant efforts to assure the survival, at least in the form of documentary records, of Indian cultures. Around the middle of this century began a resurgence, first in Native American populations, then in pride, self-awareness, and assertion of red

---

1. Since it is generally accepted that the aboriginal peoples of the New World arrived here from Asia by crossing a land bridge where the Bering Straits are today, one can say that all the inhabitants of North and South America are immigrants—leading to Russell Baker's happy suggestion of describing Americans as either bridge people or boat people, and, more exuberantly, to Gerald Vizenor's playful investigations into where Columbus really began, and whether the Chinese might be a tribe the Indians had lost.

2. Contemporary "declarations of Indianness," of course, derive from various motives, but they do seem generally contrary to the spirit of earlier official legal acts of assimilation, such as the Citizenship Act of 1924, which rather cynically welcomed Indians as citizens so as to evade the real problems posed by the Indians' refusal to vanish.

cultures as distinctively different from those of white society. This resurgence has been steadily accelerating, and it seems inevitable that American Indians will play an increasingly important role in this country's life during the twenty-first century.[3]

Little need be said about the more than three centuries of conquest except that it was, with a few minor exceptions, a process of destruction bordering on genocide, including the use of biological warfare—the deliberate infecting of Indians with diseases to which they were not immune. Hundreds of treaties were ceremoniously signed and then consciously violated by the federal government. This darkest chapter of American history needs to be recalled not merely on grounds of moral integrity but because it highlights the distinctiveness of the American Indian experience from that of all other "minorities" in the United States. Not only was no other group native to United States territory, but no other group was the object of genocidal warfare. Our popular histories are correct in recounting how the Indians, at first friendly and accommodating to European invaders, fought valiantly and skillfully, when driven to armed resistance, from the swamps of Massachusetts to the Sierras in California. It is worth remembering Solzhenitsyn's observation that losing a war is usually disastrous for a government but that such defeat may strengthen and ennoble a people.

Writing Indians

What I have called the ethnological phase of Indian post-Columbus experience began to emerge in the first quarter of the nineteenth century, when Washington Irving wrote sympathetically of King Phillip in his war with the New England colonists in the seventeenth century; when Henry School-

3. Changes in minority populations recorded by the census were reported, for example, in the *New York Times*, 11 March 1991, pages A1 and B8. The growth of this segment of our population is astounding in places: in 1970, 2,443 people in Alabama identified themselves as American Indian; in 1990, 16,506 Alabamians so identified themselves. A comprehensive survey of Indian adaptation to the encroachment of whites is Robert Berkhofer's *The White Man's Indian: Images of the American Indian from Columbus to the Present* (New York: Knopf, 1978). Valuable in a different way is the essay by J. Anthony Paredes, "The Emergence of Contemporary Eastern Creek Indian Identity," in *Social and Cultural Identity*, ed. Thomas K. Fitzgerald, no. 8 of the *Proceedings of the Southern Anthropological Society* (Athens, Ga.: University of Georgia Press, 1974), 63–80. Instead of an overview, Paredes details the specific history of the Escambia County Creek Indians from contact until the early 1970s, providing illuminating insight into local manifestations of responses (and nonresponses) to national changes.

craft, after composing an epic poem on the Creek wars, began something like scientific research into Indian lifeways; when artists such as Bodmer, Caitlin, and Charles Bird King painted Indians and scenes of Indian life; and, above all, when James Fenimore Cooper's *Leatherstocking* novels were enthusiastically received throughout Europe, as well as in America. Cooper's work spawned literally thousands of stories—right down to the film *Dances with Wolves*, an almost exact replica of the Cooper paradigm, especially its underlying nostalgia: the red man, like the wilderness, is inevitably being extinguished by the inexorable advance of Western civilization.[4]

Cooper is an often inept writer, pretentious but bumbling, in his plots, uncouth in his sentence structure, horrendously improbable in his dialogue but at times astounding in his imaginative prescience. He became the most influential proponent of the myth of the noble savage. Indeed, Mark Twain's condemnations of him may have been motivated less by revulsion at Cooper's literary offenses than by disgust with his admiration for Native Americans, since Twain's contempt for Indians seems to have been unbounded.[5] But Cooper's romanticizing of Indians was entangled with enough realistic criticism of white Americans to dramatize some parts of the essential tragedy of the Indians' victimization and that victimization's countereffects upon the Indians' destroyers.[6]

Cooper's novels are both aesthetically and factually preferable to many nineteenth-century literary representations of Native Americans, for example, Longfellow's popular midcentury poem *The Song of Hiawatha* (which sold nearly 40,000 copies the year it was published, 1855). Longfellow reveals the absurdly sinister underside of his nostalgia when, in the final episode, he has his Ojibwa hero, burdened with an Iroquois name,

4. Cooper's fiction brings to concentrated focus very old traditions of attitudes toward indigenous people, traditions that the Puritans brought with them and that tended to crystallize in an equation of Indians = heathen = past as the antithesis of Whites = Christianity = future.

5. The villainous Injun Joe of *Tom Sawyer* (whose original, Twain admitted, was a harmless town drunk) is a fairly mild example of Twain's racism, more uninhibited, for instance, in his description of the Goshoot Indians in *Roughing It*, and in his unfinished sequel to *Huckleberry Finn, Huck and Tom among the Indians*, which features a lovely blond woman abducted by swarthy, evil, corpse-mutilating Indians for purposes Huck says "it would not do to put in a book."

6. Cooper's literary and moral strengths can be appreciated if one contrasts his work to that of his most successful imitator, the phenomenally popular German writer Karl May, whose incoherent romanticizings of the American Indian suggest a severe cultural pathology.

order his people to welcome the black-robed fathers who arrive from across the ocean as bringers of truth and the good life. Whereupon Hiawatha hops into his canoe and paddles himself off into the sunset. Although Cooper's cultural importance should not be underestimated, nor his literary innovations disregarded, it may be that, in the long run, all such self-conscious American literary efforts (such as Lydia Child's *Hobomok* [1824], analyzed by Priscilla Wald in this volume) to assimilate red peoples into white literature will need to be evaluated against the first appearances of works in English by Native American writers—an idea that twenty years ago could not gain a formal hearing in the Modern Language Association convention. (I speak from personal experience.)

In 1854, John Rollin Ridge, a Cherokee, became the first American Indian to publish a novel, *The Life and Adventures of Joaquin Murietta, the Celebrated Bandit.*[7] This blood-and-thunder potboiler will never supersede *Madame Bovary* as an object of stylistic analysis. Its literary interest, in fact, lies in its journalistic character. Ridge wrote the novel to take advantage of the celebrity of its protagonist, a Robin Hood figure who never existed, though a man who claimed to have killed him earned a substantial reward, proving that one should never underestimate the value of myth. For California readers, some of the interest in the "bandit Murietta" may have centered on the bounty hunter who reported shooting him—and who certainly did shoot some Mexicans. At any rate, Ridge exploits every hyperbolic resource of language to render his protagonist Byronically attractive, even providing him a consort as faithful as she is beautiful.

7. Ridge published this novel, and a good deal of his other work, under the name of Yellowbird, a translation of his Cherokee name. He was known to California readers as both an "Indian" and an "American." His novel is available through the University of Oklahoma Press reprint of 1955 (sixth reprinting, 1986) with a valuable introduction by Joseph Henry Jackson. My simplified sketch of Ridge's early career should be supplemented by the biography by James W. Parins, *John Rollin Ridge: His Life and Works* (Lincoln: University of Nebraska Press, 1991). On the Ridges' place in Cherokee history, one may consult (besides the sources cited in Priscilla Wald's essay in this volume) Gerald Reed, "Postremoval Factionalism in the Cherokee Nation," in *A Troubled History*, ed. Duane H. King (Knoxville: University of Tennessee Press, 1979), 148–63; and Thurman Wilkins, *Cherokee Tragedy: The Ridge Family and the Decimation of a People*, 2d ed. (Norman: University of Oklahoma Press, 1986). That John Rollin Ridge's situation in California was not solely determined by personal psychology and circumstances is interestingly revealed by the essay of Carolyn Thomas Foreman, "Edward W. Bushyhead and John Rollin Ridge, Cherokee Editors in California," *Chronicles of Oklahoma* 14, no. 1 (1936): 295–311.

The chief attraction of the book appears to have been the bandit himself. Murietta was a Mexican who, like many of his countrymen, had come to California to mine gold. Some were successful, and, when California became one of the "united" states, these "foreigners" were brutally and illegally dispossessed of their property, an aspect of the "gold rush" that tends to slip out of our history books but that Ridge brings to the fore. The Californians' treatment of the Mexicans parallels the Georgians' treatment of the Cherokee, whose expulsion was in part precipitated by a discovery of gold in their territory. I hesitate, however, to praise Ridge for subversively encoding a condemnation of the Americans' treatment of Indians. For one thing, his novel includes a passage of scathing ridicule of California Indians that sounds like Twainian racism. To me, *Murietta* seems more interesting in that it illuminates a complicated sociohistorical situation in which the theme of a foreign Robin Hood could be seized on as a way to make money from American readers by a Cherokee, ambitious to succeed as a California journalist. One aspect of the confusing circumstances is highlighted by the volume of Ridge's *Poems*, the first such collection by an American Indian to be published in this country. These are, with a couple of slight exceptions, typically Victorian romanticizings in rhyme, sweet sentimentalizations that include such conventionalities as reference to a Cherokee girl's "white hand."[8]

These verses (unlike the exuberant brutalities in *Murietta*) seem inappropriate for an author whose father, grandfather, and cousin were victims of savage murders that he long dreamed of avenging—some of that bloodcurdling biography being related in the preface to his innocuous poems. In different ways, both Ridge's poetry and his novel urge us to attend to the intricacy of how acculturative forces have worked among Native Americans, an intricacy that seems (at least to someone of my limited knowledge) to distinguish the Native American experience from that of most other "minorities" struggling with dominant white culture in the United States. Central to this peculiar play of forces, I believe, is that the Indians so consciously resisted and literally fought; though physically defeated, therefore, they were able to retain a more than merely defensive commitment

---

8. John Rollin Ridge, *Poems* (San Francisco: Payot, 1868). The description of Ridge's mother and grandmother with his father's corpse is from the introduction to this volume, a depiction that scarcely prepares one for the mildness of the verse. Ridge was not a major poet, but some of his poetry breaks free from the worst conventional sentimentalizing; his best-known poem, "Mount Shasta," which he inserted in *Murietta*, derives not unworthily from Shelley's "Mont Blanc."

to their values, even while adapting shrewdly in other ways to Anglo-white society. In materially poor and relatively small societies, any individual's existence as an embodiment of a specific culture is continuously experienced with extraordinary force. So far as the culture is a vigorous one, a firm, yet flexible, system of vital processes (as many Native American ones, in fact, were and are), new ideas and practices can be translated and structured into traditional attitudes without extreme stress and without creating too much fear or guilt in individuals engaged in this acculturative activity. George Sword's more subtle, complicated, and more significant accomplishments within this boundary situation are examined in Elaine Jahner's essay in this collection.

Something of this intricate interplaying may be suggested by a summary of Ridge's familial-tribal background. His grandfather, Major Ridge (the title bestowed by General Andrew Jackson for his service in fighting against the Creek), was a full-blooded Cherokee who did not speak English. He sent his son John to a school in Cornwall, Connecticut, where he was a successful student and wooer of Miss Sara Northrop. Her mother was amenable to their relationship, but his father objected to it—he had expectations of a local Cherokee for a daughter-in-law. There were even more violent objections to the match in the Connecticut community. John's will prevailed, however, and he married Sara in Connecticut and brought her back to Georgia as his wife. His son, John Rollin, was born in 1827 in the large house of his father's plantation, which included slaves and a schoolhouse with an imported white teacher.

In the 1830s, the Cherokee were forcibly and, according to Supreme Court Justice John Marshall's famous decision, illegally "removed" from their prosperous farms in Georgia. John Ridge, like his father, had vigorously resisted this usurpation and believed that President Jackson would not permit it. When this hope proved illusory, and the Cherokee became increasingly subject to harassment without any legal redress, he decided it would be best to accept the unfair judgment and relocate to Indian Territory. Although he finally persuaded his father to accept this view, a majority of his people, led by John Ross, another distinguished Cherokee, continued to resist for some time. At Honey Creek, in Indian Territory (close to present-day Southwest City, Missouri), to which the Ridges traveled, John built a new house and school, and employed the same teacher whom he had employed in Georgia. In 1839, a group of Cherokee associated with the Ross party who had been forced to emigrate to Indian Territory decided to satisfy the Cherokee blood-law, which prescribed death for anyone ceding tribal land. The plotters determined to assassinate the Ridge family, who were, besides being political rivals to John Ross, convenient scapegoats for the newcomers' difficulties in the territory, especially with older Cherokee settlers. On the night of June 22, 1839, four men dragged John Ridge from his bed and stabbed him to death, while others assassinated Major Ridge and a cousin the same day. John Rollin never forgot the scene of his father's body "with blood oozing through his winding sheet, and falling drop by drop on the floor. By his side sat my mother, with hands clasped in speechless agony. . . . And bending over him was his own afflicted mother, with her long, white hair flung loose over her shoulders and bosom, crying to the Great Spirit to sustain her in that dreadful hour."

John Rollin's mother took her surviving children out of the Cherokee Nation into Arkansas. There, John Rollin received a good education, and, in 1847, he married a white woman. Two years later, within Cherokee territory through the instigation of the Ross faction, he was deliberately provoked so that he could be murdered, but he succeeded in killing the *agent provocateur* and escaped back to Arkansas. Although he was ready to stand trial for this killing, his family persuaded him not to risk putting himself in the power of his enemies. He joined a party of gold-seekers and moved to California, where he worked as a miner, a trader, an auditor, and a county recorder. Here, he also began to make money, finally, as a writer, though he was slow to give up the idea of returning to the Cherokee Nation to avenge his father's and grandfather's murders.

In the early 1850s, John Rollin became editor of the *Grass Valley Journal* and thought he might have realized a handsome sum from the *Joaquin Murietta*, had not its publisher failed.[9] Ridge did achieve something of a literary reputation in California, and his success as an editor enabled him to establish a good home for his family in the Sacramento Valley. At this time, he conceived the idea of setting up, with a surviving cousin in Arkansas, a periodical devoted to Indian concerns. Ridge's idea was that the journal

> would be a medium not only of defending Indian rights, and of making their oppressors tremble, but of preserving the memories of the distinguished men of the race. . . . Men, governments, will be *afraid* to

9. So Ridge claimed; Jackson, in his introduction to the novel, throws doubt on this idea, and Parins accepts Jackson's view. The success of subsequent "versions" of *Murietta*, however, proves that Ridge had indeed struck a popular topic that did make money for others.

trample upon the rights of defenseless Indian tribes, where there is a power to hold up their deeds to execration.

Asserting that he would bring to the paper not only the "fire of my own pen" but also that of "leading minds in the different Indian nations," Ridge hoped to do "justice to a deeply wronged and injured people by impressing upon the records of the country a true . . . account of the treatment they have received at the hands of a civilized and Christian race!" He immediately added: "If I can once see the Cherokees admitted into the Union as a State, then I am satisfied." [10] Here is displayed a paradoxical capacity of Native Americans to make use of the encroaching culture they resist. Ridge's ideal, which his father had also cherished, of the Cherokee fully realizing their tribal destiny by becoming part of the "united" states at whose hands they had suffered so unjustly, is difficult for most of us to understand today, since the possibility of sincere belief in the United States as representing a permanent advance toward political liberty has been so successfully eroded by the contrastive efforts of jingoistic patriots and academic intellectuals. [11] The overwhelming attention to problems of African Americans in our society, moreover, has obscured the very different situation of Indians, who are not necessarily afflicted with that "double-consciousness" so famously formulated by W. E. B. DuBois. As Ridge/Yellowbird, with a kind of spectacular simplicity, illustrates, for some Indians at least, indigenous and European cultures could be complexly reinforcing rather than simply divisive. Our current tendency, an unconscious heritage of the Cold War, is to think of political emotions in solely oppositional terms, but it seems arguable that the

10. These ideas are discussed by both Jackson and Parins, though my quotations from Ridge's correspondence are from the essay by Angie Debo, "John Rollin Ridge," *Southwestern Review* 17, no. 1 (1932): 59–71. On pages 66–67, Debo, although sympathetic, judges (in contrast to my opinion) the weakness of Ridge's literary work as deriving from his abandoning his true Cherokee heritage. In this volume, Priscilla Wald, examining this situation from the perspective of American social history, demonstrates how conflicts among the Cherokee helped to precipitate the State of Georgia's move against them, a focal point being the creation of a Cherokee constitution, supported by the Ridges as leaders of the "Americanized faction." One understands how the Ridges might have conceived of a "constitutionally" established Cherokee nation subsequently becoming a state, but Wald seems correct in demonstrating how such "mimicry" blocks "acceptable" assimilation.

11. Ridge's situation interestingly suggests the value of Edward H. Spicer's discussion in the following pages of how *every* state contains two or more peoples, as well as validates Spicer's important point that "hidden" peoples are not peoples who are hiding.

strength of Ridge's loyalty to his Cherokee heritage (scarcely "blind," since his family had been victimized by his own people) could give power to an idealized Americanism, and such Americanism supports his native culture. This interplay of conflictive reinforcements, rather than a merely divided consciousness, appears throughout Ridge's life and his written work, which in several ways anticipates much subsequent Indian writing in English. For example, although *Murietta* is rather overtly fiction pretending to be history, it takes on the style and attributes of genuine history as it progresses toward its conclusion. Surprisingly, but revealingly, *Murietta* became the basis of what were claimed to be genuine historical accounts by white American historians.

What happened, briefly, was that Ridge's novel was pirated six years after its publication, and that popular piracy spawned others, so that three years after Ridge's death, his novel was reissued in a "third" edition, which then was used as a documentary source by California historians. This inventing of history was possible in part because of Ridge's mixing of history, biography, and fiction, a mixing that has continued to be a notable characteristic of subsequent Indian literary productions. Under modern conditions, writing produced by a member of any marginalized group is likely to be "journalistic." But this "impure" mode that allows for an individualistic perspective on some clash of diverse social forces has been peculiarly congenial to Indians—for instance, Simon Pokagon, Will Rogers, D'Arcy McNickle, and, in our own time, Gerald Vizenor. As the second and last of these names remind us, a "journalistic" approach also facilitates humorous satire, a very powerful element in much traditional Indian discourse.[12] Ridge's humor in *Murietta* is of a frontier style that jars our more delicate sensibilities. This humor, however, manifests a fundamental self-confidence underlying not only the work of writers I have just mentioned but also that of men such as LaFlesche and George Sword, who, in different ways (as discussed in the

---

12. The pervasive quality of humor in Indian oral tellings has impressed most students of Native American life, and what Bakhtin calls a carnivalesque quality, especially in its fondness for generic "impurity," is a marked characteristic of traditional Indian discursive modes, toward which many contemporary Native American writers seem naturally to gravitate. It is worth noting that American ethnology, in contrast to European, has emphasized native humor, in part, one suspects, because American anthropologists lived more intimately with their native hosts. A magnificently hilarious example is Keith H. Basso's *Portraits of 'the Whiteman'* (Cambridge: Cambridge University Press, 1979), whose first dedication is "For three Apaches, now gone away, who encouraged me to laugh at myself." Basso has worked and lived with the Apache for more than thirty years.

essays by Ramsey and Jahner in this collection), used writing to come to terms with the complexity of their lives on the precarious boundary between traditional, oral Indian cultures and technologically advanced, "scientific" American culture.

The importance of Ridge's writings (which include a broader range than my concentration on his novel has suggested), then, lies in their revelation of the flexibly powerful sense of cultural identity that continues to undergird even recent writing in English by Indians. That strength permits Indians to confront with surprising frankness and adroitness challenges to (and even radical transformations in) what provides them with the "native" identity they articulate against Euro-American preconceptions. It makes possible the extraordinary assimilation of diverse elements from competing social entities that enables the protagonists of modern novels by Indians such as Leslie Marmon Silko's *Ceremony* and N. Scott Momaday's *House Made of Dawn* to survive. Ridge's work may also help us understand the spiritual appeal of the autobiography of Black Elk. This best-seller reconstitutes "Indian" religiosity effectively enough to make *Black Elk Speaks*, in the opinion of Vine Deloria, Jr., a kind of Bible for modern young Indians. As Raymond DeMallie and others have demonstrated, however, this reconstituting involved, for Black Elk, transmuting into his tradition elements of white religion absorbed through his participation in Christian services.

What is most impressive about the survival of American Indians, their success in not vanishing, is that they resist not merely by clinging to the past but by changing, accepting, even welcoming at least part of the present. Their persistence should provoke us (though so far it has not done so) to realize to what a large degree culture *is* transformation. Like homo sapiens' "big brain," every culture provides a group of human beings with supranatural means for accommodating, in an original fashion, to "random" circumstances, what cannot be accomplished by creatures without our complex brain structures and the systems beyond biology it produces. Better recognition of culture's dynamically adaptive values, offered by an understanding of the ways in which Indians managed *not* to disappear (either through genocide or assimilation), offers us, were we willing to recognize it, an escape from the banality of such currently popular enterprises as theorizings on the "poetics of culture."

Native American Anthropology

Poetics of culture are usually carried on by means of anecdotes of ethnology supporting hypotheses about such abstractions as *discourse* and *otherness*. Such generalizing anecdotalism necessarily spends little time on historical distinctions, but attention to the current moment of Native American history requires at least a rough discrimination of American anthropology from European modes. The most powerful American anthropological "school" was the Boasian school, although, significantly, its founder, Franz Boas, disavowed the ideal of anything like a "school."[13] In contrast to English anthropology and the chief American variety it superseded, the Boasian school had a taproot leading back to Germany, its ultimate origin to be found in traditions of which Johann Herder was the most important articulator. This tradition was responsible for the modern conception of culture.[14] The essence of the Herderian view is that cultures are precious because diverse, and significantly interesting because unassimilable into any essentializing, unitary definition of "culture" (for example, one that abstractly contrasts it against "nature").

The empiricist, dialogical, and historical orientation of Boasian anthropology distinguishes it from European theoretical, imperializing ethnology. Illustrative of the difference is the recent *The Writing of History* by Michel de Certeau, which includes a chapter analyzing one of the earliest (and most fascinating) commentaries on New World cultures, that of Jean de Léry on the Brazilian Tupinamba in his *History of a Voyage to the Land of Brazil* (1578). The characteristic bias of European ethnography appears in Certeau's first paragraph: "In primitive society, a timeless land as it were is displayed before the observer's eye ('Things have always been

13. The most conscientious and responsible historian of American anthropology remains George W. Stocking, among whose several works probably the most useful is *Race, Culture, and Evolution: Essays in the History of Anthropology* (New York: Free Press, 1968), along with the introduction to his collection, *Selected Papers from the "American Anthropologist," 1921–1945* (Washington, D.C.: American Anthropological Association, 1976). The latter is a kind of supplement to *Selected Papers from the "American Anthropologist," 1888–1920*, ed. Frederica de Laguna (Evanston: Row, Peterson, 1960), prefaced by a hundred-page essay on "The Beginnings of Anthropology in America" by Irving Hallowell.

14. The most comprehensive analysis of the topic appears in the monograph of A. L. Kroeber and Clyde Kluckhohn, *Culture: A Critical Review of Concepts and Definitions* (Cambridge, Mass.: Papers of the Peabody Museum, vol. 47, 1952).

like this,' remarks the native)."[15] "*The* native"—not a Tupinamba, or a Zuni, or a Japanese, but an abstraction, an appropriate participant in that notorious colonialist abstraction, "primitive society." As revealing of Certeau's Eurocentrism is the remark attributed to "the native." I have never in the anthropological literature of the New World encountered such a statement, but I could cite hundreds of Indian mythological tellings referring to a time when, according to the teller, "things were different." In analyzing Léry's work, Certeau never considers that the Tupinamba might have arrived on the Brazilian coast not very long before the French, although from the opposite direction, having only recently driven out the previous inhabitants. For the European historian, "primitives" are "timeless"; only Europeans have history.

The resistance of Boasian anthropology to the European ethnological tradition kept alive by Certeau is embodied in the races and genders of practicing American anthropologists. From its earliest days until the present both Native American and women anthropologists have played a large and distinguished role in American ethnology. Such participation helps to explain why contemporary Indians have been able so successfully to exploit ethnological research in their legal battles, social activism, and literary art.

It is scarcely accidental that the historicist conception of culture as a set of essentially arbitrary systems relativistically distinguishing one human society from another took shape in Germany during the last years of the eighteenth century, since the conception is antagonistic to the imperialistic universalizing tendencies of the French Enlightenment. The opposition was carried forward in the work of Barthold Niebuhr, whose *Romische Geschichte* (1811–1812) is often cited as decisive in the turn from neoclassic historicism. The idea of culture as existent only in diverse cultures took hold slowly throughout Europe, not penetrating into English thought, for instance, until near the end of the nineteenth century, and often being distorted in the process. Why the relatively pure form propagated by Boas at the beginning of this century was inspiring to so many young scholars in the United States is explained by my mother's summarized description of

15. Michel de Certeau, *The Writing of History*, translated by Tom Conley (New York: Columbia University Press, 1988), 210. Certeau's style and purposes are radically different from those of Léry, whose unpretentiousness has sustained the value of his report for four centuries. *A Voyage* is frequently very funny because of Léry's delight in the New World as a spectacular source of *nouvelle cuisine*, but it is ethnographically far superior to the works of Léry's more learned and self-aggrandizing contemporary commentators on the New World.

his appeal. She imagines Boas standing on the Parnassus of Morningside Heights pointing to the New World lying below,

> its shadowed parts and its sunny places alike virgin to the ethnologist. Virgin but fleeting—this was the urgency and poetry of Boas' message. Everywhere over the land were virgin languages, brought to their polished and idiosyncratic perfection of grammar and syntax without benefit of a single recording scratch of stylus on papyrus or stone: living languages orally learned and transmitted and about to die with their last speakers. Everywhere there were to be discovered Ways of Life, many, many ways. There were gods and created worlds unlike other gods and other worlds, with extended relationships and values and ideals and dreams unlike anything known or imagined elsewhere, all soon to be forever lost—part of the human condition, part of the beautiful, heartbreaking history of man. The time was late; the dark forces of invasion had almost done their ignorant work of annihilation. To the field then! With notebook and pencil, record, record, record. Rescue from historylessness all languages still living, all cultures. Each is precious, unique, irreplaceable, a people's ultimate expression and identity, which, being lost, the world is made poorer as surely as it is when a Praxitelean marble was broken and turned to dust.[16]

Among the notable effects of this Herderian-Boasian vision upon the American academy, I single out only a cluster that is helpful in explaining why the ethnological phase of Indian-white relations could produce some redemptive effects for Indians. The preeminent feature of North American Indian life before Columbus arrived was the extraordinary number— perhaps as many as five hundred—of distinct cultural units among a relatively small population, perhaps two million souls. In the Herderian view, size and physical power of a culture is not paramount; what matters is distinctiveness. The tribal peoples of North America, therefore, provided a splendid manifestation for Herderian thinking, and probably not by a funny coincidence. Herder's thought had been influenced by some knowledge of American Indians.

The large number of distinctive cultures among a relatively small population in North America also rendered inescapable, in an unusual fash-

---

16. Theodora Kroeber, *Alfred Kroeber: A Personal Configuration* (Berkeley: University of California Press, 1970), 51.

ion, the importance of language in ethnological study. From its very beginning, American anthropology had to grapple with linguistic configurations not identical with cultural layouts and displaying distributional irregularities that challenged any easy explanation.[17] Professional anthropology in this country, unlike that in European countries, evolved in an inextricable symbiosis with the development of new kinds of linguistic analyses and systematizations. This union consistently acted as a check on schematic, universalist theorizing, while favoring historicist and empiricist approaches, and, just as important, it reinforced the American tendency to de-emphasize "primitivism." From its very beginning, historical linguistics had to recognize the lack of valid criteria for defining any given language as more "advanced" than another. Linguistics, therefore, strengthened American anthropology's emphasis on variety rather than hierarchy, as is illustrated even in Edward H. Spicer's comments in this collection on the relations of language to culture and political philosophy. Boas's own ethnological work, for example, cannot be evaluated in isolation from its involvement with his linguistic discoveries and systematizing descriptions. Again, there was a fortuitousness in the large number of distinct language/culture groups of small populations in North America: Confronting a new language, a linguist first needs one or two speakers, not masses.

Boasian anthropology, then, could justify itself as an intensely personal study of small societies whose astounding distinctiveness the anthropologist celebrated merely by describing. It produced an unparalleled gathering of ethnological material coincident with linguistic and archaeological data from an enormous range of contiguous, yet diverse, cultures. Such a special complex of anthropological data helped to provide grounding for the later resurgence of Indian self-awareness and self-assertiveness. There is almost no Native American, however alienated by American civilization from his tribal background, who cannot recover a considerable body of knowledge about his tribal roots not only from his own people but also from ethnographic records of American anthropologists, records still being added to, as the Parks-DeMallie contribution to this volume demonstrates. Sometimes ethnographic records may be more accessible than tribal histories. This "advantage," of course, may put a peculiar burden on the contemporary young Indian, a special burden reflected in some recent Indian writing.

17. Traceable in *The Sapir-Kroeber Correspondence*, ed. Victor Golla, no. 6, in *The Survey of California and Other Indian Languages* (Berkeley: University of California, 1984) is the evolution of Sapir's new conception for classifying North American language families fundamental to most subsequent anthropological linguistic study.

What could be worse than having to learn of one's own traditions through the work of a foreign ethnographer, a member of the group that has decimated one's native heritage? Some outcries of resentment against anthropologists are motivated by the discomfort a Native American naturally feels at having to recover his or her heritage through the aid of American scientists, exacerbated, of course, by an understandable desire not to admit having recourse to such information.

Another consequence of Boasian anthropology was the fundamentally inadvertent respect, even honor, it bestowed on the culturally devastated and isolated. Contemporary Indians are justified in ridiculing the antiquated idea that Indians are vanishing. Yet, their valid assertions ought not to obscure the fact that American anthropologists—unlike most of their European counterparts—repeatedly recorded languages, stories (mythical and historical), and descriptions of cultural practices from the last survivors of tribal peoples destroyed by American civilization. A whole array of Native American cultures has truly vanished, except for the records made by Boasian ethnologists, who not infrequently gained information from literally the last living member of a tribal nation. The most famous of these final survivors is Ishi, a Yahi Indian, but we possess a body of Clackamas literature, for example, which we owe to the tellings of one woman, and there are many analogous cases. Because a genuinely Herderian approach inhibits simplistic idealization of noble savages, the inadvertent, if inevitable, effect of such "salvagings" was to enhance the impressiveness of minute and "unimportant" cultures, and even to enlarge the significance of particular individuals who otherwise would have been ignored by our history, as they, in fact, are by most recent theorists of "ethnographic discourse" and "otherness."

In the contribution of Parks and DeMallie, this collection presents evidence of how salvage anthropology evolves toward ethnohistorical approaches that increase the interplay between Indian and white forms of thought. Just as Indian novelists have adopted, but adapted, Euro-American fictional forms, so white academics have been adapting their systems of recording and re-presenting the nature of native materials. Thus, the general form of the Parks-DeMallie project is very similar to that of the great collections published at the end of the last and the beginning of the present century, epitomized by the unwieldy annual reports of the American Bureau of Ethnology. Yet, that form now serves as a means for articulating native perceptions of the nature of indigenous history. One result of this transformation is immediately to open such texts to increasingly complex interpretations. Jahner's reading of Iron Hawk's rhetoric as an instance of Indian resistance to white power, for example, takes on added interest in the light of DeMallie's presentation of the speech not as personal (though couched in the first person) but as a memorization of a communally agreed-upon position. Thus, ethnohistory advances the ideal of Boasian anthropology of recovering the full temporal and spatial specificity of cultural events of preliterate societies but does so through the development of systems of editorial and rhetorical analysis no longer dependent solely upon Euro-centric preconceptions of the social and psychological functions of dis-course.

It was helpful to the Native American resurgence after the Second World War that the Indians' defeated and dispossessed ancestors had already been accorded, by the triumphant culture, a peculiar kind of honor, made all the stronger because it was more an inadvertence of scholarship than an exercise in nostalgic sentimentality. This is why it is reasonable to regard Indian attacks on the discipline of anthropology, and outrage at being treated as subjects of study, as symptoms of a real recuperation of Indian cultural strength, not the blind defensiveness of the enfeebled.

Such resistance should remind us that American anthropologists have studied primarily Native Americans. Unlike the Europeans, who stud-ied exotic colonials, American anthropologists studied other Americans. My father's principal Yurok informant, Robert Spott, was a native Califor-nian—as I happen to be. It was frequently possible, moreover, for American anthropologists, as was the case with my father and Robert Spott, each visiting in the other's home, to establish a long-term relationship, spanning many years, a relationship producing a very different ethnology, and a very different response to ethnology by the informant, from that resulting from short trips to far-off colonies. Contemporary anthropologists such as Keith Basso, Barre Toelken, and Gary Witherspoon have continued this tradition, devoting decades to interactive study of particular cultures. As Kipling's *Kim* so memorably dramatizes, British and French ethnology was, from the first, a branch of the "great game" of spying and exploitation. In the United States, the two principal "battles" among professional anthropologists arose from revelations after World War I and the Vietnam War that ethnologi-cal work had been "perverted" to military-political purposes by agencies of the federal government. To say this is not to absolve American ethnolo-gists from all charges of racism and intellectual arrogance, but it does force recognition that these evils necessarily took a special form among schol-ars conscious of "sharing" the same country with their informants. Few

American anthropologists were blind to the fact that they studied people devastated by their own culture's demolition of Indian life, that their own houses stood on what had been Indian land. Throughout human history, however, invading peoples and native inhabitants have worked out various accommodations to joint occupancy of territory, and these accommodations, however vicious or benign, set up very different relations from those of, say, a British or French visitor temporarily camping in a colony far from "home" and participating (either officially or unofficially) in a governmental program of "pacification," "assimilation," or "cultural development" (this last being a favorite French euphemism). American anthropology was never ideologically innocent; its ideological slant is obscured, however, if its radical differences from European ethnology are ignored.

The special American Indian–ethnologist relationship was enhanced by another peculiarity of American anthropology too often ignored by recent theorists of "cultural studies": its inseparable linkage to archaeology, from which Europeans such as Malinowski remained detached.[18] Archaeology does make some of the demands of the physical sciences (though the key is the intuitive knowledge of where to dig), and this bias appears in the fact that in its earliest years American ethnology was often associated with geological surveys. Archaeology also, however, concentrates attention on historical change, as is obvious, say, in the Southwest, where contemporary Indians occupy sites distant from abandoned cliff dwellings.

Archaeology also tends to focus attention on artifacts, but artifacts that are concretely, rather than abstractly, "meaningful," especially when possessed of significant aesthetic qualities. The archaeologist's concern is with restoring an artifact's specific situation, spatially and temporally, in a culture. The artifact uncovered by the archaeologist is "displaced" (physically, it is likely to have been broken); the task is to restore its wholeness, chiefly by "replacing" it in its original spatiotemporal context. This is why a concrete aesthetic component is often of special concern to the archaeologist. It is by discovering a system of stylistic evolution/devolution that one can establish a historical order for what now lies contemporaneously confused in the same ground. This dependence on specifics of style as means

18. Stuart Piggott, *Ancient Britons and the Antiquarian Imagination* (London: Thames and Hudson, 1989), points out that in the Enlightenment tradition of history "there was no place for the study of the past by means of material culture" (23). Archaeology, like anthropology and historical linguistics, emerged as a feature of what Isaiah Berlin has called the "counter-enlightenment." George Stocking notes that the majority of early Boasian anthropological research was financed by private museums, as the Pawnee material described in this issue by Douglas Parks was gathered for the Field Columbian Museum.

to reconstruction tends to concentrate attention on the nature of a culture in itself as an empirical historical entity. Of course, anyone who works with, say, Mimbres pots is unlikely to think of the people who made them as "primitive."

An oddity of American ethnologists' involvement with archaeology is that North American Indians were predominantly hunting and gathering, rather than sedentary, peoples. They moved, they traveled, and their cultures also were mobile. Some Plains Indians, when first encountered by Europeans, had but recently relocated from northern woodlands. Of course, what we think of as typical Plains cultures depended on the introduction of the horse to the New World by the Spanish. Every circumstance of the Indians' situation, therefore, led American anthropologists to attend consistently to processes of historical transformation, which is why their work could become helpful in making the revival of Native American peoples a genuine reemergence, not a pseudoreturn to an irrecoverable past.

Resurgence: Tribalism and Pan-Indianism

To appreciate not only the character of the Native American resurgence of the past forty years but also its considerable promise for the future, then, one ought to recognize the peculiar nature and role of anthropological studies in North America as helping to foster it, even its rejections of and hostility to ethnographic attitudes and work. From very early, for example, Indians learned to act as ethnologists. The "revolutions" in ethnology during the past generation, especially in the direction of "dialogical anthropology" in America, draw strength from at least a century of significant Indian participation.

Hence Jarold Ramsey's essay in this volume is of special importance, drawing attention to Francis LaFlesche's complex role as Indian ethnographer. Though LaFlesche has good claim to being the first professional Indian ethnologist, there is a whole array of Indians who became involved—Juan Dolores, William Jones, George Hunt, Ella Deloria, George Sword, William Beynon, and Alfonso Ortiz, among others—as ethnographers of their own people. Here, too, the fact that Boasian anthropology so often centered on "native" peoples and favored long-term relationships is significant. This phenomenon is paralleled by, indeed, intertwined with, developments in literary culture, wherein perhaps the most important and interesting precursor of the Native American "literary renaissance" may be said to be (without disrespect to writers such as Charles Eastman and J. J.

Matthews) D'Arcy McNickle, one of those who founded the National Congress of American Indians in 1944, an artistically and intellectually gifted man, the diversity of whose accomplishments still awaits adequate description and assessment.

Almost everything about McNickle's life is complicated. His ancestors, Metis and Cree, were involved in the Riel rebellion in Canada, and his family, who had fled southward after the rebellion's suppression, was granted a tribal allotment by the Salish, among whom they settled. McNickle sold that allotment to pay his way to Europe in 1925, after three years at the University of Montana. An early version of the novel he eventually published as *The Surrounded* is an assimilationist biography of a young Indian, including decisive experiences in 1920s Paris. Two major experiences seem to have been decisive in leading McNickle to discard his red version of Hemingway and Fitzgerald and to transform his novel into a realistic picture of contemporary Indian life in the American West. First, writing for the *National Cyclopedia of American Biography* to support himself, he became fascinated by the work of Professor William Gates, a scholar of Central American cultures. Recognizing his lack of scientific training, McNickle proposed himself as an assistant who could present Gates's anthropological material in an attractive fictional form. Although Gates was intrigued by the idea, it came to fruition only years later in McNickle's second novel, *Runner in the Sun*. Later, McNickle accepted a job on the staff of John Collier, the celebrated reforming Commissioner of Indian Affairs, and McNickle's work in this position deepened and extended his understanding both of the range of Native American problems and of the difficulties added on top of these by white bureaucracies trying to control Indian lives.

The results of these experiences make *The Surrounded*, published in 1936 with little success, artistically one of the finest novels written by a Native American, and they go far to account for its establishing the pattern for the early fiction of the Native American "literary renaissance" beginning more than thirty years later, to which notable contributors are N. Scott Momaday's *House Made of Dawn*, James Welch's *Winter in the Blood* and *Fools Crow*, Leslie Marmon Silko's *Ceremony*, and Louise Erdrich's sequence, *Love Medicine*, *The Beet Queen*, and *Tracks*. Unlike most of the later novels (with the exception of Welch's *Jim Loney*), however, McNickle's is unflinchingly tragic, a perspective reemphasized in his even more powerful posthumously published novel *Wind from an Enemy Sky* (1978). The darkness of McNickle's clear vision arises from the profundity with which he probes, from an Indian perspective, the question of whether specific

Indian cultures can survive in any meaningful way in the modern world. The depth of his questioning derives from his extensive practical knowledge of bureaucratized contemporary life and from an acute sensitivity to the complexities of the tensions between any particular Indian cultural system and the possibilities of sustaining its existence through a modern pan-Indianism, a political movement that McNickle himself helped to bring into being.

McNickle's fiction thus focuses attention on one of the distinctive problems of resurgent Indian life today: the validity and viability of pan-Indianism, since the outstanding feature of traditional Native Americanism is the multiplicity of diverse, and often mutually hostile, cultures. It is the deep tension between these two contradictory forces that distinguishes the contemporary Native American situation. Two contrastive examples may suffice to define this struggle as it acts upon Indian imaginations. N. Scott Momaday's Pulitzer prizewinning novel, *House Made of Dawn*, the publication of which, in 1969, is generally taken to signify the onset of the Native American "literary renaissance," begins and ends with Indian words, but not words in Kiowa, the tribal group with which Momaday associates himself. In fact, his father, a Kiowa, married a Cherokee, and his tribe's hostility to her was one factor in the couple's moving to the Southwest, where Momaday grew up monolingual in English, though he associated with Navajo and Jemez Pueblo Indians. The title of his novel, of course, is taken from the American army doctor Washington Matthews's translation of a Navajo hymn. Much of Momaday's career has consisted of rather torturous efforts to reclaim his links to his Kiowa heritage, his difficulties in doing so making him a peculiarly fitting representative of many contemporary Indians, who are forced to use a nontraditional pan-Indianism for accommodating to a tribal heritage to which their personal relationship has become tenuous.

Gerald Vizenor, both politically and intellectually more sophisticated than Momaday, has adapted techniques of postmodern fiction to render this peculiar Indian problem. Novels such as *Griever: A Monkey King in China* and *The Heirs of Columbus* are distinct from, say, the somewhat formally similar fictions of Ishmael Reed, because Vizenor is so complexly engaged not merely with the conflict of white American culture against Indian cultures but also with the pan-Indian/specific Indian culture tension. Although Vizenor has written extensively about his people's (the Ojibwa) history and traditions, he has made use of a pan-Indian trickster-transformer figure as an organizing principle for most of his fiction—one aspect of which is commented upon by Jonathan Boyarin in his essay in this volume. Because among Native American cultures trickster figures so frequently also function as creators of social practices, they cannot be classified as simple jokesters or buffoons, nor as victims, although often victimized. Vizenor develops this duality. His trickster-transformers are usually not Ojibwa-specific, yet they have a habit of setting up local communities, or separate "states," that seem to be adaptations of Indian separatism to the conditions of postmodern technology and life, of which the recent history of the Soviet Union and Eastern European nations forcibly reminds us.

Even before these startling events, however, Edward H. Spicer, at the end of his distinguished career, became fascinated with the problems of such real nations within states. This interest began in his fieldwork with Indians but steadily expanded into many different societies. What he intended as an introduction to a book-length monograph, therefore, seems an appropriate opening essay in this volume, for it establishes a context within which to view the difficulties of inter-Indian relations underlying white-Indian relations as the central feature of the contemporary Native American resurgence. Another characteristic of Spicer's approach, his tentativeness about embarking on theoretical generalizations, illustrates an empirical bias of American anthropology, which has concentrated not only on the diversity of Indian cultures but also on recognition of them as self-transformative rather than static entities. One peculiarity of Indians' claims against our larger society lies in their predilection for simultaneously asserting general aboriginal rights without diminishing a demand for recognition of the integrity of particular tribal characteristics that are not frozen in an artificial archaism. In the world of the twenty-first century looming ahead, this peculiarity seems deserving of particular attention. Priscilla Wald's essay, for instance, dramatizes several self-contradictions involved in the Marshall Supreme Court's decision in favor of the Cherokee against Georgia, not the least of which involved states-rights advocates denying to the Cherokee the very political autonomy they wished to assert for themselves against the federal government. Wald thus illuminates a kind of ideological inconsistency perceivable in much nationalistic rhetoric resounding around the globe today. Historians such as Alden Vaughan and James Axtell have documented a wide range of shifting patterns of interaction between whites and peoples only belatedly identified as "red" (as Vaughan has shown). Such scholarship may well turn out to be a useful model for a variety of social and historical studies in the twenty-first century, which promises to be one combining social homogenization through technology with revived demonstrations of localized cultural independence. It has been claimed that the Iroquois League was a model for the American Constitution, the kind of unexpected cogency that gives validity to Vizenor's delightfully healing suggestion in *The Heirs of Columbus* that the great explorer was just trying to find his way back home. It seems not inconceivable that what Native Americans are able to make pan-Indianism do and not do for their tribal identities may have lessons for the many other peoples currently trying to fit nationalistic particularism into our technologically unified world.

Something of the ramifying particularities of this kind of challenge to urbanized cosmopolitanism are suggested in the conversation with Jack Salzman, which follows Spicer's essay in this volume. Salzman, the director of Columbia University's Center for American Culture Studies, which, along with its regular academic and publishing programs (the Center is currently engaged in preparing the multivolume *Encyclopedia of African American Culture*) has in the past decade offered many public programs focusing on issues of race, ethnicity, and minority problems, a significant number of which have involved Native American concerns and Native American participants, even though Indians constitute only a tiny portion of the seemingly infinite variety of ethnic groups in New York City. Since it is extraordinarily difficult to develop dialogues between diverse ethnic or cultural groups, there may be a useful lesson in contemporary American Indians' relatively successful mode of adjusting between the fragmenting tendencies of a traditional tribal particularism and the dangers of a subtly too-assimilative "pan-Indianism," as Salzman suggests.

Complementary to the Center for American Culture Studies' interest in Indians is a growing awareness among at least a few scholars of the potential impact on literary criticism of new kinds of analyses of traditional Native American literatures, what we may consider under the rubric of "ethnopoetics." In essence, ethnopoetics challenges the underlying Eurocentricism of dominant critical approaches. In the field of linguistics, to cite a somewhat analogous situation, the many, very diverse American indigenous languages have, for the past quarter of a century, offered themselves as a significant testing ground for universalist theories in that discipline, and have provided, as well, specific challenges to critical generalities about how language constructs and creates reality.[19] Likewise, students of Indian social structurings have increasingly questioned Marxian and Freudian interpretive models that explain all individual and all social actions in terms

19. An excellent example of such concretizing is found in Gary Witherspoon, "Language in Culture and Culture in Language," *International Journal of American Linguistics* 46, no. 1 (1980): 1–13.

of some superpowerful, metacultural principle.[20] Less spectacular, but in the long run perhaps more important, may be developments in literary criticism deriving from the evidence of American Indian accomplishments. The intersecting essays in this collection by Parks-DeMallie and Jahner suggest how Eurocentric presuppositions may have led us either to ignore or to miscomprehend the subtlety of much Indian discourse, especially along linguistic "boundary" conditions. It is no diminution of the accomplishments of Roy Harvey Pearce and Frederick Jackson Turner that their works now seem one-sidedly simplified in terms of the archives that ethnologists and ethnohistorians are beginning to create—a one-sidedness to which Pearce himself called attention some time ago.[21]

Since I have written elsewhere on the significance of ethnopoetics,[22] I will only mention here one of its methodological implications. Ethnopoetics is devoted to identifying and describing the artistic accomplishments of preliterate peoples. Major pioneers were Barre Toelken, who demonstrated the creative role of audiences in oral performances; Dell Hymes, who detected systematic formal structures in materials collected by ethnologists and linguists who had ignored the possibility of such aesthetic form; and Dennis Tedlock, who sought to demonstrate the artistic significance of various elements in oral performance, including changes in a speaker's pitch, volume, speed, and ordering of pauses in delivery. I should stress that these are patient scholars who have dedicated years to infinitely painstaking and detailed linguistic and cultural research through the cooperation of longtime informant-friends. Their results are worthy of attention precisely because they have been so carefully "excavated" from beneath an ethnological overlay that concealed the artistries they delineate. In contrast to much contemporary literary criticism, which announces a familiar text as suddenly illustrative of some new, abstractly prefabricated concept, ethno-

20. See Calvin Martin's critique of Eric Wolf's Marxist assumption of essential identity between European and Indian societies in *The American Indian and the Problem of History*, ed. Calvin Martin (New York: Oxford University Press, 1987), 12–13.
21. Roy Harvey Pearce's important book *Savagism and Civilization: A Study of the Indian and American Mind* (Baltimore: Johns Hopkins University Press, 1967) brilliantly argues the thesis that American civilization, to a significant degree, shaped itself in contrast to its perception of Indian "savagery." Just a few years after its publication, Pearce identified as his book's principal weakness his failure in it to consider adequately the relationship from the Indian perspective. See his "From the History of Ideas to Ethnohistory," *Journal of Ethnic Studies* 2 (1974): 86–92.
22. Karl Kroeber, "American Ethnopoetics: A New Critical Dimension," *Arizona Quarterly* 45, no. 2 (1989): 1–13.

poetics seeks to identify, through meticulously detailed research, specific artistic forms within works where the possibility of such formal skill had previously seemed inconceivable.

A useful illustration of how ethnopoetic attitudes might act renovatively for general criticism is the analysis by Ives Goddard of some Fox uses of the third-person pronouns.[23] Goddard observes that the Fox language differentiates through the use of *proximate* and *obviative* forms (as English does not) its representations of third persons in terms of those persons' functions in a sentence, and in terms of the presence or absence there of other third persons. A crude analogy of this proximate/obviative usage would occur in English if one could, in certain circumstances, say or write *ho* instead of *he*, *sho* instead of *she*, *hom* instead of *him*. Although there are some invariant grammatical rules in Fox about the use of *he* or *ho*, there is also enough latitude for choice that a specific use of proximate or obviative can define a special intersubjective function or unique situation of the character thus referred to. A given sentence might, for example, dramatize a sudden, particular change in relations between a man and a woman if, say, *sho* were used instead of *she* but *him* did not shift to *hom*.

The chief value of this example for a literary critic is the fact that English does not possess the kind of discrimination in the third person that the Fox language offers for exploitation by a gifted artist. One's imagination is boggled, considering what Shakespeare or Jane Austen might have done with the tool of proximate and obviative pronouns. The difference, however, should give some pause to the glibness with which today's critics tend to pronounce on "universal" characteristics of language and literature. More important, though, is the invitation such a revelation offers to meditation, for instance, on the impoverished condition of our critical thinking about how pronouns are used in our own literary texts. An encounter with something so genuinely new, so genuinely "other" as this feature of Fox storytelling ought to be an enormously stimulating experience for critics. Such newness and otherness is the primary contribution of ethnopoetics.

Ethnopoetics, however, offers more than insights into formal characteristics of oral literatures. It enables us to practice—instead of talking abstractly about—multicultural criticism, as is illustrated by Linda Ainsworth's

---

23. Ives Goddard, "Aspects of the Topic Structure of Fox Narratives: Proximate Shifts and the Use of Overt and Inflectional NPs," *International Journal of American Linguistics* 56, no. 3 (1990): 317–40. My discussion shamefully oversimplifies Goddard's presentation, which is, incidentally, one in a series of analyses of Fox texts he has carried out.

contribution to this volume. Her essay demonstrates how a mythic narrative represents not only cultural practices but also the needs giving rise to them, thereby opening to question their efficacy. Such exemplification of another culture's self-awareness gives us a vantage point from which better to understand the causes and consequences of idiosyncratic configurations in our own cultural structures, at the same time that it enhances our capacity productively to appreciate "alien" systems of being human.

In literary criticism, then, as well as in other disciplines, traditional Native American cultures and literatures are becoming provocative of valuably reflexive analyses of Eurocentric modes of thinking. Indian literatures are particularly useful in sharpening critical processes by compelling scholars to take multiculturality seriously, that is, to confront it as a highly specific reality, not a faddish generalization. A different kind of example is provided by Stephen Tyler, who has argued that, contrary to what deconstructionists claim, there has been a pervasive tendency in Western European thought since before Plato to conceive of thinking in terms of representation rather than communication, oversimply, in visual rather than oral terms. In his analysis, contemporary emphasis on signifiers or Derrida's arguments about writing, therefore, are continuants of, rather than deviants from, a central focus of Western thought, one distinctively contrary to the habits of Dravidian peoples he has studied.[24] Whether Tyler is correct on the particular issue, there is no doubt that traditional Native American literatures, buttressed by the research of ethnohistorians such as Parks and DeMallie and critics such as Ainsworth, Ramsey, and Jahner, all of whom make examination of moving boundary conditions of cultural interfaces possible, now offer fertile terrain for challenging fundamental assumptions of Western critical thinking. More than a decade ago, I observed in *Traditional Literatures of the American Indians* that it was not Indian literatures that were primitive but our critical methods. The essays in this volume suggest that in various disciplines that kind of challenge posed by American Indian cultures is increasingly being recognized and welcomed in what—belatedly—is becoming a genuinely post-Columbian world.

---

24. Stephen A. Tyler, "The Vision Quest in the West; or, What the Mind's Eye Sees," *Journal of Anthropological Research* 40 (1984): 23–40.

The Nations of a State

Edward H. Spicer
Preface by Rosamond B. Spicer

Preface

Edward H. Spicer wrote copiously about the Yaquis of Arizona and Sonora, about many aspects of their culture and their history. In due course, his interest in Yaqui ethnohistory led him to examine the history of all the tribes of the Southwest United States and Northwest Mexico and led to his writing *Cycles of Conquest*.[1] This, along with other studies, directed him to think about peoples whose cultures had endured over long periods of time, "persistent cultural systems" as he called them in his article in *Science*.[2]

As noted in the preface, this piece constitutes the first half of a chapter as written by the late Edward H. Spicer. The second half, though further developing his ideas, is not specific to the American Indian and so is not included here. The final section printed here, which offers a pungent statement, is Spicer's conclusion to that chapter. The book was never completed because of his untimely death.

1. Edward H. Spicer, *Cycles of Conquest* (Tucson: University of Arizona Press, 1962).
2. Edward H. Spicer, "Persistent Cultural Systems," *Science*, 19 Nov. 1971, 795–800.

In the final chapter of *The Yaquis: A Cultural History*,[3] he expanded further on this idea, including not only Yaquis as an enduring people but extending his ideas to other American Indian tribes and to various European peoples, as well.

While writing this final chapter of *The Yaquis*, he already had in mind another volume, a volume that would detail the history of the peoples— he had carefully selected ten—on whom he had already touched and that would, through those ten, illustrate a grand design of the relationship of nations and states and how nations survive within states. It was to be called *Enduring Peoples; or, Ten against the State*. This work would have been the summation of his fifty years of scholarship.

He plunged enthusiastically into the writing of this book and completed five of the histories: The Basques, The Catalans, The Irish, The Welsh, and The Hopis, in addition to what he first thought of as chapter 1, "The Nations of a State." He was considering that this might, instead, become the concluding chapter. Planned were a new introduction and five more chapters: The Senecas, The Cherokees, The Yaquis, The Lowland Mayas, and The Jews.

I would like to quote a paragraph that he wrote as a possible introduction:

> This book is about people who, against great odds, have for long periods maintained their identity. It is about people who have refused to let military conquest and political domination remove them from the stream of human history. It is about people who have insisted on holding to their own view of the world and their place in it despite heavy pressures to give up their individuality and allow themselves to be blotted from the human scene. In short, it is a book about people who have resisted conquest and attempts by people more powerful than they to absorb and assimilate them. It is, therefore, a book about ideals held to in the face of forces applied to destroy them. It is a book about the triumph of moral over other kinds of power, over military, economic, and political power.

This quote enunciates the argument of the following article. In spite of the fact that it was intended as a chapter, it stands on its own merits as a contribution to our understanding of world history. The ideas set forth here,

---

3. Edward H. Spicer, *The Yaquis: A Cultural History* (Tucson: University of Arizona Press, 1980).

in 1981, foretell events that have actually taken place since 1988, in what was the USSR, in Eastern Europe, and, in fact, in the United States and in countries around the world.

The nature of the nation-state, of the enduring ethnicity, including symbols, languages, and cultures, of the nations within the state, is clearly laid out here. These pages, however, are only the first half of the full chapter. The second half, with sections entitled "The Consequences of the Blindness" (because of the limited monolithic view of the rulers of the state) and "The Emergence of Nations" (a forecasting of what has actually taken place, particularly in Eastern Europe), is not included in this essay because the focus of this issue of *boundary 2* is the American Indian. Most of the numerous American Indian tribes within the United States consider themselves to be autonomous nations. Like so many other nations within states today, they are strongly asserting their nationhood in no uncertain—though mostly peaceful—terms.   R. B. S.

• • • •

When Daniel Corkery, an Irish schoolmaster, in 1925, named a book *The Hidden Ireland*, he called attention to a phenomenon of great significance in the world of the twentieth century. His study described the life of a people with deep cultural roots who were a part of the British Empire and yet whose existence, in the terms in which Corkery made them known to us, was utterly unknown to the English. By describing in eloquent terms the writings of Irish authors during the eighteenth century, Corkery demonstrated that there existed in Ireland a rich and distinctive intellectual and literary life. This cultural life, however, was carried on in Gaelic, the native language of the Irish. Few, if any, of the English people were aware of the Irish language, and those who were aware during the eighteenth and nineteenth centuries associated it only with illiterate and backward peasantry. Almost no Englishman seemed to know that Gaelic had been, a few centuries before, a major language of Christian thought. That it had continued into the nineteenth century as a medium of literary life in Ireland was simply beyond the pale of English consciousness. Matthew Arnold sensed something of the special quality of what he called Celtic literature, but for him it was a thing of the past, to be appreciated as one did Greek or Latin. He seemed unaware of the gulf that separated him as an Englishman from the Irish actually living in his time. John Stuart Mill analyzed with great acumen the economic causes of that gulf in the nineteenth century, but his attention was confined to economic and social conditions. Mill remained ignorant, insofar as his works tell us, of the continuing life of Ireland through the Irish language. Thus, it was not only during the 1700s, as Corkery tells us, that Ireland was hidden; it was even more deeply hidden through the nineteenth century from England's most sensitive men and women, not only from the politicians and businessmen who made England's policy for the continuing subordination of Ireland.

The hiddenness of Ireland was no isolated phenomenon, no simple expression of a special English obtuseness. For Spaniards, for the French and other Western Europeans, for Russians, for Americans, North and South, the peoples who were part of their empires or nation-states were equally hidden from their awareness. By "hidden" we do not, of course, mean that the dominant peoples in these states were unaware that their territories included a variety of peoples. The English were thoroughly, and usually unhappily, aware that a different kind of people from themselves lived on the island of Ireland, along with other somewhat similar people in Scotland and in Wales. Spaniards who made state policy during the nine-teenth century were quite aware of Basques, Catalans, and even Galicians. The white Americans who controlled the United States were aware of blacks and, in a general way, of American Indians. What remained hidden from the makers of state policy was that these peoples were living cultural lives of their own, that they had developed languages, or even that they spoke anything worthy to be called a language. As in eighteenth-century Ireland, there had grown up a strange impassable barrier that enabled the domi-nant peoples to believe that others within their nation-states were justly subordinated. Either, it came to be believed, the subordinated peoples were inherently inferior or they might demonstrate their worthiness as human beings by discarding their outworn ways and becoming like the dominant peoples.

Hidden Nations

It is important to realize that when we refer to the phenomenon of the hiddenness of nations, we are not pointing merely to the obvious situation of colonial dominance by Western states that surged through the world from the sixteenth through the nineteenth centuries. We are not referring only to the condition of very great cultural differences that suddenly appeared within the same state as a result of colonial expansion. The European colo-nial empires are a special instance of a much more general phenomenon. What we say here is relevant for understanding colonial growth and disintegration, but it well may be that we should look at what we are concerned with as a fossilized colonialism.

The causes for barriers to mutual understanding that result from recent colonial contacts between markedly different peoples are obvious. On the other hand, the barriers that exist for centuries between peoples living side by side within the same political structure are a different kind of phenomenon. It is not obvious that they should be there. It is not obvious why they should persist. It is not obvious why they should grow stronger with time and become less and less assailable. The hidden Ireland existed at a time some eight centuries after the first political contacts between the Irishmen and the Saxons. What were the causes of the deep gulf across which the English could not see after eight hundred years? In the United States, the Iroquois and the "Americans" had known each other for more than two hundred years, but the Americans who made policy for New York State in the 1960s[4] knew nothing of the language, the cultural history, or the religion of the Seneca. Similarly, in Spain, during the nineteenth century, the people of Catalonia and the dominant Castilian-speaking people of the peninsula had known each other for something like a thousand years, yet Castilians believed that the Catalan language was a degenerate dialect of Castilian. How had this come about? There was no question in the minds of Castilians that the French had a language distinct from Castilian, but they had not learned this about their own immediate associates. What kept them in a world apart from people within the same state? It is not obvious why higher barriers grow up between members of the same nation-state than between different nation-states. It is answers to questions of this sort that we must find if we are to understand the phenomenon of the hiddenness of nations as it developed during the centuries between 1500 and 1900.

Perhaps the first point to be clear about is that the people who are hidden are not hiding. They do not originate the cocoon that hides them from the dominant people. The cocoon is spun around them by other peoples, namely, the people who dominate the state apparatus within which all live. Here, we must be clear about the political environment in which the hidden people have their being. This environment is currently labeled *the nation-state*. This is a term of doubtful utility, even though it calls attention to the important fact that the entity with which we are concerned has two major

4. During the 1960s, the Seneca suffered relocation due to the building of the Kinzua Dam on the Allegheny River and were also subject to the concomitant pressure by the United States government for "termination."

kinds of components—the state and the nation. The term does not, however, indicate that the nations are plural while the state is single. It is in that fact that we have the basic clue to understanding this environment that breeds the hiddenness of nations.

That fact, so deeply hidden from most of us in the modern world, is that every state (the exceptions are too trivial to dwell on) is a plural entity. Every state contains within itself two or more nations. This is fundamental; yet, the term *nation-state* tends to perpetuate the obscuring of this fundamental fact, because it suggests that a modern state is composed of a welded unity—a single nation within a state. Insofar as it suggests this kind of entity, the term perpetuates misunderstanding and obfuscation.

What is essential is to understand that a state, no matter what those who control it think and publish, consists of several entities that we are calling nations and that have been called that for the last several centuries in most European languages. A nation, in simple language, consists of people who have in common a historical experience that they symbolize in ways giving them a common image of themselves. It might help, for clarity, to shift our terms from the long-established ones to others and call the entity to which we refer *a* people, rather than a nation. It is very important in making use of this term that we emphasize the *a* before *people*. We are not talking about people in general, about any collection of individuals that one might put together for statistical purposes; rather, we are talking about *a* people, and included in the concept is *boundedness*. A people is bounded in a quite different way from a state. A state maintains the privilege of defining a territorial boundary around itself, a boundary that can be marked as a relatively fixed line on a map to enclose the territory within which the legal citizens of the state reside. The boundary of a people is not that simple, because it depends on the sharing of meanings among individuals. People are citizens of a state regardless of how they feel about the state's government; they are citizens by fiat of the state. The citizen of a state is so, because the state defines him or her as a citizen and has forms filled out in courthouses, or elsewhere, to testify to that fact. A member of a people, on the other hand, is so by virtue of identifying with others who share his or her feelings about certain symbols and about one another. In a basic sense, the individuals who identify as a people do so by their own choice. The self-identification, which is the effective foundation of the existence of a people, rests on the sharing of meanings associated with various symbols. The boundary, therefore, may often shift, and it is this possibility for great instability in a people's boundaries that has led to the cloud of confusion that surrounds the solid reality of the existence of peoples in the modern world—and in the past.

We have said that a people's existence depends on the symbols of historical experience that the individuals composing a people share. The nature of such symbols we shall henceforth call *ethnic* symbols. They exhibit a tremendous variety, ranging from heroes such as William Tell of the Swiss and Crazy Horse of the Sioux, through the Brehon Law of the Irish and the Fueros of the Basques, to the Sardana dance of the Catalans and the Kachina dances of the Hopi Indians. As symbols, they have a very concrete existence—as words spoken or written, as human or mythical figures, as dance steps and rhythms, as songs, and so on. As symbols, they stand for something besides their own concrete forms. That is simply to say that individuals associate them with events in their historical experience that give rise to emotions, feelings of pride, or a desire to emulate, because of the demonstration of courage or wisdom or nobility in the event symbolized. If the symbol is a dance, for example, associated with defiance of attempts to suppress or overcome a people, performing the dance may give a sense of actual participation in the historic defiance. At the least, it puts in a historically defined frame current feelings of solidarity with others. The associations of ethnic symbols are manifold, but they have in common the capacity for stimulating in some degree the sentiments and the ideas felt and believed in by the people for whom the meaning exists.

The boundaries of peoples are at the limits of the domains of meaning of symbols. The symbols, such as their own names for themselves, may be unknown to, and therefore wholly without meaning for, neighboring peoples who learn only their own and not their neighbors' languages. The word *Yoeme* was unknown to Mexicans at the beginning of the nineteenth century. Yet, *Yoeme* was the name that this people called themselves. Unaware of the word, the Mexicans called them *Yaquis*, even though they had known them, lived beside them, and fought with them for more than two centuries. For Yaquis, the word had intense meaning and embodied their sense of pride in themselves and in their long proprietorship over fertile farmland that the Mexicans coveted. Repeatedly, a people's own name for themselves has remained hidden for hundreds of years from neighboring peoples. It remains a symbol without meaning for enemy or friendly neighbors, but it is rich in meanings for the people who use it. Such a term marks a part of the boundary between two peoples; here, a domain of meaning begins for one of the two peoples, and here it also ends, because it has no meaning for the neighbor. To trace the boundaries of peoples, it is necessary to discover the symbols and the domains of meaning for each, a process not difficult if one remembers that a people's own language is the major vehicle for perpetuating the domains of meaning. Without the learning of that language, the search for ethnic symbols is sure to be frustrated, but with it a new world opens up.

The domains of meaning mark the boundaries of peoples and do not require governments to declare them. Peoples come into existence and go on existing without benefit of state intervention. There is, to be sure, a process within a state that is essentially similar to the process by which a people maintains itself. A government adopts a flag, names official heroes, and seeks to stimulate loyalty to the state and its purposes by getting people to make common identification through those symbols. States have been very successful in establishing domains of meaning for a limited number of symbols, such as a flag, and in this degree they are like peoples or nations. A state, however, never has the rich array of symbols, ranging through all aspects of life, that characterizes a people.

This brings us to the heart of the matter with respect to the composition of a nation-state. Every state is composed, with very minor exceptions (the tiniest of states in Western Europe, such as Monaco or, perhaps, Denmark), of two or more nations, two or more peoples. In most twentieth-century states, only one of these peoples controls the government. It usually has been a conquest state that, by a process of military domination, has gained control of a territory and set up a government to manage the affairs of the peoples within that territory. Thus, for some six hundred years, Great Britain existed as a conquest state that had incorporated Wales, Scotland, and Ireland into a territory over which the English maintained control until 1922, when Ireland separated. Thus, also, the United States conquered one Indian tribe after another across the North American continent, as well as the Mexicans of Texas and the Southwest, and incorporated all these many peoples into a single political whole. Likewise, an Iranian government incorporated Kurds, Turkmen, Balochis, and others into a government controlled by the family of the Shah Pahlavi. And so, throughout Europe and the Americas, as well as Asia, we can discern the process of the formation of conquest states.

Essentially, what we mean by a conquest state is a political organization with an established territorial boundary that has, by means of military power, incorporated other peoples under the control of the conquering people. There are all sorts of subprocesses by which the conquest states of Western Europe had taken form by the twentieth century, including marriage alliances and some voluntary associations. While recognizing the essential character of their formation, what we are concerned with here, rather, is their basic composition. This rests on the establishment by one people of control over the governmental apparatus of administration, lawmaking, judicial procedure, and taxation, in terms of which the other peoples in the territory are required to organize their lives. A variety of arrangements exists through which, in various degrees, other peoples take part in the different aspects of government, but, regardless of the kind of participation, the institutions in which they work together with the dominant people are those of the dominant people. If the nation-state was a monarchy, of which there were so many until the twentieth century, all governmental management was in the hands of the original dominant people. If it was a democratic republic, there was often a spread of public office among the various peoples composing the whole. It was a rare state, however, in which the forms of governmental activity exhibited characteristics derived from the cultural traditions of any but the dominant people.

During the twentieth century, new forms of the state began to appear, some modeled on the federative tradition of the Swiss and some newly invented, but until that new era began, there prevailed a simple structure of dominance—subordination; one people's way of doing things established the mold for the lives of all other peoples in the state. Educational institutions, legal and judicial procedures, modes of election of officeholders, banking and financial institutions, and so on were all in the patterns of the dominant people. The dominant people maintained itself in a superordinate role and subordinated the other peoples within its political and cultural framework. This was the essential structure of the nation-state.

Once we understand this structure, it becomes easier to appreciate the phenomenon of the hiddenness of nations described by Daniel Corkery for Ireland. We must recognize, however, that this was merely one well-described instance among thousands that could have been chosen. In general, the dominant peoples of the nation-states of the nineteenth and twentieth centuries governed peoples whom they believed were like themselves already, peoples who could be made into images of themselves, or peoples who were hopelessly inferior and could not be changed. They did not seek to learn about the peoples whom they had subordinated in the various forms of the state. The dominant peoples wove cocoons of official policy and bureaucratic words around other peoples and hid them from view. They induced blindness in themselves about the real nature of the subordinated peoples.

The case of the English has become notorious, especially since the descendants of the rural Irish have made something of themselves in America different from the nineteenth-century English image of the Irish. It is difficult to believe now, in the late twentieth century, that the Irish were depicted in English periodicals as inferior, ape-like beings, stupid and frequently depraved. That ugly image grew out of the poverty-stricken condition to which most Irish had been reduced by the centuries-long English policy of land confiscation. In the early nineteenth century, the English laughed at a stage-Irishman, who was something like the minstrel-show black in the United States—an ignorant and happy-go-lucky figure worthy only to be laughed at and kept at work. It is not, however, that aspect of the attitudes engendered in dominant peoples that we wish to stress. Extreme economic subordination with its degrading consequences is a serious matter, but at least as serious is the self-induced ignorance among dominant peoples about the cultural life of those they subordinate. It was perfectly true that during the early nineteenth century there were Irish in Ireland and blacks in the United States who lived at the edges, as it were, of fully human society. They accepted an inferior role and played the fool for the enjoyment of their acknowledged superiors. This kind of behavior, however, in all cases, represented only an outer fringe among the subordinated people. There was, at the same time, a deeper cultural life and a richer expression of the human spirit—among the Irish, among blacks in the United States, and among the thousands of other hidden nations.

It was this coexisting life that remained entirely, or almost entirely, unseen by the dominant peoples. For centuries, in Ireland, there was a distinctive cultural tradition maintained in the Gaelic language. It flourished as early as the eighth century, when it received tremendous impetus and vitalization through the work of Christian missionaries. It became a bulwark of Christianity during the Dark Ages in Europe. It fostered a tradition of learning and produced poetry and other literature. The Irish, however, fared badly from the 1400s on against the Norman and the English invasions of their island. They became a subordinated people during four hundred years and as such were submerged within the whole of the English nation-state, or, as it became, the British Empire. At first, in an effort to protect themselves from assimilation by the vigorous Irish culture, the Norman English created a Pale of settlement within which they stayed. They sought, through segregation from the native Irish, to maintain their own racial and cultural characteristics. They then extended the boundary of the Pale in unison with their military successes against the Irish, and the commitment to a segregation policy intensified. English people living in Ireland refused to learn the Irish language and disdainfully rejected Irish ways, but they had to work hard to do so because the Irish culture was deep and strong. Meanwhile, they enforced their dominance with greater and greater completeness. As they did so, their isolation from the Irish who behaved in the Irish manner, speaking their own language, for example, became more and more complete. With that isolation went an increasing ignorance of Irish ways of life and an intensification of feelings of English superiority.

By the beginning of the nineteenth century, English ignorance of the deeper life of Ireland was, as Corkery pointed out, just about complete. Not only were the Irish economically and politically subordinated under the state system that the English bound them to but there was a concomitant subordination of the language and the Irish cultural traditions. That is to say, more and more of the Irish were forced to assimilate English ways in order to live decently and so were forced to reject the Irish culture and language. Those who maintained the Irish ways suffered one of two consequences: they were either ground into poverty under the imposed land and trade system, or they simply existed in total isolation from the dominant trends within Ireland. Learned men steeped in the old literary tradition struggled in miserable poverty to teach it to handfuls of rural children in the illegal Hedge Schools. Outside of this great effort, the language became chiefly a language of peasant people. The rural people of the west of Ireland preserved it in songs and sayings as an oral literature that had now become a folk remnant rather than the literature it had been, expressing the culture of a learned class and a people generally.

This long history of decline remained hidden to the English. Very few became aware of it until shortly after the middle of the nineteenth century, when some Anglo-Irish, as residents of Ireland maintaining English ways came to be called by Irish, began, like Douglas Hyde, desperately to collect and to preserve the Irish folk literature in, to use Yeats's phrase, the "Celtic twilight." We are concerned here not so much with what happened to the Irish and their tradition as with what happened to the English. We are concerned with the English, along with the dominant Americans, in the same kind of situation that engendered blindness in the United States and, as well, the Castilian-speaking Spaniards, from whom the growth of Basque literature remained hidden. We will consider these three and, through them, call attention to a thousand other cases of what we may call cultural blindness,

which attacks a people who become the dominant people in a nation-state.
The phenomenon is so general over the world that it cries out for better
understanding, and we must not ignore it if its consequences, so serious
for humanity, are to be avoided.

The blindness of dominant peoples is rooted in the power situation
in which they dominate. Dominant peoples control the institutional relationships of nations in their state. The dominant people do not have to adjust
to others; they can require the subordinated peoples to adjust to them. Out
of this springs their inability to bring the subordinated peoples into ordinary
focus. The dominant people do not ordinarily experience any pressures to
see the subordinated peoples as the subordinated peoples see themselves.
Everything in the environment, to be understood as the nation-state, is con-
ducive to the development and confirmation of an ethnocentric view of the
world. It was ethnocentrism that infected the English to the point where they
were unable to see the nature of Irish life and culture. Intent on conquest of,
and then on separation from, the Irish, who at first subtly penetrated their
image of themselves, the English wove a veil around the Irish through which
ultimately they could see almost nothing. From outside such veils, the view
of the world, and of the peoples in it, is limited by the dominant peoples
themselves. The blindness of ethnocentrism has consequences both for
the dominant peoples and for the subordinated ones. It has consequences
for all of us, and, therefore, we must deal with cultural blindness for what
it is.

How the State Became Blind

The nation-state, it is sometimes said, has had its heyday. That may
be true, as multinational corporations accumulate power, the United Nations
deals more or less effectively with world issues, and nation-states struggle
with seemingly irresolvable internal conflicts. Nevertheless, we still live in
the era of the nation-state, in that period of human history in which the
nation-state has steadily risen to the position of being the most widespread
and the most taken-for-granted form of large-scale politico-economic organization. All the peoples of the world in the late twentieth century live within
nation-states. Some are very small, such as Israel, and some are very large,
like the Union of Soviet Socialist Republics. But everywhere in Asia, Africa,
and Oceania, as well as in Europe and the Americas, the still-dominant
model, the generally accepted political unit in terms of which we all think,
is still the nation-state. A new era may be dawning in which the nation-

state will recede as the dominant political model, but that era cannot yet be clearly seen.[5]

The era of the nation-state may be regarded as having a beginning during the 1400s and continuing through the 1900s. It may have a longer life than that, but we shall treat it as having lasted for about six hundred years, possibly a little longer. Its origin-place most certainly has been Europe, primarily Western Europe. It may be regarded as growing directly out of the ruins of the Roman Empire, by way of the Holy Roman Empire. The nation-state was a new creation, quite distinct from the ancient empire type of political structure, by at least the 1600s. It reached its climax of development during the early nineteenth century and may be considered to have declined since then—for the past 150 years.

It may be questioned that the states of Western Europe that became organized during the 1500s, 1600s, and 1700s constitute something actually different from the Roman, the Persian, the Egyptian, or other ancient empires. Our contention is that the nation-state is something quite different, even though it has obviously made use of many of the empires' means of organization and concepts of political process. The difference lies in the conception of the relationship between the constituents and the whole of the political structure. In the Roman Empire, the ruling conception was that of a paternal, protective power drawing tribute and military manpower from fully distinct—that is, non-Roman—political and cultural units, or congeries of peoples. In return for tribute and levies of soldiers, the Roman organization provided protection for trade routes, from internal civil disorders, and from conquest by other peoples. These reciprocal relationships and the resulting unity of the whole Empire depended on continuously functioning military power, resident legions throughout the whole vast length and breadth of the Roman territory. The peoples who lived under Roman rule maintained their own political and cultural life in their own traditional ways. To be sure, they supported within their own territories centers of Roman administration and, indeed, of cultural influences. Throughout the Empire, there were Roman cities, where Roman Law prevailed, in the midst of native cities, where it was not expected that Roman Law should govern peoples' lives. Any individual of the "tribes," as they were usually called, could, if he pleased, come to live in a Roman city, acquire Roman citizenship, live under Roman Law, and, thus, become Roman. There was, however, no organized program for

5. At the time this essay was written, in about 1980, the USSR was still very much in existence. The dissolution of the USSR did not occur until 1988–1989.

the assimilation of natives, other than this. The Britons, the Iberians, the Franks, and the Teutonic tribes outside the Roman cities went their own ways. Rome had no intention at any time of setting up levels of government, from local to provincial, for all the hordes of people who contributed taxes and manpower to the Empire's organization. Outside the Roman administrative network, the peoples ran their own affairs. This was the basic pattern of each ancient empire—tributary peoples continuing their own traditions, religious and otherwise, living under the protection of continuously active, usually Roman-commanded, military companies.

The structure of the nation-state developed along very different lines, although the conquest origins of many may be seen in forms descended from imperial administration. Out of very diverse forms of organization, the nation-state steadily defined and put into practice a much more unitary structure than was ever conceived by an ancient empire. Sometimes beginning as an actual confederation of nations, such as the Spanish state, or a paper confederation, such as the United States, nation-states have steadily centralized administration and have increasingly allocated all varieties of power to the central government. This tendency was most marked in Europe between the 1500s and the early 1900s but has continued thereafter, as the bureaucratic centers have become more and more ponderous. Accompanying the centralization of administration, the managers of the states have undergone a steady growth of antagonism toward the nations composing the states, antagonism toward not only the political realm but also toward their cultural heterogeneity. This has been expressed through many means, such as centrally administered school systems, central banking systems, and central control of communication systems. Thus, the example of the ancient empire has been a powerful developing influence, the nation-state being a product of the empire's concepts and organizational means that were adopted by the state during the first couple of centuries of the nation-state's growth. Most influential in bringing this trend to its climactic expression during the nineteenth century was a general concept that seemed wholly foreign to the prevailing way of thinking in an ancient empire—the concept of internal homogeneity.

Long before the idea of centrally regulated trade and commerce was embodied in nation-state government in Europe, a tendency toward the adoption of "standard" languages became clearly apparent. The language varieties by means of which the peoples of Europe communicated were myriad. For every group of villages among which there was some form of cooperation, ranging from mutual help at harvest time to the putting on of religious dramas, there were distinctive ways of speech, phrases, and particular words that were not used in the same way beyond that group. The language varieties, or dialects, however, in a given region had a common origin in one or more ancestral ways of speech, and, thus, there were basic features that made groups of such varieties mutually intelligible over sometimes wide areas. As various peoples, or, rather, as dominant families among a given people, gained political power over others and founded dynasties of rulers, the language varieties spoken by those families were imposed everywhere within their domains. That is, in order to communicate with the rulers, local headmen, and others, had to use the language of the given feudal lord (or whatever he was called), because the lord and his representatives did not deign to use the local ways of speaking. In this way, a common means of communication, in the form of one language variety from among the many of a region, slowly spread. The growing dominant patterns of usage developed both for practical reasons and for prestige.

As "royal" families developed—that is, families who concentrated the most military power in a region in their own hands—they imposed their mode of speech, at least as an alternative, if not as a complete replacement, over their whole domain. It was in this way that a regional dialect that had been spoken in southwest London gradually became during the 1500s the "English language," the linguistic variety of greatest prestige and maximum utility wherever the dominant English royal family held sway. The process of the expansion of a variety, until it became the dominant one for many people, was initiated by political growth. It was immensely aided by the introduction of writing all over Europe, when ways of pronouncing words and modes of grammatical expression could be standardized in a form that outlasted a generation or even a whole dynasty.

The development of a standard language involved, then, both a process of imposition for practical governmental purposes and a process of emulation; it came about as a dynastic family of a particular people among all the peoples of a kingdom, or other political unit, gained great prestige. The mechanical means by which the standard language took on a more and more stable form and became singled out from the myriad dialects of a region were, first, the expansion of writing and printing and, second, the growth of cities. In Western Europe, this happened in the fifteenth and sixteenth centuries, the same period during which the political forms of organization constituting the nation-state were assuming more definite shape. The two growths went hand in hand. The records of the growing nation-states were standardized for better management purposes, and information and royal decrees were diffused in the language of the royal family. There rarely were conscious efforts to standardize the language forms (that came later), but usage was standardized, nevertheless. It was in the cities that writing developed new functions different from those that had prevailed in the monasteries. In the monasteries, the language of communication and the language in the manuscripts was Latin, in which forms of prayer had been standardized. Early monarchies also used Latin as the official language at first, but steadily during the 1400s a process of adoption of the "vernacular" as the official language of state communication resulted in the replacement of Latin. Castilian, born in the extreme northwest of the Spanish peninsula, in 1487, became the official state language of the rapidly expanding kingdom of Castile and, as a Golden Age in literature burst forth, became the standard language for all the peoples of Spain. In the British Isles, at about the same time, what had been the dialect of a part of London underwent the same kind of transfiguration, to be accepted by Shakespeare's time as the standard language for all the peoples of the Kingdom of England. Even if spelling on paper was by no means uniform until centuries later, ways of pronunciation and expression did become generally accepted. All over Europe, stimulated by the same process, standard languages emerged out of the many vernaculars—French, High and Low German, Hungarian, Portuguese, Italian, Czech, Serbian, Polish, Russian—wherever the nation-state was also emerging. The political structure of the nation-state should be considered along with standard forms of speech and writing as complementary aspects of a more general process, namely, the homogenization of culture that accompanied larger-scale human organization.

There were important cultural concomitants of the development of standard languages. As we have seen, the appearance of a standard language was an aspect of the growth in power of a dynastic family. As the holders of power in a nation-state practiced their own language variety as the means of communication with their subjects, all other dialects were downgraded. The standard language was not imposed by force on the subjects of a kingdom. Rather, the royal usage acquired high prestige because those with power used it; many individuals sought to enhance their prestige by adopting the dominant forms. Moreover, the instruments of writing in the cities gave a mechanical advantage to the dissemination of the standard language. Under these circumstances, many language varieties were rapidly and completely displaced. Not all varieties succumbed, but most did, and those that remained were evaluated by the people of the cities and by those who had adopted the dominant usage as inferior, as of low quality.

As the written form became more and more used, and as schools began to employ the dominant variety, the fate of the vernaculars considered inferior was sealed.

In regions such as what came to be known as France, the standard language, once confined to small areas, became dominant everywhere in a short period; nevertheless, a language of southern France, Provençal, and of the northwest, Breton, continued in existence. In the Iberian peninsula, although Castilian also spread widely and rapidly, the languages of the Basques, the Galicians, and those of the east in Catalonia, Valencia, and the Mallorcan Islands continued to exist. Where tongues other than the standard one continued to be used, some also developed written forms and so employed that mechanical means to aid in their standardization and continuance. Important all over Europe was this continuation, under the conditions of language standardization in the nation-state, of dozens of languages alongside the one that had become standard.

As an accompaniment of this phenomenon, we must emphasize that the nation-states were hostile to languages that rose and challenged the standard form. Every nation-state encouraged or adopted aggressive measures for replacement of those "inferior" languages that had not been eliminated by 1600. This was an expression of the tendency toward cultural homogenization that was integral in the environment of the nation-state. The blindness of the state took the form of not seeing any of these language varieties as vehicles of respectable cultural development. They were perceived, rather, as enemies of the state, because they went contrary to the dominance of the standard language. The state may be seen as in the service of the process of homogenization of culture. It—that is, its spokesmen—devised various arguments in support of the exclusive use of the standard language within the borders of the state territory.

The growth of standard languages gave rise to other standardizations. One of the most far-reaching in its effects was the uniformity brought to law and legal procedures. Nation-states, in general, became deeply hostile to variation in legal procedure and, therefore, were strongly inclined to eliminate court and legal usages of local origin, the product of local experience and local cultural orientations. The reason for the elimination of such local law was held to be that identical laws and penalties were necessary in order to provide equal justice for all. It was believed that part of the function of a state was to provide this for all its citizens equally, and, therefore, a centralized and uniform legal system had to be imposed from the capital city of the nation-state.

Another concomitant of the standard language that contributed to the blindness of nation-states with respect to the existence of their constituents was the writing of history from an ethnocentric point of view. The dominant nations naturally were interested in their own histories. As standard languages began to take form, histories began to be written in those newly standardized vernaculars. The writers of history of a nation-state were first chiefly those for whom the standard language was their native tongue or who felt the standard language to be prestigious and, therefore, most likely to gain recognition for the writer if he or she used it. It is not surprising that the first written histories of nation-states were histories of the dominant nations within each state. Not only citizens of England but also literate French, Dutch, and citizens of other European states came to look on the history of England as the history of the English. They did so because this is the way it was written by Englishmen. Aside from the recounting by the English of their military conquests of other peoples, such as the Irish and the Scots, the historical accounts were exclusively concerned with the English. These accounts dealt with events in which the English participated in Ireland or Wales or Scotland, but not with the events as they were seen and understood by Welsh, Irish, or Scottish people. The nation-state came to be *the* unit of historical scholarship and presentation—that unit as understood by the dominant people. Just as most of the dialects that had been spoken in a nation-state became lost to history, so even the nondominant peoples who made up a state began to undergo a process of becoming lost to history, because they were mentioned only in passing or as adjuncts to the process of domination by the dominant people. Only as some nondominant peoples, whose languages persisted and had been reduced to writing, took steps to write their own histories from their own points of view did the historical record acquire some degree of completeness. Participation of nondominant peoples in the writing of their own histories, however, usually came at a very late stage, in the nineteenth century at the earliest, in the development of the nation-state.

In this way, as in the case of language, the writing of history contributed to the homogenization process so prominent in the nation-state environment. Each nation-state saw itself in the center of the stage of history, and chronicles were written accordingly. As dominant peoples continued to write from this viewpoint, they became less and less able to discern the presence, even in their immediate theater of history, of any other peoples besides themselves, except as temporary obstacles to their own dominance, as disappearing remnants, or as persisting, backward peoples unworthy to be regarded as in the same category with the dominant nation.

The standardization of history was a destructive process, eliminating from the sphere of historical knowledge hundreds of peoples who, equally with the dominant peoples, had histories. It was more destructive than was the standardization of language, because it removed from general view cultural wholes, not just one aspect of a culture.

There is nothing surprising in the fact that language and law became set in the mold of dominant peoples. They were fundamentally involved in practical considerations closely connected with the difficult problems of managing large numbers of people to achieve common purposes. Taxation and the administration of courts, for example, required common means of communication and common procedures. If such means were not developed, chaos or, at best, infinitely slow and uncertain measures would result. Standard vocabularies and legal procedures were developed by nation-states much as the ancient empires had developed them; Roman Law and the Latin language, for example, were diffused over the whole of Europe under the Roman Empire. It is true, also, that we can learn little or nothing, except from Roman records in Latin, of the histories of the many peoples of Europe during the long era of Roman domination. These records give us the Roman view of the Teutons, the Franks, and other European peoples. It was not the habit of Roman writers of histories to interview native leaders and incorporate the results into the histories and chronicles that they wrote. In these ways, the processes of government bred similar results in nation-states as had been apparent in the old empires. No doubt they gave rise, also, to a similar ethnocentrism and its accompanying blindness to the realities of subject peoples and their affairs. Nevertheless, the qualities that differentiated the nation-states from the ancient empires were important and must be dwelt on if we are to gain an understanding of the era in human history through which we have been passing during the twentieth century.

A region under the control of Rome was characterized by scattered administrative centers. In these, the practical concerns of tribute-taking and military administration proceeded according to Roman tradition in the Latin language. The administrative centers inevitably became centers for the diffusion of administrative and military aspects of Roman culture, along with other such practical matters as engineering methods. They were also centers for the diffusion of more intimate ways of life, because, of course, Romans lived in those centers and built their own kind of houses and baths, dressed in the Roman way, and so on. Subjects of Rome outside the administrative centers and cities began to emulate the Romans; this was not a matter of forcible imposition. The result was a very different sort of political and social environment from that created by the nation-state.

The nation-state in its ultimate, ideal form, attained in most of its manifestations by the nineteenth century, sought a cultural uniformity never conceived by the Roman Senate, by Roman consuls, or by any other Roman officials. The diversity of peoples was an accepted fact of the Empire. Dress was different, speech was different, local government was whatever it was but surely not Roman. People might seek to imitate Roman ways in their daily lives outside the Roman cities, but that was their affair. In contrast, we may take the development of the nation-state in Western Europe in what we may call its purest form just before, and during, the 1700s.

The nation-state attained its most characteristic form in France and perhaps under the Bourbon monarchs, but it was not confined to the monarchy variant. The same traditions of government were adopted by the leaders of the French Revolution and, following that phase, by Napoleon, who spread over the whole of Europe those governmental tendencies that had been perfected in France. All the varieties of the nation-state, including the American ones, ultimately partook of this ideal type to some degree. The basic assumptions of the nation-state had led to the high valuation of a greatly centralized political structure. It was embodied in its most perfected form in the Napoleonic codes, where it took the extreme form toward which the nation-state everywhere had been tending. With Napoleon's disappearance, the basic centralized political and administrative structural principles by no means disappeared. They continued in somewhat different forms appropriate to the regional traditions wherever the nation-state spread.

The division of the territory of a nation-state into "departments," or whatever they might be called, by drawing lines on a map, epitomized the structural principles. Each department was imposed on the peoples of the state, and its boundaries bore only the vaguest relationship, if any at all, to the boundaries of nations as peoples of those nations had experienced them for centuries. The departments were imposed for purposes of uniform, and what was thought would be efficient, administration. The conception of efficiency was that of central government officials rooted in a principle of administration, namely, the convenience to them of uniform rules and regulations. The face of the nation-state was now pictured in terms of areas conceived with reference to the purposes of a central government; the divisions were arbitrary, however, insofar as the needs and interests of the people composing the departments or districts were concerned. It was in this conception of a state as a homogeneous mass of individuals that the epitome of the nation-state as a human environment was achieved.

The departmental state did not stay clear of aspects of peoples' lives other than the strictly administrative, as had the ancient empires. Perhaps an important factor in the tendency of the state to move into all aspects of life was the Christian background of the nation-state in Europe. The Romans believed in a cult of the state, but this was not a religion embracing all aspects of life, and it was merely added by the Romans as one more cult to all the forms of religious expression that they encountered in the Empire. Moreover, in Rome itself there was no uniformity of religious life. "Religion" was a diversity of viewpoints and practices. In the nation-state, however, things were different. The whole tendency, as we have seen, was toward uniformity not only of administrative procedure but also of language and of worldview, as expressed in, for example, history. Starting from a simple and to-be-expected ethnocentric worldview, as expressed in the dominant nation's writing of its own history, the nation-state moved steadily toward an all-embracing policy of standardization of language, historical knowledge, and worldview. The tendency was expressed not only in these aspects of culture but also in literature, in theology, and in philosophy. By the late nineteenth century, most nation-states were thinking about, if they had not already instituted, centralized school systems, either administered from a "national" capital or regionally managed, with content designed by teachers centrally educated in "normal schools." There was variation, but, essentially, school systems, as conceived and established in the nation-state, were vehicles for the dissemination of a common culture. They were a culminating expression of the tendency toward standardization that we have traced through language, law, and history, and they were promulgated in the name of and with the aid of the symbols of the nation-state.

This condition came about not without impact on what one might have expected would remain most aloof and remote, namely, centers of higher learning. By the early nineteenth century, philosophy itself had taken the nation-state to its bosom and developed its dominating tendency as a fundamental principle of the human mind and destiny. This was most apparent in Germany, which was still in the process of building a strong nation-state along the strictest lines of that now-triumphant conception. German philosophy began to provide intellectual foundations and guidance for the growth of the nineteenth-century Prussian nation-state. One of the philosophers who developed the philosophical basis for the concept of the nation-state and the template for the Prussian variety was Georg Wilhelm Friedrich Hegel (1770–1831). Fully accepting the process of conquest as the basis for the nation-state, past and future, Hegel offered a conception of the state as the ideal human environment. There was no mistaking that he was talking about the nation-state and accepting as his model the form it had attained in Europe by the early nineteenth century. He saw it in terms of its dominant tendency—that is, as an embodiment of human development to a completely uniform state, with no internal cultural or other kinds of differences. To be sure, he saw the nation-state as developing through a dialectical process of continuous resolution of contradictions, but the entity that so progressed was a homogeneous one that maintained its homogeneity through the dialectical process.

Hegel's state was, of course, not a real entity; it was an ideal creation of the mind; it was the supreme Idea and, therefore, an expression of God. As Hegel developed his view of the state, it was apparent that he was modeling it on the form of the absolutism found in the Prussian monarchy and that he was convinced that that form of the nation-state had come closest to perfection. It simply needed more development in the direction that it had been going. This called for the maximum in centralization and the maximum in homogenization of peoples and cultures. In Hegel, the nation-state found its greatest philosophical spokesman. He appeared at a time when there were notable signs of reaction against the kinds of blindness that the nation- state had engendered. We must take Hegel as a sign of the times, of the beginning of the decline of the nation-state. With no apparent knowledge of the human constituents of nation-states, he proceeded to formulate the nature of the central tendency of the nation-state far more definitely than anyone else. His words removed the nation-state from the arena of human action in which it had been born. They crystallized its inherent character in an ideal realm where it might be quietly contemplated, at the same time that it was being transformed into something new and different in the real world.

A major result in those nation-states that moved in the direction set by their dominant orientations was an insulation against reality. We will speak of this condition as cultural blindness. It profoundly affected the dominant nation, the one that controlled the operations of the state. In the extreme cases, it led to a total inability on the part of members of the dominant nation to perceive the existence of any but themselves within the state. Other people might be seen as poor copies of themselves, in need only of the proper influences, whether through schools or other means, for changing them from inferiors to acceptable citizens of the state. Ways for changing peoples so perceived were developed in various nation-states during the nineteenth century. One of the most comprehensive cultural assimilation systems was that set up by the United States for transforming American Indians into members of the middle-class white society. It took decisive form in the 1880s and was applied promptly to the more than 150 culturally different Indian groups. The measures were based on assumptions about which those in control of the state had no doubts whatsoever. The methods used for transforming Indians—the severing of relations between parents and children, the enforcement of schooling, the breaking up of local communities, and the replacement of religion and language, among other measures—were believed to be obvious and necessary steps to a desirable end. What the Indians might have had, if anything, in the way of their own kind of life, was rated as worthless and dying, if not dead. The valuation of existing Indian culture was totally negative, and, therefore, it was only just and right that Indians be provided with the culture of the dominant people. The application of these measures seemed especially easy because of the smallness and powerlessness of the Indian groups. They were brought entirely under the control of the dominant people through the reservation, or land control, system. If any dominant people's program of cultural assimilation could have worked, this should have been it. Yet, it did not work, even though it was applied unswervingly for more than fifty years, and less rigorously for another fifty. The colossal failure of this program for realizing cultural homogeneity must go down in history as the ultimate in products of cultural blindness. The remarkable story of the American dominant nation's failed program emerges in the history of many American Indian peoples.

The Problem of the State

In our review of human experience during the era of the nation-state, we must accustom ourselves to the adoption of a standpoint that removes us from the limitations of seeing, or failing to see, things only from the angle of the dominant nations. This is not an easy frame of reference to adopt, because for centuries our worldview has been dominated by the writers of history, the users of language, and the judgment of laws as developed by the dominant nations of the nation-states. Where they have accustomed us to speak and think in terms of the "Irish question" in Britain, the "Negro problem" and the "Indian problem" in the United States, and the "Jewish problem" everywhere but in Israel, we must attempt to ask questions about the "English question," the "white problem," and the "Gentile problem." It is only by combining the viewpoints of dominant and nondominant peoples that we can penetrate the cocoons of confusion that have been woven around these most vital problems of mankind.

An Interview with Jack Salzman, Director of the Columbia University Center for American Culture Studies

Karl Kroeber

KK: Let me begin by asking you to explain the rather odd title of your Center for American Culture Studies.

JS: The primary significance of the title is to distinguish the American Studies we practice from more traditional American Studies. We focus on interrelations of various cultures that make up the United States by providing a forum through which each of these can display its particular forms of expression.

KK: You don't believe in the melting pot?

Besides regular academic offerings, an extensive publishing program, and residencies for artists and writers, the Center for American Culture Studies, under the leadership of its founding director, Professor Jack Salzman, has sponsored more than sixty public programs focusing on issues of race and ethnicity. Of these, a dozen have centered on, or have significantly involved, Native Americans and their concerns. I interviewed Professor Salzman to elicit his special perspective on Indians in their relation to both urban problems (a majority of Native Americans now live in cities) and current debates about multicultural curricula.

JS: We question the validity of the concept of the melting pot, if you define the melting pot as producing one big stew in which everything is assimilated and loses its distinctive characteristics. But the Center isn't founded on simple oppositionalism. Because we explore American society in ways that traditionally haven't been used doesn't imply that other approaches are useless or obsolete. We try not simply to replicate what goes on in classrooms or what universities have seen as their traditional academic functions; we raise questions and pose issues that normally get bypassed. We test, for example, the possibility of enabling the academic community and the larger public community to work together in addressing public policy matters affecting the many diverse groups and peoples making up New York City. To the degree that we're successful, perhaps we can be a model for analogous centers in other places. As you know, I've been abroad a good deal advising on that, because the British, French, and Germans are very interested in our structure.

KK: My interest, and the reason for this conversation, is that, though its focus is New York City, the Center has not ignored Native Americans. Is that symptomatic of the Center's unusual approach?

JS: I'd say so. Many of the traditional divisions in American Studies are artificial. There may not be as many Native Americans in New York City as in the western states, but there are, for example, museums here with large collections of Indian materials. I know you remember our program on the return of relics and skeletons.

KK: That bringing together of Indians and museum directors was impressive—particularly because of the extraordinary number of Indians who came here, many of whom spoke so effectively.

JS: Especially because so many people in the audience, including university people, had never had the opportunity to see and hear Indians making their case for themselves. As you know, one of our poets in residence was a Native American, and we've had quite a few Indian artists and writers working and talking here. We hope the Center can, in the future, address the simple, but overwhelming, fact that not only were Indians genocidally attacked in the past but now they don't exist.

KK: They claim they are flourishing.

JS: Physically—numerically—that's true. Even so, they are now perhaps even more excluded than ever from the conception of what America is for people in power. Take George Bush, for example: His rhetoric so completely eliminates Indians. For him, Native Americans are the Puritans. Bush adopts the language of the Puritans, the language of morality: America will bring morality to the world, because we are enacting God's goodness.

In this rhetoric of white messianic control, there isn't any place for history—such as who owned the land in the first place. We will bring a new world order of righteousness and goodness. I think this comes about because, as such writers as Gabriel García Márquez and Carlos Fuentes insisted, the United States largely exists as a product of the European imagination. The European immigrants imagined what America was going to be for them. Their fantasies were not always fulfilled, of course; but many people found America providing what they wanted, or what they came to believe they wanted. Whatever that might have been, it consistently excluded Native American cultures.

KK: Is it possible that the violence of the Bush rhetoric reflects an unconscious awareness that such imagination is changing?

JS: That could be. What we see today are immigrants not from Europe but from Latin America and Asia, and, of course, in the last half century we have begun to hear more publicly from African Americans, who were never voluntary immigrants. Many of these "new" Americans, of course, buy into the old imaginings of their European predecessors. Like the earlier immigrants, they destroy their "native" cultures as fast as they can. It is self-genocide, not something that is done to them. But now there are voices among these new and "minority" groups that are arguing against throwing away their original culture. That is the focus of the struggle about multiculturalism. It seems to us that Native Americans are especially relevant to this issue: Does America mean the single, world-powerful new order that Bush claims to speak for, or is America a more complex, even self-conflicted, interplay of diverse cultures, which would include the interaction of native and immigrant?

KK: You make the United States sound a little like the Soviet Union.

JS: There is a connection. Principally, I suppose, they aren't superpowers in the old sense any longer, whatever Bush's rhetoric. But the Soviet situation is the opposite of ours in one way: They have a huge "native" population compared to ours, and not our immigrant tradition.

KK: So how does the Center address multiculturality?

JS: I think we address the issue most simply by providing a place where multiculturalism can be debated and argued in concrete and specific terms. We do that not to arrive at some "objective" view, some academic generalization, but to get people to talk. We particularly want to involve people who belong to at least two "cultures," people who have a vested interest in becoming part of—or resisting—the superculture, people who are engaged in struggles with other cultures or ethnic groups. Such debates and discussions, as I think you've seen, bring a very specific historical past, or pasts, to bear on the present. Or, they show people where they need to know something about history, as when the Koreans on one of our programs during the African American boycott of a Korean produce store in Brooklyn were asking me—asking the Center—to give them information they could translate into Korean on the history of prejudice against African Americans in the United States. That's an example, incidentally, of why I think it is important for centers such as ours to exist. We provide a place where issues can be confronted by people who normally don't enter the consciousness of the academic community.

KK: Do you think that consciousness-raising can have any effect on how we teach literature or on the kind of literature we teach?

JS: Let me suggest just one thing. The Center's activities help put all our arguments about the canon and core curriculum in a more realistic context. If nothing else, it forces us to see those debates within the university as related to what kids are taught, or not taught, in elementary and secondary schools. That should help us to recognize that what we teach and how we teach ought not to be separated from the practical consequences of fulfilling—or not fulfilling—our obligations and responsibilities to the public community.

KK: I'm not sure I see the relationship.

JS: Let me put it this way: The choice of books taught in any course seems to me always to result primarily from political choices and only secondarily from educational choices. The prime responsibility most universities recognize is to give a body of knowledge to the students. That's very different from choosing books to teach students how best to use the minds they have, to teach them how to think. The latter I'd call educational rather than political. All our current discussions about the canon boil down to what body of material ought to be taught, which essentially is a political decision. The political character of our discussions about canon and curriculum—and the importance of *who* has the decision-making power—is unmistakable.

I know I'm saying the obvious, but we often overlook the fact that decisions in universities, as well as in the public schools, are made by committees, which nowadays have to have "representative" voices. Think a moment about how you and I teach literature. Isn't the thing we teach above all else that we speak for no one but ourselves? We represent nobody but ourselves. That's our authority as teachers in a classroom. And we try to get the students to speak the same way, not as representatives of anything, just for themselves.

KK: You're right; that is the way I teach.

JS: I think that "unrepresentativeness" is a major reason some of us care passionately about literature—whether we're reading Jane Austen or Toni Morrison. Most of us ultimately feel somewhat confused about who we are. Great literature always does two things at once. It makes us feel a bit less certain about who we are, and, at the same time, it makes us feel just a little bit better about that uncertainty.

Most core programs or demands for or against a canon are the result of pressure groups insisting that individuals cannot go into a classroom and speak for themselves. Even if you—the teacher—don't see yourself as being a representative voice, you are perceived by others as representative, so the books you assign are representative of an ideological position. Every academic knows that line, but too few have followed it back down to the pre-university level, where its implications stand out clearly. There, the political character of who makes the decision about which books are to be read becomes obvious. The Regents? E. D. Hirsch? Al Sharpton? Whoever they may be, they are not speaking solely for themselves.

And that sets up the intriguing issue of community control. How much curricular power should any "expert" have? Aren't "experts" just representatives of particular political constituencies? So, the question arises: Should parents be allowed to determine what texts ought to be taught? Or, Should parents be denied the right to have a say in the education of their children? In the practical life of pre-university education in a city such as New York, that is an enormously difficult and delicate question. But if we ignore it, as most academics do, our discussions of canonicity become, well, academic—they become socially irresponsible and open the door to people, from Bush to Leonard Jeffries, who *claim* to speak for others. What literature and the teaching of literature ought to foster is the power of speaking only for oneself, which means not letting other people usurp the right to speak for you.

KK: Since you mentioned her, I can't resist saying that Jane Austen's novels are about just that—young women learning to speak for themselves. But you can't teach everything, so the university has to recognize certain practical limits, and that becomes the basis of canons and core curricula.

JS: You are absolutely right. If you want to talk about what ought to be in a core curriculum today, you should start with the practical problems, not the abstractions. At Columbia, as at most other universities, there are efforts to "expand the core," to introduce Third World literatures. At the same time, American literature ought to include some notice of Native American literatures. But from what you tell me, study of Native American literatures is very complicated. There are a hell of a lot of them!

KK: Three to five hundred.

JS: And they function in ways that are strange to us. Just the fact that they are oral literatures makes them difficult for us, leaving aside problems of translation and the rest. But there is also important African American writing, the Asian literatures, and so on, and so on. How can one possibly deal adequately with any of these, let alone with all of these, on top of the tradition of Western European literature? If we really mean what we say about the importance of recognizing our world to be multicultural, we have to face the fact that maybe four years for an undergraduate education aren't enough any longer.

KK: But four years of current tuition rates surely are!

JS: Exactly. Yet, we must avoid the simplistic views of a Roger Kimball or an Allan Bloom, on the one hand, and the trend toward tokenism, on the other. Any discussion of what we teach that doesn't start with the practical difficulties of taking into account the true complexity of our multicultural society—and, of course, I haven't even mentioned the need to provide an increasingly important scientific education—is idle and irresponsible. I don't know of any of our professional academics who genuinely have confronted this problem.

KK: How does the Center help us confront it?

JS: Very quietly, I'm afraid. By holding the programs we do, the Center tries to get the academic community to face the facts and difficulties of living in a multicultural society. By doing that, we try to get academics to recognize that they increasingly are talking to themselves and among themselves in ways that have very little relation to the reality of the lives of most citizens in this country outside the academy, which leaves the field open to the Bushes and the Sharptons. By focusing on multicultural issues, we try to make connections between the university and the real lives of people who don't belong to the academic community.

KK: Is there any way in which the Native American situation has a distinctive role to play in that connecting?

JS: The answer to that, of course, is that every group is distinctive and contributes in a particular way. But—and you know more about this than I do—my sense is that American tribal peoples were, and still are, quite ethnocentric.

KK: That's true.

JS: Therefore, a major issue today is what can be the nature and contribution of pan-Indianism.

KK: I think that's the central problem facing Native Americans five hundred years after Columbus. It's a major mistake of people who speak about Native Americans as if their situation were exactly equivalent to, say, that of African Americans.

JS: That supports what we see every day at the Center. Any single model is inadequate for American multiculturalism. Yet, still, here we all are interacting together. One sees what I'm tempted to call an equivalent of the ethnocentrism of the Indians in the way in which people belonging to different groups, national, ethnic, whatever, are not only ignorant of other peoples but even happily ignorant. What first astounded me here was the lack of interest that people in various ethnic communities have in other ethnic communities. If I do a panel, whether fairly low-keyed or high-powered, let us say on the African American community, the audience will be, for the most part, African Americans. There will be very few Hispanics, very few Asians. If I do a panel on Asian Americans, almost no one who is not Asian American will show up. We use terms such as *discourse* and *dialogue* all the time, but, in fact, there seems to be relatively little interest in dialogue between and among various communities.

This has made me think about my own life, growing up in a quasi-ghetto, Williamsburg, in Brooklyn. It wasn't until my late teens that I realized there was any reason to think of it as a ghetto. One tends to take one's culture for granted as the standard. If somebody is a Sioux or a Navajo and thinks that is the best culture in the world, fine. But it seems to me that that person will be a better Sioux or Navajo if he or she develops a better understanding of how Sioux or Navajo culture differs from—or is like—other cultures. It is that kind of understanding that makes a person not representative of, but an individual in, a particular cultural group.

That can't happen without conversation, at least, between and among communities—not just between a so-called minority and the dominant cultural group. Getting such conversations going is harder than most academics realize. When I was nineteen or twenty years old, I was dating Cecily, who is now my wife, and one of her uncles took us to a Chinese restaurant. I had never been in a Chinese restaurant. I ordered an egg-salad sandwich. Cecily's uncle looked at me with absolute horror. All he knew was that I was Jewish and from a fairly religious family. But when I looked at the menu in that Chinese restaurant, I had no idea what to do with it, and—this is the important part—I didn't want to find out. I lived in a world so circumscribed that I had no reason to think that I ought to want to know something like that.

That's just a trivial story about my foolishness, but I find remembering it a good antidote to the disturbing professionalism of so many academics who claim to be concerned about otherness. It is difficult, to say the least, to see what the jargon-laden obsession with theory—will we ever get away from the influence of Foucault, Derrida, and Lacan?—has to do with the lives of the diverse peoples of our country, many, maybe most, of whom have to struggle just to survive. If the Center does nothing other than challenge some of the current academic pretense, it will do good service to lots of Americans—including native ones.

The Navajo Nightway and the Western Gaze

William Overstreet

On a Saturday night after the first frost has settled over the high desert, turning the cottonwoods and aspens in the washes and along the streams to golds and yellows, and after the rainy season has ended, the lightning no longer threatening to break the afternoons open, the snakes no longer likely to emerge from the rocks until next spring, on such a night you can follow the red taillights of the pickup trucks and gas-guzzlers and vans down a well-traveled dirt road, such as the one heading south from Black Hat, New Mexico, just past the Pittsburg and Midway strip mine, which is lit spectrally by the floodlights on the crane and cab of a massive shovel that chews up the ground in truck-size gulps. You can trace the red taillights for mile after mile, eating dust, dodging ruts carved into what only weeks ago had been tractionless mud, your car now bouncing along roadbeds that resemble corrugated roofing more than roads, until ahead you see the glow cast against the stark blue sky by piñon and cedar bonfires, and off to the

Book Reviewed: James C. Faris, *The Nightway: A History and a History of Documentation of a Navajo Ceremonial* (Albuquerque: University of New Mexico Press, 1990); this work is hereafter cited as *NW*.

side of the road, amid the bare brown clumps of rabbitbrush, saltbush, and sagebrush, the gathered Navajo, hundreds of them. Leaving your car behind, you follow the beam of your flashlight across the rugged ground and join the crowd massed about the line of Yei, the masked impersonators of Holy People, as they chant in their eerie falsetto and dance in the firelight.

As the night wears on, gets colder deep in the high desert (you're at well over six thousand feet elevation here), and as your breath begins to materialize, spiritlike, in gray clouds on this, the last night of a nine-day Nightway, a burly Navajo standing beside you under the startlingly bright Milky Way feeds one of the bonfires, which has been pleasantly toasting your legs through your pants and long johns. Meanwhile, three or more alternating teams of dancers, six male Yei and sometimes a parallel line of six female Yei (often accompanied by the mischief-making Water Sprinkler), have continued the repetitive dance, illuminated by the fires and, overhead, a string of bare light bulbs suspended from rough-hewn wooden poles. The Navajo men watch in their cowboy hats or caps, waist-length jackets, jeans, and cowboy boots. The younger women and girls tend to favor jeans and parkas and Reeboks, while many of the grandmothers, the gray-haired *sáaniisání* (old women folks), are draped in their traditional long skirts and in multicolored Pendleton shawls and blankets. Most of the People stand silently or chat quietly. Others sit in lawn chairs or on logs covered by old folded rugs and blankets. Off to the side, Navajo entrepreneurs man makeshift concession stands, where they sell coffee, burgers, styrofoam bowls of mutton stew with posole, fry bread, and Navajo tacos.

Maybe a handful of other Anglos, *bilagáanas*, have found their way to this Yei Bichei, drawn by word of mouth or a roughly lettered sign that appeared, a day or two earlier, by the side of the main road to Gallup. You don't feel unwelcome here, but you can't help feeling apart, an outsider at this healing ceremonial, on the last night of which, if over the preceding eight days all the prayers and songs have been performed correctly by the medicine man and his assistants, and if the proper words have been spoken and prayersticks offered and sand paintings created on the floor of the hogan, the Holy People are inevitably drawn to sanctify the healing process, the restoration to mental and physical health, to a sense of balance and harmony and completeness—to *hózhǫ́*—of the person for whom this Nightway is being offered. It will go on until near dawn, when the final prayer will be offered, the final song sung.

This is as much of the Nightway, the *Yé'ii Bicheii*, as most Anglos ever see, and one can easily forget that it is a *curing* ceremonial for a range of ailments that includes paralysis, blindness, hearing loss, and mental disturbances.[1] It is in this context—one of superficial public knowledge, one of not knowing—that James C. Faris's recent work on the Nightway, the first extended research on the ceremonial in nearly half a century, may serve not so much as a starting point as a turning point in our understanding of the Nightway, and perhaps of *hózhǫ*.[2]

For a ceremonial of such significance, and with the events of the final night of the Yei Bichei having been mentioned so frequently in newspapers,

1. The Navajo word for the Nightway ceremonial is *Tł'éé'jí*, but it is also frequently called *Na'akai* or *Yé'ii Bicheii*. The English appropriation of the latter name has been rendered in countless ways: Yehbechai, Yebitsai, Ye-Be-Chai, Yei-bet-chei, etc. Robert W. Young and William Morgan, Sr., in *The Navajo Language: A Grammar and Colloquial Dictionary*, 2d ed. (Albuquerque: University of New Mexico Press, 1987), prefer "Yei Bichei"; where it seems helpful to cite Navajo words, transcription will be according to Young and Morgan's orthography except where direct quotation requires other forms.

Often among Anglos, Yei Bichei is used to refer just to the final night of the Nightway, when Talking God (*Haashch'ééłti'í*), the grandfather (*bicheii*) of the Yei (*Yé'ii*)—otherworldly beings, "fearful ones"—presides over ceremonies that include dancing by masked Yei impersonators. Neither the Yei nor the Holy People are "supernatural." In traditional Navajo thought, all natural phenomena—animals, plants, rocks, mountains, the sun, the cardinal directions, etc.—have inner animated presences; the Holy People (*Diné diyinii*), of whom the Yei are one form, are such spirit-force-people: invisible, in-dwelling, powerful, potentially dangerous, but most often either indifferent or benevolent toward the Earth-Surface People (*Nihookáá dine'é*).

2. Many abstract concepts crucial to Navajo are not easily translated into English. Gary Witherspoon discusses *są'ah naagháí bik'eh hózhǫ*, or as it more commonly appears, simply *hózhǫ*—a concept that Navajos consistently identify as central to their thought—in "Language and Reality in Navajo World View," in *Handbook of North American Indians*, vol. 10, ed. Alfonso Ortiz (Washington, D.C.: Smithsonian Institution, 1983), 570–78 (subsequent references to articles in the *Handbook* will be abbreviated *HNAI*). *Są'ah* derives from the past tense of "to grow, to mature" and "refers to the completion of the life cycle through death of old age." *Naagháí*, a form of the verb "to go"—of which there are some 356,200 distinct inflected forms in Navajo—"refers to continually going about and returning," "to the continuous reoccurrence of the completion of the life cycle." *Hózhǫ* encompasses "concepts such as beauty, perfection, harmony, goodness, normality, success, well-being, blessedness, order, and ideal." In sum, "The goal of Navajo life in this world is to live to maturity in the condition described as *hózhǫ*, and to die of old age, the end result of which incorporates one in the universal beauty, harmony, and happiness described as *są'ah naagháí bik'eh hózhǫ*" (571–73). The ethnographer Gladys Reichard and others have suggested that *hózhǫ* represents the end toward which supernaturals, time, space, and nature, as well as man, tend, and perhaps "the utmost achievement in order" (see Gladys Reichard, *Navaho Religion: A Study of Symbolism* [Princeton: Princeton University Press, 1970], 45).

popular magazines, and guidebooks, scholarly documentation of the Nightway remains surprisingly sparse. On the other hand, it shouldn't seem *that* surprising, given that much about Navajo history in general remains conjectural. Most archaeologists and anthropologists place the Navajo in the Southwest shortly before the Spanish arrival in the first half of the sixteenth century. Others, however, including many Navajo, have argued for their presence in the Four Corners area dating back to A.D. 1000 or earlier, before the abandonment of the great Anasazi cities—Chaco Canyon and Mesa Verde, for example—in roughly 1200–1300; some have contended that Navajo raids contributed to the disappearance of the large Anasazi communities, but that interpretation fell into scholarly disfavor early in this century.[3]

The conventional view has also been that while many Navajo ceremonial practices derive from rites performed by their Athapaskan ancestors, many can be traced to, or were adapted after contact with, the Pueblo peoples. There can be no argument that the Hopi, Zuni, and other Pueblo tribes profoundly affected Navajo agriculture and culture, especially during the period after the 1680 Pueblo Revolt against the Spanish, when many small groups of Pueblos lived with bands of Navajo to escape Spanish retribution for having slain so many missionaries. But, Faris cautions, this orthodox view derives, to the detriment of the Navajo, at least in part from "very powerful Western conventions of Navajo and Pueblo relations, of the inscription of savagery and civilization, and of the tropes of nomadism and sedentation, and the mechanisms by which some views are dismissed and others are privileged" (*NW*, 18).[4]

The problem is that very little archaeological evidence exists—and its interpretation remains in dispute—for placing the Navajo in the Southwest before the 1400s, and Faris, while legitimately calling for the question to be reexamined, offers no convincing rebuttal except his conviction that

3. For a brief summary of Navajo prehistory, see David M. Brugge, "Navajo Prehistory and History to 1850," in *HNAI*, 489–501.
4. Faris's cautionary comments about orthodoxy in interpreting Navajo-Pueblo interrelations are reinforced by picking up virtually any book-length history of the Navajo written before, say, 1970. See, for example, the once highly regarded and still widely available history by Ruth Underhill, *The Navajos*, rev. ed. (Norman, Okla.: University of Oklahoma Press, 1967), especially the first seven chapters, which cover the same period as Brugge's essay. A reader can't help noticing her reliance on the "conventions" and "inscriptions" to which Faris refers.

Navajo views of their preliterate past should be weighed more heavily.[5] Preliterate time frames are, of course, notoriously unreliable according to social-scientific standards. As many anthropologists and ethnographers have noted, oral traditions frequently collapse decades and even centuries into far shorter time frames. In the case of the Navajo, for example, the many versions of their origin myth and many of their ceremonials, including the Nightway, contain references not only to topographical features of the Southwest but to maize and domesticated sheep, neither of which the Navajo possessed prior to contact with the Pueblo peoples and the arrival of the Spanish, respectively.[6] To date, anyway, no one has proposed how to differentiate between those elements of Navajo-told chronology that reflect a linear (Western) history and those that reflect a process of accretion, revision, adoption, adaptation.

Even after the appearance of the Spanish and then, in 1846, the Americans, little documentation about Navajo ceremonialism exists. Faris dates the first account of a Yei dance, held at Zuni Pueblo, to late 1881, while the first published description of a full Nightway, by James Stevenson, appeared in 1891; Stevenson's summary remains, in Faris's estimation, the best account of a single Yei Bichei. By that time, Washington Matthews, a physician, had already completed the research that led in 1902 to the publication of his classic *The Night Chant: A Navaho Ceremony*, which continues to be regarded as the most thoroughly detailed—although necessarily incomplete—composite version of the ceremonial. Subsequent accounts include those of Edward S. Curtis, in the first volume (1907) of his twenty-volume *The North American Indian*; Alfred Tozzer (1909), who may be largely responsible for general acceptance of the notion that many features of Navajo ceremonialism were borrowed or adapted from Pueblo tribes; and Clyde Kluckhohn (1923), whose description, Faris claims, plagiarizes the work of Stevenson and an unpublished account by Brother Simeon Schwemberger (1905). Stevenson, Tozzer, and Kluckhohn offer the only extensive firsthand accounts of an individual Nightway, while Matthews, Curtis, and Father Berard Haile (1947, but largely based on research

---

5. Faris presents, in passing, an etymological claim, translating the Navajo word *'anaasází* as "enemies of the old ones" (*NW*, 24)—that is, presumably, enemies of the old Navajo—rather than the more conventionally accepted translation of "ancient ones." I suspect Faris might agree that debatable derivations offer limited insight.
6. Paul G. Zolbrod, *Diné Bahane'* (Albuquerque: University of New Mexico Press, 1984), offers the most complete version of the Navajo creation story.

notes from the first decade of the century) have written generalized compilations of Nightway practices and materials.[7] Although more recent research has been done on specific aspects of the Nightway—prayers, songs, origins, material culture, and so on—most later work has been secondary, analytical, or interpretive, trying, for example, to fold the Nightway into a Jungian or structuralist or functionalist framework. It is precisely the theoretical underpinnings of much of this analytical work that Faris questions in his commentary. I'll have more to say about this later.

• • • •

The principal purpose of Faris's book is to make available Nightway materials that have not been published before, including the complete text of the Nightway origin story told by the medicine man (*hataałii*: chanter, singer) Hosteen Klah and twenty-two sand painting reproductions from three other Nightway medicine men: Slim Curly, Red Woman's Son, and, most importantly, Speech Man. The most comprehensive version of

7. Faris cites Edward Sutherland, "The Diaries of John Gregory Bourke: Their Anthropological and Folkloric Content" (diss., University of Pennsylvania, 1964), as the source for the 1881 date. The other references in this paragraph are as follows: James Stevenson, "Ceremonial of Hasjelti Dailjis and Mythical Sand Painting of the Navajo Indians," *Bureau of American Ethnology Eighth Annual Report, 1886–1887* (Washington, D.C.: GPO), 229–85; Washington Matthews, *The Night Chant: A Navaho Ceremony*, Publications of the Hyde Southwestern Expedition, Memoirs of the American Museum of Natural History, whole ser. vol. 6 (Anthropology ser. vol. 5), (1902; reprint, New York: AMS Press, 1978); Alfred M. Tozzer, "Notes on Religious Ceremonials of the Navaho," in *Anthropological Essays Presented to Frederic Ward Putnam in Honor of His 70th Birthday* (New York: G. E. Stechert, 1909), 299–343; Edward S. Curtis, "The Night Chant," in *Selected Writings of Edward S. Curtis: Excerpts from Volumes I–XX of "The North American Indian,"* ed. and introd. Barry Gifford (Berkeley: Creative Arts Book Company, 1976), 29–36; Clyde Kluckhohm [*sic*], "The Dance of Hasjelti," *El Palacio* 15 (1923): 187–92; Berard Haile, *Head and Face Masks in Navaho Ceremonialism* (1947; reprint, New York: AMS Press, 1978), 40–76. Faris's statement that Kluckhohn plagiarized from Stevenson and Schwemberger appears on page forty of *NW*; he subsequently cites twenty-seven instances of "verbatim copies" from Stevenson (*NW*, 69) but also notes that Kluckhohn's attendance at the Nightway was apparently "the final episode in a summer adventure" and that the resultant essay—his first publication—was written before Kluckhohn became a trained anthropologist (*NW*, 47). Since this essay was written, Schwemberger's account, accompanied by some two dozen of the four dozen photographs he took of events surrounding a Nightway held at St. Michaels, Arizona, in November 1905, has been published in Paul V. Long, *Big Eyes: The Southwestern Photographs of Simeon Schwemberger, 1902–1908* (Albuquerque: University of New Mexico Press, 1992), 41–75.

the Nightway's origin, the Klah text was taken down in English transcription only, handwritten in three notebooks totaling about 188 pages; it was retold and shortened to twelve printed pages by Mary C. Wheelwright and initially published in 1938, some ten years after being transcribed.[8] The eleven Slim Curly sand painting reproductions, from the Father Berard Haile Collection at the Museum of Northern Arizona in Flagstaff, were painted in the mid-1930s, perhaps by one or more Franciscans, based on rough sketches drawn under Slim Curly's supervision. The six Red Woman's Son reproductions, from the Robert C. Euler Collection of the Museum of Northern Arizona, were apparently based on old crayon sketches used by Red Woman's Son and reproduced between 1949 and 1950 by Elsie Spangler, an artist, with the assistance of Robert Euler, then an anthropology student. The other five sand paintings, attributed by Faris primarily to Speech Man, constitute the earliest known Navajo-made reproductions, dating from 1902–1905; they were obtained from the Father Berard Haile Collection of the University of Arizona Library's Special Collections. As reproduced in Faris's book, the five Speech Man sand paintings are wonderfully vibrant and dynamic, avoiding the rigid geometric precision apparently imposed on the other reproductions by the Anglo copiers.

If *The Nightway* contained only the Klah text and the sand painting reproductions, it would still constitute a valuable resource for Navajo studies, but Faris also includes detailed charts as well as text documenting the "Euro-American history of the Nightway" (*NW*, 3) from the 1880s on, and a chapter tracing the genealogies and apprenticeships of Nightway medicine men beginning in the 1860s, a task for which Faris interviewed all living Nightway medicine men.[9] In addition, Faris has written a chapter on

8. Hosteen Klah, *Tleji or Yehbechai Myth. Retold in Shorter Form from the Myth by Mary C. Wheelwright*, House of Navajo Religion [subsequently renamed the Museum of Navajo Ceremonial Art and then the Wheelwright Museum of the American Indian], Bulletin no. 1 (Sante Fe, 1938). Other versions of the Nightway origin story can be found in, for example, Matthews's *The Night Chant*, 159–212, and Edward Sapir and Harry Hoijer's *Navaho Texts* (Iowa City, Iowa: Linguistic Society of America, 1942), 136–259.
9. The chapter on the *hataałii* was coauthored by Linda Hadley, a former director of the Rough Rock Demonstration School's Training School for Medicine Men and Women, which was started in 1969 with support from the National Institutes of Mental Health but then was forced to close when the Reagan administration canceled the funding. Mrs. Hadley also served as Faris's translator during many of the conversations with the medicine men.
    I had the privilege of meeting Mrs. Hadley quite by accident in February 1991 in the waiting room of a Gallup automobile dealership where my car was getting an oil change

ceremonial material culture, especially Nightway medicine bundles (*jish*)—
bags of corn pollen, feathers, stones, rattles, masks, medicinals, ground
pigments, and the like—and how they have been gathered and transmitted, sometimes through generations of medicine men.[10] Of most interest to
the nonspecialist, this chapter charts the history of how various Nightway
masks have been collected by museums and galleries. A similar account-
ing of sand painting reproductions is contained in his chapter "Organizing
Vision," as is a chronology of sand painting photographs. In sum, Faris's
research efforts and attention to detail can hardly be slighted.

For some readers, however, Faris's critical approach may be more
problematic. On the first page of his introduction, he states his intention:
"Details of the ceremonial episodes of this extensive narrative text [Klah]
and of these sand paintings reproductions are vital evidences in one of
the central arguments of this work: that Nightway *practices*—those healing procedures which order, harmonize and re-establish and situate social
relations—*are in local knowledge prior to other concerns*. And it is only
in careful attention to *local beliefs* and *local knowledge* that Navajo conceptions of order and beauty can be understood" (*NW*, 3). In support of
this contention, he adopts a critical stance that he himself characterizes
as "distinctly political" and "polemical." To begin with, he says, "Anthropology does not present, it represents—and in this intellectual motion, great
displacements and distancing occur" (*NW*, 4). Moreover, many of the perspectives that have made the Nightway an object of "anthropological gaze"
over the years have been "largely misplaced or unfortunate—not that they
are necessarily 'incorrect' so much as they are simply so characteristically
Euro-American." They represent an ethnographic tradition that, "despite a
patronizing relativism, succumbed to the speculations and deceits of an
anthropology convinced of its own truths and self-consciously grounded in
Western epistemologies" (*NW*, 5–6). In contrast, his own study, he claims,

> seeks no underlying symbols, no essential themes or even core con-
> cepts, no central metaphor, and no precocious dialogue. There are

and she was having her pickup repaired. We happened to strike up a conversation, and
that was when I first heard of Faris's book. I was looking forward to meeting her again
when she died on 1 October 1991, at Rough Rock, Arizona.
10. The most authoritative work on *jish* is Charlotte J. Frisbie's 627-page *Navajo Medicine
Bundles or "Jish": Acquisition, Transmission, and Disposition in the Past and Present*
(Albuquerque: University of New Mexico Press, 1987). In view of the exhaustive nature
of Frisbie's book, Faris devotes only twelve pages to the subject.

not assumed meanings to be revealed, or rationalist truths to be teased out by appropriate method. It assumes that the Nightway does what Navajo say it does, and in a preliminary fashion examines how people can hold these truths. . . . By examining these truths, of course, this study scrutinizes in ways Navajo would probably not. But it does not do so in any particular brief for an anthropology nor any other Western inscription. It attempts simply to look at a specific knowledge as a knowledge. (*NW*, 6)

Some might find these comments somewhat disingenuous. After all, Faris himself is a professor of anthropology at the University of Connecticut, and his book has been published by one of the largest academic presses in the Southwest. In addition, his work arises from the same critical impulse that, in the poststructuralist era, forged a space for itself in the Euro-American academy by deconstructing other Western blindnesses.[11] The resultant discourses are themselves, of course, "Western inscriptions," even if of a different character than what preceded them. Faris cannot be unaware of all this, although I don't recall his making it explicit in *The Nightway*.

In a sense, Faris hearkens back to the progenitors of Navajo studies (1885–1920). The work of Matthews, Haile, and others was replete with "the inscriptions and historic tropes of Western encounter: vague racism . . . , evolutionist assumptions . . . , and incredible myopia to issues involving social relations, effectivity and self-awareness. But," Faris adds, "they were still remarkably free of developed theoretical baggage and the debris of anthropology's later epistemologies, or at least these were not explicit and did not interfere with the presentation of descriptive material as much as they did later." By the post–World War II period, "careful description and texts drop away and presentations are in aid of establishing some theoretical position or another. The Navajo have ceased to be heard, seen, or certainly felt at all except through dense theory-laden filters" (*NW*, 6). Among those coming under criticism for their "metaphors of social scientific truth" are such noted ethnographers of the Navajo as Mary Wheelwright, Clyde Kluckhohn, and Karl Luckert.

Wheelwright is characterized as a leader in efforts to situate Navajo practices and conceptions within a universal schema, seeing them col-

---

11. As the reader has probably already realized, the term *Western* in the context of Navajo studies is unavoidably loaded with tropes—metonymy, synecdoche, irony, etc. I leave it to the reader to reflect on the meaning of the Western (regional) in the Western (Euro-American) tradition.

lectively as "a prime exemplar of an ideal Jungian system." Such "motions," Faris comments, "are still popular and continue to be attractive to both romantics and humanists" concerned with reducing the "rich logic" of Navajo belief "to but variation and fodder for a truth derived from Western arrogances—even if their motivations are to elevate it" (*NW*, 12). Kluckhohn is described as "the dominant early practitioner" of "a gathering anthropological synthesis—the functionalist hegemony that has characterized anthropological studies of Navajo belief to the present." He, "like most anthropologists, could not admit alternative belief systems on their own terms, but only on anthropological terms (here, rationalist functions [e.g., economic determinism, psychological determinism]), as the Jungians had earlier (and later) admitted them to their own more banal universalist schemes" (*NW*, 13). Luckert is described as descending from a Western epistemology characterized by

> evolutionist inspiration, a sort of Frazerian magic-religion-science continuum popular at the turn of the century. . . . Curiously, this general form of explanation, stemming from comparative religion studies, is still seen in some contemporary work . . . which seems to view Navajo texts and belief as part of a greater whole appropriate to specific stages of development. Perhaps coincidentally, Luckert is in particular one of the leading proponents of a liberal view that continually attempts to support Navajo belief with rational proofs—rather like theologians working out the gynecological technicalities of the Virgin's pregnancy. (*NW*, 11)

Excessive rhetoric aside, Faris has been working toward a central thesis, one that goes a long way toward explaining his insistence on returning priority to the detailed circumstances of the Nightway ceremonial as practiced. Namely, too many anthropologists cannot accept Navajo truths *as* truths and reveal an implicit arrogance in their language: They state that Navajo belief "reflects and symbolizes rather than constitutes, that actions 'express,' that illness is cured 'through symbolic manipulation'" (*NW*, 13).

Perhaps no Western interpretation is more denigrating than the "commonsense" view that the documented success of healing ceremonials such as the Nightway can be explained as psychosomatic curing, faith or symbolic healing, the placebo effect. Faris responds to this presumption by contending that "the Navajo account of *how* and *why* it works is rarely taken seriously, or only in patronizing collapse of the West's inability to fit it into their own project" (*NW*, 11). Leland C. Wyman, who dedicated himself to gathering sand painting reproductions and publishing the texts of numerous Navajo ceremonials (Beautyway, Red Antway, Windway, Mountainway, Blessingway), exemplifies this "collapse" in an essay he wrote late in his career for the Smithsonian's *Handbook of North American Indians*:

> No doubt the Navajo's predisposition to worry over health (it is his "type worry"), exacerbated by the prevalence of actual disease, caused him to combine his religious and medical practices. . . . Curing ceremonials often do cure the patient, especially when the ailment being treated is largely of psychosomatic origin. A few of the procedures in Navajo ceremonials may have actual organic effects, but above all the ceremonials constitute a powerful system of suggestive psychotherapy, which relieves psychosomatic ills and enables the patient to bear organic troubles with more fortitude. . . . Moreover, the psychotherapy extends to all the spectators, while the ceremonial reaffirms the basic tenets of their faith and, by providing a fixed point in an existence of bewildering change, gives them comfort, societal security, and something to hold to in an unstable world.[12]

Questionable assumptions abound: that the Navajo have a "type worry," that this "type worry" is sufficient to explain why traditional Navajo do not distinguish between religion and medicine, that the basis of any "cure" must be "suggestive psychotherapy," that ceremonials help the Navajo collectively buck up in the face of what (for *them*) must be "bewildering" change. Such maddening condescension reveals the misplaced sense of (Western) superiority that Faris rails against.

John R. Farella, writing only a year after Wyman's essay appeared, notes in the preface to his study of Navajo thought, *The Main Stalk*, that while he had originally intended to examine the "psychosocial aspects of illness etiology" among the Navajo, he soon discovered that Navajo considered psychosomatics to be obvious: "They knew that all illness had a psychosocial etiology and, further, they found it trivial."[13] He goes on to

12. Leland C. Wyman, "Navajo Ceremonial System," in *HNAI*, 537–38. In support, Wyman cites a 1942 Kluckhohn essay, "Myths and Rituals: A General Theory," *Harvard Theological Review* 35, no. 1 (1942): 45–79, but he could have cited other works by Kluckhohn, such as his still widely available joint effort with Dorothea Leighton, *The Navaho*, rev. ed. (Cambridge: Harvard University Press, 1962). Kluckhohn and Leighton's research predates World War II, and the sections of their book dealing with psychology may best be read today as a portrait of a previous generation's mindset toward the Navajo rather than as a source of insight into Navajo behavior.

13. John R. Farella, *The Main Stalk: A Synthesis of Navajo Philosophy* (Tucson: University of Arizona Press, 1984), vii; hereafter cited as *MS*.

say that too often observers have viewed preliterate or native systems as belonging to a different—inferior—order of truth and that they have also tended to take what natives say literally: "Natives have been assumed to be fundamentalists. Along with this has gone the assumption that they are cognitively operating at a very literal level. Metaphor, or interpretation, has been the job of the ethnographer and, I think, presumed to be either an entirely different sort of thing than what the native does, or a different level of abstraction than how the native conceptualizes" (*MS*, 8). Partly as a result, the West has often failed to recognize that native observations can be both metaphorically sophisticated and empirical. Farella adds,

> The scientist, the Western epistemologist, and the Navajo philosopher are all saying, "This is the way the universe is"; they are presenting facts and truth, not opinions or beliefs.
>
> Facts or truth are debated, accepted, denied, or modified. They require active participation in the form of judgment on the part of the observer. Beliefs, on the other hand, can be passively collected, but, in doing so, the entire basis of the philosophy (that is, that it is empirical and true) is denied. It is the difference between knowledge as artifact and knowledge as interaction. (*MS*, 7)

And it is toward knowledge as interaction—local truth, local knowledge—that Faris, too, tries to redirect the reader: "To consider [Navajo ceremonial practice] on its own terms requires not only very careful attention to the ceremonial details, prayers and songs, but a commitment to the integrity of local discourse—to accept its subjecthood and its healing potential *in Navajo cognition*, rather than judge its effectivity from a non-Navajo view of how it works as it does" (*NW*, 11).

• • • •

Having established his polemic in opposition to how the Nightway has been recorded and analyzed during most of the twentieth century, Faris directs his argument toward the sand painting reproductions and the Klah text. A Nightway typically incorporates between four and six sand paintings—some comparatively small, though large enough for the patient to sit on a central figure or design, and some big enough, ten to twelve feet in diameter, to cover much of the free floor space of the ceremonial hogan. When it has served its purpose, each sand painting is destroyed, with the medicine man or his assistants disposing of the ground stone, pollen, and any other compositional materials.

The accuracy of any sand painting reproduction, including those of Speech Man, is problematic, given strong proscriptions against their secular use or, for that matter, against recording any aspect of a ceremonial by sketch or tape or photograph. Any such attempt violates the sacred purpose of the ceremonial: to attract the Holy People, whose presence is required to sanctify the cure.[14] At least when it comes to sand paintings, however, the most common—but not the most traditional—view is that making even minor graphic changes serves to evade the dangers of exact re-creation.

In the chapter entitled "Organizing Vision," Faris makes the case that Euro-American statements about Navajo art emphasize functionality— "that is, assumptions of fixed symbolic meanings, of methodologically derived correlations, of art as reflection" (*NW*, 109). Sand paintings do have "a vital aesthetic component, because the creation is an *attraction* and invitation" to the Holy People and employs "many mechanisms of situating and constituting graphically, . . . not unlike the rhetorical mechanisms . . . for songs and prayers. There is elongation, repetition, redundancy, contrast, balance, symmetry, rhythm, coherence, consistency, orientation, elaboration, and direction" (*NW*, 121). Nevertheless, "the activity itself is paramount, the ceremony—the action—carries significance, not the product as such," and, accordingly, "the aesthetics of Nightway sandpaintings . . . cannot be, as in the West, based on the vision of gaze nor the static and fixed and cultivated aesthetic so vital to Western concepts of beauty and value" (*NW*, 120–21).[15]

14. Most Navajo accept that misfortune, including death, may result if sacred materials are misused or reproduced for secular purposes. Nevertheless, as Faris documents, sand paintings and entire ceremonials have been photographed and even filmed. A Nightway recorded in December 1963 near Lukachukai, Arizona, by the American Indian Films Group Project was followed in less than a year by the deaths of three principals—the medicine man, the person sung over, and a still photographer. Others, including Washington Matthews and Father Berard Haile, are believed by some Navajo to have suffered "Yei Bichei sickness," a condition that involves progressive paralysis and blindness. Indeed, some medicine men regard the Nightway as so powerful, and so unsafe if behavior is even inadvertently improper and procedures not precisely followed, that they limit the number of ceremonials they perform in a given year (*NW*, 79). As for the 1963 footage, no detailed analysis has yet been undertaken, according to Faris, and at least some Navajo leaders want it destroyed. Still photographs from the ceremonial have, however, been published, including several that accompany Leland Wyman's essay "Navajo Ceremonial System" (see note 12).

15. Sand painting as an "art" continues to grow in popularity, judging by the stacks of sand paintings found in Southwestern gift shops. Most are knockoffs for the tourist trade, consisting of overly simplified colored-sand designs and figures glued to particle board,

The Klah Nightway text is, even more fundamentally than sand painting reproductions, the object of Western intentions. As Faris points out, all Nightway narrative texts merge with the history of their recording, "for the collection of narrative by non-Navajo establishes a corpus of material which never existed as a unified genre, specific coherent discourse, or certainly not in any regular Navajo practice" (*NW*, 25). Such texts are "artifacts of anthropological insistence"—in the case of the Klah text, Mary Wheelwright's "naively assuming the existence of a unified, single, authoritative, and original 'version' of the Nightway 'myth' " (*NW*, 176–77). In other words, the text, recounting the events of twenty-seven ceremonials (some fragmentary) performed by or under the supervision of the Holy People, is, undeniably, pieced together, a composite, an artificial concatenation of episodes that apparently attempts to relate, perhaps even justify, as many variations in Nightway practice as possible.

All Nightway narratives describe how a young man called the Dreamer, or the Visionary, chances upon and is taught the Nightway ceremonial by the Holy People. He then transmits this knowledge to his brother before leaving his family to dwell with the Holy People. Two points should be clarified. First, one must distinguish between description of an actual Nightway and the Nightway narrative, although there are many parallels in that each Nightway is, in theory and largely in practice, a recapitulation of what the Holy People taught. Second, as far as anyone knows, the Nightway narrative does not belong to the Navajo oral tradition. Of course, individual episodes have been transmitted orally through the generations and have undoubtedly even been performed, but the totalizing character of the Klah text and of other versions of the narrative sets them apart from this tradition. To reiterate, the Klah narrative never existed as a piece until Klah sat down, at Wheelwright's instigation, and began speaking through a translator. As might be expected, the narrative contains little of the repetition, assonance, alliteration, dissonance, and other features usually associated with oral literature:

> After the sweating ceremony they sent a dog messenger to Taos . . .
> on a Rainbow which was around his neck. When he arrived at
> Taos they held a great feast, with thirty-two plates of food and the
> Taos people said that if the dog could eat all these thirty-two plates
> of food they would give him much food to take back with him to the

---

and they bear only passing resemblance to the twenty-two reproductions in Faris's book, let alone to the "real thing."

ceremony and he ate all of it, beginning at one end of the plates and eating until it was all eaten and then he ran around . . . collecting the crumbs. The Taos people said they would send much food which all of them would give and that they would come later to the ceremony, and they gave the dog the food and he went back to the people and gave the gifts and told about his adventures. (NW, 194–95) [16]

This episode, from the fourth day of one of the ceremonials recounted by Klah, is probably as "literary" as the narrative gets. A more typical passage might recount, for example, the making, painting, significance, and disposition of dozens of prayersticks used on a particular day of the ceremony:

The next morning they made eight Keht-Ahns [K'eet'áán] for the four dancers, one black, one blue, one white, and one yellow and the other four were offerings to the Mountain Sheep, white, blue, yellow and black. After this they made eight . . . other Keht-Ahns which were tied together in pairs. These were called Keht-Ahn-Bih-Yah. . . . They were tied together in pairs, one blue Keht-Ahn which was female and one black, the male. They had faces on them and were tied together with four cotton strings with a white eagle tail feather tied to them at the back, and one spruce twig in front and one behind. (NW, 190)

The fact that the Klah narrative has little "literary quality" is, in the most fundamental sense, irrelevant. It is, of course, Faris's contention that the Nightway succeeds as a healing ceremonial precisely because the medicine man and his assistants reproduce the incredibly intricate details, the full range of "situating practices," that have been transmitted through generations of medicine men. (The ceremonial is so complex that the medicine men Faris and Linda Hadley interviewed for The Nightway required between three and fifteen years, and averaged just over seven years, to complete their Nightway apprenticeships [NW, 98]; Hosteen Klah claimed to have studied for over twenty years before performing his first Nightway.) Although narrative episodes can be strung together, "the ability to articulate them in narrative form has little to do with successful Nightway practice" (NW, 29). As others have noted before Faris, most Nightway medicine men know only parts of the narrative "behind" the individual ceremonies. They may learn

16. Note the reference to Taos, which would seemingly place the Navajo in contact with Pueblo people before the Nightway was created. It is unlikely, however, that the ceremony is of such recent origin, and one should keep in mind that Western conceptions of linear time have little bearing on the narrative.

fragments in conjunction with learning the practice, but if the Nightway is performed properly, knowing or not knowing the complete narrative, which is never spoken as such during the ceremonial, has no bearing on the cure.

The whole thrust of Faris's commentary is that anthropologists studying Navajo ceremonials should restore primacy to *practices* rather than focus on elicited texts or concoct synthetic formulations. The fundamental value of the Klah text lies in its wealth of ceremonial detail, not in some virtually shapeless "plot" that fulfills "the Western sociopolitical as well as religious demand for constituting 'myths,' central mandates, archetypes and cardinal themes." Any such "reduction to a rationalist universal not only denies the particular and the integrity of the specific, but also establishes the universality of Navajo social relations from its own assumptions" rather than from the local knowledge of the Navajo themselves (*NW*, 30).

· · · ·

To redirect the reader to the Nightway itself, to its practices and effectivity, to its local truth, Faris has adopted what he has characterized as a political, polemical stance. And *polemical* is certainly the correct term, as evidenced by his word choice, both in criticizing preceding work ("variation and fodder," "banal universalist schemes," "theoretical baggage and . . . debris") and in pushing a particular set of in-vogue terminological buttons: "Western arrogances," "functionalist hegemony," "anthropological gaze," "hegemonic positivist epistemologies" (*NW*, 17), "Euro-American projects of exotic gaze" (*NW*, 11). . . . He even manages to work in single, passing references to Foucault's *Archaeology of Knowledge* and Derrida's *Of Grammatology*. As a result of his lingo, his tone sometimes comes across as unnecessarily strident, his arguments as a bit too facile. This, however, is a relatively minor quibble, even if some readers, especially those with a more traditional orientation toward Navajo studies, may be put off.[17]

On reflection, another difficulty with Faris's central argument emerges. That is, if close attention is paid to Nightway practices, one is apt to find oneself, in John Farella's words, "standing too close to a pointillist painting" (*MS*, 4). Citing Haile's "immense" output, Farella faults that branch of the ethnographic tradition that presents details and fails to perceive "how it all fits together." Superficially, this difference in approaches

---

17. I have one even more minor quibble with *The Nightway*—namely, that it has been sloppily proofread. It is filled with annoying typos, stylistic inconsistencies, and sometimes misplaced words that, fortunately, obscure Faris's meaning on only a few occasions.

would seem to put Faris and Farella at odds, but what is needed, of course, is both a return to the "richness and integrity of each individual action, practice, and ceremonial detail" (*NW*, 14) *and* a sensitive reassessment of how such details coalesce and shape the broader culture. To extend Farella's metaphor, in examining the points of paint/light, one must, at some point, draw back, look at the whole from the right and the left, from across the room, from the doorway to another gallery.

• • • •

In reviewing for the *New Yorker* recent additions to the contemporary collections of the Museum of Modern Art in New York, Adam Gopnik describes an installation by Bruce Nauman that consists of "a darkened room in which video projectors cast enormous, wall-size images of a hairless man who shouts out, in affectless, electronically distorted speech, 'Hit me, hurt me, feed me, eat me!' and 'Sociology!' and 'Feed me, eat me—anthropology!' "[18] For Gopnik, the installation is deliberately farcical, although some critics, he notes, apparently accept "Feed me, eat me—anthropology!" as a valid contribution *to* anthropology. More fundamentally, he sees the Nauman installation and its companion pieces as raising once again the false opposition between the engaged and the aesthetic—between, if you will, the lived fact and the artifact, for this is an opposition played out again and again in all discourses, anthropology as much as art. If, as Gopnik contends, the politics of a Cubist collage—"its insistent reclamation of lived life"—can't be separated from its aesthetics, neither can the lived fact from its artifact, for once the prayersticks have been offered, the sand paintings erased, the prayers and songs repeated, the dance danced, the cure accomplished, we talk in artifacts.

Gopnik goes on to say, "The point in having a domain of art that, in some rough way, you demarcate from other kinds of thinking is not that you believe art to be specially excluded from the world but that you believe there are ways of access to the world which no activity other than art provides."[19] If we replace each occurrence of "art" in Gopnik's sentence with "local knowledge," this, I think, is what Faris might say was covered over and forgotten by ethnographers for much of the twentieth century and what his political, polemical commentary seeks to rediscover on behalf of the Navajo. Giving priority to local knowledge, or local truth, becomes "an

18. Adam Gopnik, "Empty Frames," *New Yorker*, 25 Nov. 1991, 116.
19. Gopnik, "Empty Frames," 118–19.

insistent reclamation of lived life," both providing a way of access to the world that no other activity offers and offering to a revitalized anthropology the chance to bear witness to the Nightway's search for balance, harmony, completeness, order, beauty.

Postscript

There's a postcard for sale at the Navajo Nation Museum in Window Rock, Arizona, that reproduces one of Edward Curtis's photographs, taken in 1904 (Figure 1).[20] The portrait carries the name recorded by Curtis— *Haschógan*, or Navajo House God, though today the more common English name for *Haashch'éé'ooghaan* is Calling God. The photograph, courtesy of the Library of Congress, is one in a series of "Edward Curtis Indian Classics" published by Beautyway of Flagstaff, which is identified on the back of the postcard as "Cooperative Publisher with Museums, Parks, and Travel Organizations." In small print running vertically up the middle of the back of the card (which was printed in Hong Kong), one reads, "Small Prints to Send, Give, Frame or Hang As Is." A brief explanatory note says, "Edward Sheriff Curtis is without peer as the photographic chronicler of the fading ways of the native North American. For thirty years, 1898 to 1928, he traveled the Plains, Southwest, Northwest, and Alaska for images that will be treasured for a millennium." (Forget, for the moment, that Curtis's account of the Nightway in *The North American Indian* was apparently told to him by Charlie Day, one of a family of early traders around Chinle, Arizona, and that Curtis wasn't even in Navajoland during the fall or winter, when he could have witnessed a full nine-day Nightway—he visited the area only during the summer of 1904. Forget, too, that the costumes and masks in his Nightway photographs may have been manufactured above the Day store; that the Yei Bichei dance and other Nightway events were staged, danced in the daytime, and in violation of the proscriptions against recording sacred events; that non-medicine men made the sand paintings he photographed; and that the costumed impersonators of the Fringed Mouth God and the Humpbacked God are not even Navajo, but Charlie Day and his brother Sam, respectively [*NW*, 54].)

---

20. The photograph is from the first volume of Curtis's *The North American Indian*, opposite page 94, but has been reproduced elsewhere, including in *In a Sacred Manner We Live*, introduction and commentary by Don D. Fowler (Barre, Mass.: Barre Publishing, 1972), 69.

Figure 1. Edward S. Curtis's *Haschógan*, courtesy of Beautyway, Flagstaff, Arizona

It's a good reproduction—sepia-toned, framed, as if matted, in rectangles of dark brown, burnt sienna, and white. Face-front, the masked figure appears to be sitting, judging by the bend of his forearms, which the photo cuts off just below the elbows. He wears what looks like a velveteen shirt and a heavy silver squash-blossom necklace with a cast naja pendant. Also around his neck, but sitting on his shoulders, lies a spruce wreath. On his head, a fan of ten or twelve eagle feathers is set in a wig made from horse mane, and a deer tail dangles from the peak of his forehead. The face of the head mask, buckskin, is painted white, with small round holes for eyes and mouth, but there is no evidence of the gourd tip and surrounding kit fox fluff that typically accentuate Calling God's mouth. The deer tail hangs almost to the mouth hole and appears to cover a design—could it be a corn stalk?—that extends upward, to the forehead. Sets of mostly indistinct painted lines decorate the eyeholes and mouth, each set forming three sides of a square, two squares for each hole: a smaller, inner square open at the top, and an outer one facing down and capping the other.

Then it becomes clear: This is not *Haashch'éé'ooghaan*, Calling God, whose mask always bears a blue face with black triangles around the eyeholes. No, this is Talking God—*Haashch'éélti'í*, the maternal grandfather of the Yei, who presides over the Nightway—posed against a neutral background, lit by the camera's flash, captured but lost, misidentified, preserved for posterity, unrecognized.

Terms of Assimilation: Legislating Subjectivity in the Emerging Nation

Priscilla Wald

In the United States during the nineteenth century, debates concerning the status of indigenous tribespeople and slaves register unresolved legal conflicts that troubled claims of national unity. In particular, two Supreme Court cases—*Cherokee Nation v. Georgia* (1831) and *Scott v. Sandford* (*Dred Scott*, 1857)—demonstrate the genesis of these debates in the territorial expansion that similarly added urgency to the potent issue of states' rights. Both cases attempt to legislate the disappearance of the "Indians" and the "descendants of Africans," respectively, by judging them neither citizens nor aliens and therefore not legally representable. In so doing, however, these cases call attention to the symbolic processes

I wish to thank Sacvan Bercovitch, Joseph Donahue, Robert Ferguson, Jay Fliegelman, Elaine Freedgood, Barbara Gelpi, Howard Horwitz, Amy Kaplan, Karl Kroeber, and Michael Tratner for extraordinarily helpful suggestions for revising this essay. I am also grateful for a summer research grant from the Council for Research in the Humanities of Columbia University and a Mellon Fellowship from Stanford University, both of which afforded me the time to research, write, and revise the essay.

through which the United States constitutes subjects: how Americans are made. The Courts' decisions turn the Cherokee and slaves into uncanny figures who mirror the legal contingency—and the potential fate—of all subjects in the Union, a fate made all the more plausible by the instability of the Union and the tenuousness of national unity.

Efforts to promote national unity did not originate in the nineteenth century. Nations typically derive their legitimacy from a unity that is presumed to give rise to an independent political entity; Thomas Jefferson's "one people," for example, declares the colonies' independence from England.[1] The Declaration of Independence must not only convert kinship ties into "political bands," a connection that can be "dissolved," but it must also convert political alliance into cultural identification, a more enduring connection. Rhetorical strategies designed to promote a collective identity emerge with particular clarity in the congress's emendations of Jefferson's draft. In the edited version, for example, the King incites the suggestively vague "domestic insurrections" rather than the more problematic "treasonable insurrections." *Treasonable* names a crime committed against an independent political entity, a charge that countermands the Declaration's claims to be calling forth such an entity. At the same time, *treasonable* too nearly calls attention to the colonists' own treasonous activities—and therefore to their political ties with England. *Domestic*, on the other hand, lays claim only to a locale, although its resonance with *home* suggests a familial collectivity. By implication, the colonies form a homeland that predates and justifies the political entity. "Domestic insurrections" has the added advantage of referring at once to the uprisings of British Loyalists and to those of slaves. Thus, the congress excises a lengthy passage in which Jefferson, assailing the King for inciting slave rebellions, raises the hotly contested issue of slavery.

The Declaration must point the way to an ongoing association among the "one people" who are renouncing the former ties. In the last paragraph, Jefferson's "good people of these states" becomes the Declaration's "good people of these colonies," and it is from these "good people" that the document derives its authority to turn those colonies into "free & independent

1. With E. J. Hobsbawm, I would maintain that "nationalism comes before nations" (*Nations and Nationalism since 1780: Programme, Myth, Reality* [Cambridge: Cambridge University Press, 1990], 10). See also Benedict Anderson, *Imagined Communities: Reflections on the Origin and Spread of Nationalism* (London: Verso, 1983), and Ernest Gellner, *Nations and Nationalism* (Oxford: Oxford University Press, 1983).

states."[2] The Declaration defines the "one people" through contrasts—with the English, for example, or with Loyalists, or with the "merciless Indian savages" whose hostility is allegedly encouraged by the King. But once the political bands are dissolved, what new ones will be put in their place? Who will comprise the "one people" of the emerging political entity? And how can it provide for an expansion—through territorial acquisition or through immigration—that will not challenge that unity?

At stake in both Supreme Court cases is, quite literally, the fate of the Union, the status of the political entity constituted in the name of "the people." Debates surrounding the federal law's extension into unincorporated territories generate both cases. *Cherokee Nation* concerns Georgia's right to violate federal treaties and to extend its legislation into Cherokee territory that was contained within the state's borders but exempt from state law. *Dred Scott* considers the status of slaves taken to dwell for an extended period in free territory. Both cases, therefore, involve a conflict between state and federal law, and both immediately precede federal crises—the Nullification Crisis of 1832–1833 (entailing South Carolina's right to nullify the federal tariff of 1832) and the sectional conflicts leading to the Civil War. In the liminal spaces of territories neither foreign nor quite domestic, legal ambiguities resurface.

What begins as a question of territoriality ends in the Cherokee's and Dred Scott's exclusion from legal and social representation as the Courts strive to resolve or obscure those ambiguities. The decisions in both cases, however, disclose as much as they cover up when they make available the conventionality of the natural rights through which citizenship and, by implication, I will argue, cultural subjectivity is constructed. As G. Edward White also argues in his detailed analysis of *Cherokee Nation*, the legal treatment of both the indigenous tribes and the slaves profoundly troubled the concept of natural law—particularly the rights to own and inherit property, including property in the self.[3] The dispossessed subjects thus embody—or

2. Thomas Jefferson, *The Papers of Thomas Jefferson*, vol. 1: 1760–1776, ed. Julian Boyd (Princeton: Princeton University Press, 1950). Subsequent references to the Declaration are from this work.

3. G. Edward White, *The Marshall Court and Cultural Change, 1815–35: The History of the Supreme Court of the United States*, vols. 3–4 (New York: Macmillan Publishing Company, 1988), especially 703–40.

   I am also indebted, in this discussion, to James Kettner's theoretical formulations of United States citizenship in *The Development of American Citizenship, 1608–1870* (Chapel Hill: University of North Carolina Press, 1978). According to Kettner, "the posi-

disembody—an important representational threat: human beings to whom *natural* property rights do not extend. The rhetoric of erasure evoked to justify this exclusion images the rhetorical process of a subject's translation into a citizen (largely a rights discourse). Ironically, the legal unrepresentability designed to deflect the political issues itself ushers in the return of the cultural repressed, what is entailed in (and covered up by) the making of Americans. By positing human beings whom the law cannot represent, in other words, the Marshall and Taney Courts actually return to the (repressed) legal ambiguities and, by extension, to the legal genesis of United States subjectivity. Positive law distinguishes among subjectivities, but *all* subjects depend on that law for their *natural* rights. I invoke the uncanny here, because I want to stress that the threat that the indigenous tribespeople and descendants of Africans come to pose to the anxious confederation inheres at least as much in their resemblance to as in their differences from other cultural subjects.

• • • •

Cherokee Nation demonstrates significant contradictions within both states' rights and nationalist arguments. Since the case turns on Georgia's violating federal treaties by legislating within Cherokee territory, which is itself circumscribed by the state of Georgia, the relative authority of state and federal legislation is in question. The interesting twist of the case is that an actual victory for Georgia entails the Court's upholding the state's integrity against the coexistence of sovereign governments within shared boundaries, which coexistence in effect echoes the states' rights argument. Conversely, a victory for the national government conceptually upholds that principle of coexistence. At deeper issue, then, is just what kind of entity the "Cherokee Nation" describes.[4]

---

tion of the Negro—and, to a lesser extent, of the Indian—contradicted the Republic's fundamental principles of equality and consent. And Americans could not resolve these contradictions without either destroying central components of the concept of citizenship or facing the potentially explosive question of whether nation or state was supreme" (286). Departing somewhat from Kettner, I argue here that unresolved constitutional ambiguities underwrote the *connection* between a paradoxical concept of citizenship and the *inherently* explosive question of the nature of the political entity of the Union. Also unlike Kettner, my focus is primarily on the *rhetoric* of two Supreme Court cases wherein, I maintain, attempts to cover up the legal genesis of United States subjectivity are both made and made visible.

4. An interesting analogue to this twist is the split in the Cherokee nation between those

The Court's decision, as explained by Chief Justice Marshall, turns on the unique "condition of the Indians in relation to the United States [which] is, perhaps, unlike that of any other two people in existence." [5] Marshall rejects the designation "foreign" that characterizes "nations not owing a common allegiance" when determining

> the relation of the Indians to the United States. . . . The Indian territory *is admitted* to compose a part of the United States. In all our maps, geographical treatises, histories and laws, it is so considered. In all our intercourse with foreign nations, in our commercial regulations, in any attempt at intercourse between Indians and foreign nations, they are considered as within the jurisdictional limits of the United States, subject to many of those restraints which are imposed upon our own citizens. . . . [I]t may well be doubted, whether those tribes which reside within the acknowledged boundaries of the United States can, with strict accuracy, be denominated foreign nations. (*CN*, 11–12; my emphasis)

The representational bind that Marshall expresses grows out of the expanding borders of the United States, which bring the Declaration's "merciless savages" on "our frontiers" within national boundaries. Once used to delineate geographical boundaries, these "savages" threaten to define the limits of a natural rights discourse. Marshall responds with an erasure marked by the (elided) subject of the passive construction in the phrase "is admitted." He assumes a consensus that has already refused the tribal nations representation: "In all *our* maps . . . it is so considered." The "Indians" are comprehended within an *American* discourse, just as the Cherokee nation is circumscribed by Georgia's boundaries, a colonizing gesture that inscribes both collective identity and geographic totality. While national policy, articulated especially in treaties, had distinguished among the tribal nations, many legal cases had obscured such distinctions in the service of the cogently articulated national terms into which the growing number of immigrants and rapidly expanding national boundaries could be readily

---

(generally slaveholders) who sided with the Confederacy and those who fought with (or at least ideologically supported) the Union during the Civil War. Slaveholding, however, was not the only determinant in this division; many argued that the Confederacy was more likely to allow tribal self-government. See Theda Perdue, *Slavery and the Evolution of Cherokee Society, 1540–1866* (Knoxville: University of Tennessee Press, 1979).

5. *Cherokee Nation v. the State of Georgia, United States Reports*, vol. 30, 11. Subsequent references are cited in the text as *CN*.

translated. By the 1830s, the terms are set for the simultaneous, and often contradictory, policies toward the indigenous tribespeople: assimilation (in the service of appropriations of both land and identity) or removal.[6] In both instances, the pretext of United States legislation of the indigenous tribespeople inheres in the struggle to construct a collective identity, "We the People," that sanctifies the independent political entity uttered into existence in the founding texts.

The nation's expanding borders generate a great deal of legal activity, but *Cherokee Nation* and *Dred Scott* demonstrate the larger relevance of property disputes to the construction of subjectivity. In a government based on what C. B. Macpherson calls "possessive individualism," the natural right to own property is a critical component of the definition of personhood.[7] The Declaration offers the right to property as both an

6. Lucy Maddox offers an especially rich analysis of Indian legislation in light of the "persistent otherness of the Indians," who "continued to frustrate white America's efforts . . . to include them within the discourse of American nationalism and, concomitantly, within the structure of the country's laws and institutions" and of how that dilemma shaped the culture of the early Republic. See *Removals: Nineteenth-Century American Literature and the Politics of Indian Affairs* (New York: Oxford University Press, 1991), 8 and 7, respectively.

  Robert Berkhofer, Jr., contends that *Cherokee Nation* made the Cherokee the point of reference for this question as well as for removal. I have benefitted greatly from Berkhofer's discussion of *Cherokee Nation*. See *The White Man's Indian: Images of the American Indian from Columbus to the Present* (New York: Vintage Books, 1979), especially "Democracy and Removal: Defining the Status of the Indian," 157–66.

7. In *The Political Theory of Possessive Individualism: Hobbes to Locke* (Oxford: Oxford University Press, 1962), C. B. Macpherson argues that seventeenth-century individualism, from which the United States Constitution's political theories largely derive, had a "possessive quality . . . found in its conception of the individual as essentially the proprietor of his own person or capacities, owing nothing to society for them." According to Macpherson, the individual's freedom lay in self-ownership—"freedom is a function of possession"—and "liberal-democratic theory" posits a society that exists to safeguard that freedom (3).

  In *Ronald Reagan, the Movie and Other Episodes in Political Demonology* (Berkeley: University of California Press, 1987), Michael Paul Rogin uses a similar phrase, "propertied individualism," to theorize a liberal American society. He offers a fascinating psychoanalytic reading of the threat that tribal communalism posed to "American" society that also considers the simultaneous threat and attraction emblematized by the "Indian savagery" onto which white aggression projected itself: "Indian threats to the self-defense of expanding white America suggest that early time when a secure self has not emerged, when it is threatened with retaliatory extermination for its own aggressive rage" (147). See especially chap. 5, "Liberal Society and the Indian Question," 134–68.

  See also Eric Cheyfitz, *The Poetics of Imperialism: Translation and Colonization*

ideological justification for rebellion and the source of human liberty. Both Supreme Court cases, however, are troubled by competing claims to property that in turn manifest competing definitions of property and personhood in the emerging nation. The legal unrepresentability of nonwhite subjects upon which *Cherokee Nation* and *Dred Scott* resolve justifies the exclusion of these subjects from the right to own property and, by implication, from personhood.

At the end of one of the two dissenting opinions in *Dred Scott*, Justice Benjamin R. Curtis asserts the symbolic—and representational—function of the law through its creation of property:

> Without government and social order there can be no property; for without law, its ownership, its use and the power of disposing of it, cease to exist, *in the sense in which those words are used and understood in all civilized States*.[8]

Here, the law names property into existence by standardizing linguistic structures if not language itself. The material fact of property is a function of owning and bequeathing, actions and relations that the law governs. The "law," in turn, expresses the terms that make experience comprehensible. By implication, the subject's desire to comprehend, to make experience meaningful, underwrites his/her obeying the law. Curtis depicts the law as a rhetorico-legal discourse that defends the subject against an implied anarchy that threatens both the physical body and meaningful experience, hence subjectivity itself.

A kinship discourse that surfaces frequently in the legislation of the early Republic explains the more symbolic importance of inheritance to cultural identity. The Naturalization Act of 1790 explicitly adds citizenship to the terms of property and inheritance governed by the patronym. This act not only "naturalizes" the children ("under the age of twenty-one years") of naturalized parents and extends the (natural) boundaries of the nation

---

from "The Tempest" to "Tarzan" (Oxford: Oxford University Press, 1991). "The burden of this book is," in Cheyfitz's words, "that translation was, and still is, the central act of European colonization and imperialism in the Americas" (104). Cheyfitz discusses the translation of "Native American land . . . into the European identity of *property*" (43). Where Cheyfitz demonstrates the translation of the other into alienating terms, I am more concerned with how that translation destabilizes the dominant group's subjectivity as it exposes the already alienating terms on which it is predicated.

8. *Scott v. Sandford, United States Reports*, vol. 60, 787–88. Subsequent references are cited in the text as *DS*.

to include children born of citizens abroad, but it also very specifically provides "that the right of citizenship shall not descend to persons whose *fathers* have never been resident in the United States" (my emphasis). By the 1830s, the trope of the family commonly represents the Union. Accordingly, from the ever more strict and complex Naturalization and Alien and Sedition Acts to the 1819 law requiring annual records of immigration, from the American Society for Colonizing the Free People of Color in the United States (founded in 1817) to the 1819 Indian Civilization Fund and the Indian Removal Policy (formalized by James Madison in 1825 and made an act under Andrew Jackson in 1830), the logic of official legislation and de facto policies of this period protects personhood and property from threatened disruptions of both metaphysical and territorial inheritance. Miscegenation legislation during these years, as Eva Saks shows, simultaneously protects a social institution that governs "the transmission of property" and "formalizes the parties' social relation."[9]

Even in legislation not specifically prohibiting interracial marriage, kinship metaphors express the anxiety evoked by nonwhite subjects in the early Republic. Justice William Johnson, in a consenting opinion in *Cherokee Nation*, pointedly excludes the Indians from "the family of nations" (*CN*, 14, 17, 18) and, consequently, from representation within the United States legal system and even, by implication, from the human family. Johnson, in fact, deconstitutes "Indians" back into tribal affiliations to support his contention that "every petty kraal of Indians, designating themselves a tribe or nation, and having a few hundred acres of land to hunt on exclusively . . . should, indeed, force into the family of nations, a very numerous and very heterogeneous progeny" (*CN*, 17).

The catalog of anti-amalgamation laws (directed as much against "Indians" as "descendants of Africans") with which Chief Justice Roger Taney begins his opinion in *Dred Scott* similarly excludes descendants of Africans from "the whole human family, . . . civilized governments and the family of nations" (*DS*, 702–3). Taney pushes the nation's natural basis through the common currency of body and family tropes:

> Citizens in the several States, became also citizens of *this new political body*: but none other; it was formed by them, and for them and their posterity, but for no one else. . . . It was the union of those who were at that time members of distinct and separate political commu-

9. Eva Saks, "Representing Miscegenation Law," *Raritan* 8, no. 2 (1988): 39–69.

nities into *one political family*, whose power . . . was to extend over the whole territory of the United States. (*DS*, 701; my emphasis)

Taney uses these metaphors to suggest the threats posed by nonwhites to the genealogy of a white "family of independent nations" (*DS*, 701). The anti-amalgamation laws "show that a perpetual and impassable barrier was intended to be erected between the white race and the one which they had reduced to slavery" (*DS*, 702); Taney's passive voice invokes what Robert Ferguson calls "the rhetoric of inevitability," establishing history itself para-doxically as a justification for and outgrowth of the laws of nature.[10] Mar-shall's consistent use of passive voice similarly characterizes the rhetoric of legal strategy, in which subjectivity is subordinated to a historical narrative that, circularly, (re)constructs it.

The family archetype evokes both the actual inheritance and the genealogical relations that legally govern it. *Cherokee Nation* enables at once the appropriation of land and the delineation of "the American people." The defense in an earlier case, *Johnson and Graham's Lessee v. William McIntosh* (1823), had appealed to the putative lack of a tribal concept of private ownership to obviate the validity of the plaintiffs' claim to contested land: "As grantees from the Indians, they must take according to their laws of property, and as Indians subjects [*sic*]. The law of every dominion affects all persons and property situate within it . . . ; and the Indians never had any idea of individual property."[11] The concentric circles of this argument geo-metrically articulate a need to circumscribe tribal property relations within an American discourse of property: The plaintiffs are within Indian domin-ion for the sake of their purchase, but the Indians are, in turn, contained within United States definitions of property. The United States government's explicit policy toward the Indians, from the aforementioned 1819 Indian Civilization Fund to its fullest articulation in the 1887 Dawes Act, had at its core the civilization (dissolution) of tribal societies through the institution of private property.[12]

10. Robert Ferguson, "The Judicial Opinion as Literary Genre," *Yale Journal of Law and the Humanities* 2, no. 1 (Winter 1990): 201–19. Ferguson thus elegantly conveys the "di-rected or selective sense of history" (215) through which the judicial opinion obscures its own arbitrariness. Legal precedent, as Ferguson suggests, restructures the present in accordance with a presumed (created) past.

11. *Johnson v. McIntosh, United States Reports*, vol. 21, 251. Subsequent references are cited in the text as *JGL*.

12. *Dawes Act, 1887*. See Appendix A of D. S. Otis, *The Dawes Act and the Allotment of Indian Lands*, ed. Francis Paul Prucha (Norman, Okla.: University of Oklahoma Press,

Circumscribed within the Euro-American community, a situation that provokes both *Cherokee Nation* and the later *Worcester v. Georgia* (1832), tribal society presents an ongoing challenge to the physical and ideological representations of the Union and its subjects. The boundaries separating a "civilized," or (re)presentable, person from a "savage" are, therefore, directly at stake in these cases. Where citizenship is defined through the natural right to own property, and, following Locke, the most basic expression of this concept rests in the citizen's *self*-ownership, members of tribes and slaves (extending, at least in *Dred Scott*, to all "descendants of Africans") constitute two ways of not owning the self: the former, in the tribal absence of an "American" concept of private property, and the latter, in their being owned by someone else.[13]

Rhetorically, indigenous tribespeople and descendants of Africans are fashioned into monsters that fit Frantz Fanon's description of "the real Other," whom the "white man . . . perceive[s] on the level of the body image, absolutely as the not-self—that is, the unidentifiable, the unassimilable."[14] But the exclusion intended to foster a sense of homogeneity among

---

1973), 177–84. The putatively progressive legislation of the Dawes Act claimed "to provide for the allotment of lands in severalty to the Indians on the various reservations, and to extend the protection of the laws of the United States and the Territories over the Indians" (177). Section 6 of the act offers United States citizenship to those Indians to whom land was allotted and who had consequently "taken up . . . residence separate and apart from any tribe of Indians therein, and . . . adopted the habits of civilized life" (182). Here, again, the relationship between citizenship and property is fully articulated. Otis's discussion of the professed and actual logic, as well as the consequences, of the Dawes Act, originally published in 1934, remains the most thorough I have found.

13. According to Macpherson, the individual is (naturally) free to enter *voluntarily* into relations with other individuals and with society at large. In thus conceptualizing the person, legislators in the early nation excluded those from cultures with different conceptions of property from personhood. It is, moreover, the inalienability of the person that these cases conceptually problematize. In *Johnson v. McIntosh*, property cannot be alienated because it is not really owned, which deconstructs a self-ownership rooted in the inalienability of the person (see Macpherson, 23–26).

G. Edward White similarly makes a distinction between African Americans and indigenes that turns on their different relations to property. He traces an evolving policy to expropriate tribal property that is similar to mine and notes that the justices' conflicting positions "functioned to exclude from discourse a third ideological point of view, that of cultural relativism"; however, he does not sufficiently consider the *representational* threat that precludes the possibility of attending to cultural relativism (see *The Marshall Court and Cultural Change*, 706).

14. Frantz Fanon, *Black Skins, White Masks*, trans. Charles Lam Markmann (New York: Grove Press, 1967), 161n.

white Americans ironically raises the more dramatic specter of the status of any "American" self without the (already tenuous) cultural identity. White America could see its own alterity, or alienation, reflected in the fate (and often quite literally in the face) of the racialized other.[15]

The Marshall Court seeks resolution to this dilemma in erasure, as in Justice Henry Baldwin's declaration that "there is no plaintiff in [the *Cherokee Nation*] suit" (*CN*, 21). This ominous (and prophetic) elision rests in the Marshall Court's reading of

> the eighth section of the third article [of the United States Constitution] which empowers congress to "regulate commerce with foreign nations, and among the several states, and with the Indian tribes." In this clause, they are as clearly contradistinguished, by a name appropriate to themselves, from foreign nations, as from the several states composing the Union. They are designated by a distinct appellation; and as this appellation can be applied to neither of the others, neither can the application distinguishing either of the others be, in fair construction, applied to them. The objects to which the power of regulating commerce might be directed, are divided into three classes—foreign nations, the several states, and Indian tribes. (*CN*, 12)

15. As Michael Omi and Howard Winant point out, in the early decades of the nation, many immigrant groups were considered nonwhite (*Racial Formation in the United States: From the 1960s to the 1980s* [New York: Routledge and Kegan Paul, 1986]). Among the best discussions of the construction of race in the United States is William Stanton, *The Leopard's Spots: Scientific Attitudes toward Race in America 1815–1859* (Chicago: University of Chicago Press, 1960), which provides an excellent overview of the scientific theories of race in the antebellum United States. See also George M. Fredrickson, *The Black Image in the White Mind: The Debate on Afro-American Character and Destiny, 1817–1914* (New York: Harper & Row, Publishers, 1971), and Ronald Takaki, *Iron Cages: Race and Culture in Nineteenth-Century America* (1979; reprint, New York: Oxford University Press, 1990).

Of the abundant examples of the binarism and nominalism of difference, the decision in *The People v. George W. Hall* (*California Reports*, 1854, vol. 4, 429–35) is among the most dramatic. The case, which was heard by the California Supreme Court, involves whether "the testimony of Chinese witnesses" can convict a white citizen of murder. The case turns on two (technically contradictory) interpretations: first, that Columbus's mistake designates "Indian" a generic term that includes Asians; and second, that "the word 'black' may include all negroes, but the term 'negro' does not include all black persons. . . . [W]e understand it to mean the opposite of 'white'" (403). As "Indians" and as "nonwhites," the Chinese witnesses cannot (do not) appear before the bar, cannot, it seems, be comprehended by the terms of the law. What cannot be comprehended must be legislated out of existence, in light of the Union's possible decomposition.

The Court's reliance on the wording of the Constitution renders the contingency of the Cherokee's legal representation on their textual representation. When Justice Smith Thompson, in his dissenting opinion, labels the Court's reading "a mere verbal criticism," he unwittingly shakes the rhetorical foundation on which, as Justice Curtis will later suggest, society and subjectivity are constructed. Thompson returns to the original act of naming to counter the "argument . . . that if the Indian tribes are foreign nations, they would have been included, without being specially named, and being so named, imports something different from the previous term 'foreign nations'" (*CN*, 41). He offers two alternative readings of the Constitution's phraseology: stylistic, "avoid[ing] the repetition of the term nation"; and practical, allowing Congress to deal separately with each tribal nation. Again unwittingly, however, Thompson taps into precisely the anxiety over heterogeneity that Johnson has evoked in "every petty kraal of Indians." At stake is the colonizing gesture that naturalizes the land as it makes the many one.

Neither Curtis nor Thompson intends to deconstruct the law. On the contrary, they offer essentially nationalist arguments, using the logic of the Constitution's regulations of commerce, currency, and naturalization to bring the individual *states* of the Union within the terms of a common law. Curtis especially argues for a common vocabulary of private property that will assimilate all who accept its terms into an American discourse. Such assimilation, however, means cultural erasure rather than integration, which entails a proportionately greater sacrifice for non-European cultures. The dissenting arguments address whether or not, rather than how, non-Europeans can, and ought to, become "Americans." Curtis wants to apply, not reform, the law, and his opinion must be understood as a response to Taney's demonstration, through an appeal to the anti-amalgamation laws with which he opens his majority opinion, that the father is not willing to give his name to his darker-skinned (or, more consistently, -blooded) progeny.

Cherokee Nation is, finally, about the incomprehensible hole in the map within the perimeters of Georgia. It is, in fact, an increasing Cherokee nationalism, evidence of the Cherokee's plan to remain indefinitely in possession of the disputed territory, that precipitates Georgia's controversial legislation. Debates within the Cherokee community had entailed whether nationalism could best be expressed in traditional Cherokee or in United States terms, but it is the traditionalists' defeat, and the adoption of a Cherokee constitution, to which Georgia would most blatantly respond. The 1827 *Constitution of the Cherokee Nation*, spearheaded by the mainly interracial (mixed Cherokee and white parentage) elite, signaled a victory for a Cherokee nationalism simultaneously modeled on and opposed to United States nationalism.[16] Andrew Jackson's political ascendancy in the 1820s encouraged, and was even largely predicated on, a federal policy that replaced the aforementioned ambivalence with a new and determined program of removal. The victorious Cherokee nationalists hoped that a demonstration of their "civilization"—this parallel Constitution, for example—would ensure their right to remain on their land. While United States policy changes guaranteed their ultimate removal, the trends signified by the Cherokee Constitution precipitated events that may actually have expedited it.

The "Americanized" Cherokee, many of whom had become farmers and even slaveholders, evoked anxious responses in their neighbors, as typified by the director of the Office of Indian Affairs at this time, Thomas L. McKenney: "They seek to be a People. . . . It is much to be regretted that the idea of Sovereignty should have taken such a deep hold of these people."[17] His common nineteenth-century use of "a People" to express a *nation* suggestively articulates the rhetorical underpinnings of personhood's contingency upon national identity during this period. The public outrage, which McKenney echoes, stems from the anxieties exacerbated by the profound threat of Cherokee separatism to the collective identity. The Cherokee's becoming like but not of the United States political entity, mirroring without acceding to its claims, seems to threaten the terms of that identity. And the threat is literally embodied by the "mixed-bloods" who trouble both white exclusionists and integrationists in their *physical*, as well as *legal*, uncanniness.

The particular nature of the threat posed by the Cherokee Constitution is complicated in precisely those ways in which, as Homi Bhabha suggests, "mimicry is at once resemblance and menace."[18] As a colonial strategy, an imposed "mimicry" mandates "a reformed, recognizable Other,

16. For a fuller discussion of the emergence of Cherokee nationalism and the nationalists' conflict with the separatist traditionalists, see William G. McLoughlin, *Cherokees and Missionaries, 1789–1839* (New Haven: Yale University Press, 1984), especially 180–265.
17. Letters from Thomas L. McKenney to James Barbour on 29 Nov. 1827 and 20 Feb. 1827, respectively. Cited in McLoughlin, *Cherokees and Missionaries*, 220.
18. Homi Bhabha, "Of Mimicry and Men: The Ambivalence of Colonial Discourse," *October* 28 (Spring 1984): 127. Subsequent references are cited in the text as MM. The Cherokee function as the colonized in Bhabha's formulation, returning "the look of surveillance as the displacing gaze of the disciplined, where the observer becomes the observed and 'partial' representation rearticulates the whole notion of *identity* and alienates it from essence" (129). Needless to say, the structural contingency of an act of mimicry at least complicates the possibility for critique. In the case of the Cherokee, the mimicry helped to promote dissent in the Cherokee nation and expedited their removal. Nevertheless, the United States government's response attests to its threat.

as a *subject of a difference that is almost the same, but not quite"* (MM, 126), which is also to say, *"almost the same, but not white"* (MM, 130). In response to an ideology that envisions Americans as cultivators, some Cherokee take up hoes and crosses, purchase slaves, and adopt a constitution, hopefully preserving whatever indigenous culture can elude the disciplinary gaze. But the nationalist Cherokee, by imitating rather than by assimilating or by otherwise disappearing, recontextualize the logic of United States nationalism. A Cherokee nation would ironically recapitulate the pre-Revolutionary colonies' relation to England: " *'imperium in imperio'* (a state within a state),'' conceptually complicating ideas of American exceptionalism, absorptiveness, and republicanism.[19] It is also worth reiterating that *Cherokee Nation* introduced complications concerning the volatile federalist debates. Only blatant racism—specifically, the assertion that the white race alone could be capable of civilization—could resolve the contradictions, and the Cherokee's mimicry (civilization in United States terms) directly countermands those assertions.

Marshall's attempt to express the Cherokee's ambiguous relation to the United States depicts the untenability of this positioning; Marshall offers an apparent compromise that works hierarchically to erase any slippage in *Cherokee Nation*: "They may . . . be denominated domestic dependent nations. . . . Their relation to the United States resembles that of a ward to his guardian. They look to our government for protection; rely upon its kindness and its power, appeal to it for relief to their wants; and address the president as their great father" (*CN*, 12). This rhetoric echoes the earlier colonial legislation of indigenous tribespeople that, as the defense argued in *Johnson v. McIntosh*, "treat[ed] them as an inferior race of people, without the privileges of citizens, and under the perpetual protection and pupilage of the government" (*JGL*, 251). Marshall responds to the Jackson government's aggressive removal policy with a paternalism that paradoxically withholds the father's name from the adopted children.

Marshall's domestic fantasy had been effectively dramatized by the future abolitionist, Lydia Maria Child, in *Hobomok* (1824). In her literary work, Child can play out a scenario that Marshall can only imply in a legal decision. Yet, their efforts to resolve an ideological predicament are strikingly similar. Set in colonial New England, the novel uses its white female protagonist's ill-advised marriage to Hobomok, chief of a neighboring tribe, to accomplish her Americanization. The fate of Charles Hobomok Conant,

---

19. Kettner, *The Development of American Citizenship*, 146–47.

son of Hobomok and Mary Conant and adopted son of Charles Brown, accomplishes for a fictitious individual what Marshall rhetorically tries, unsuccessfully, to do for the tribal nations. The novel conscientiously depicts Mary's consent to marry Hobomok as the unfortunate outcome of her maddening grief at reports of the death of her Royalist fiancé, Charles Brown, and anger at her father's unrelenting fanaticism. When she awakens to the consequences of her impulsive behavior, Mary redeems herself for her early nineteenth-century audience by accepting her exile and renouncing her inheritance. Although her father "conjure[s] her not to consider a marriage lawful, which had been performed in a moment of derangement" and enjoins her to return both to him and to the inheritance bequeathed to her by a beloved paternal grandfather, Mary "urg[es] him to appropriate her property to his own comfort," since "her marriage vow to the Indian was [no] less sacred, than any other voluntary promise."[20] Mary must stay married to Hobomok because of a contract that cannot be declared illegal. Her inheritance, on the other hand, can be invalidated by her relinquishing a legal identity that is contingent upon her (consensual) membership in a community in which those laws apply. Those laws, in other words, hold between the tribespeople and the government but have no weight within tribal society (as within the Cherokee nation). Only Hobomok can release her from her contract.

Hobomok, however, turns out to be an appropriately cooperative, noble savage. When Charles Brown appears, almost as though reborn, Hobomok concedes his entitlement to both Mary and the land and selflessly agrees to "'go far off among some of the red men in the West. They will dig him a grave, and Mary may sing the marriage song in the wigwam of the Englishman'" (*Hob*, 139). His emigration/death speaks more to the ambiguities of government policy than to any deep wish of migrating tribes, but, most importantly, his self-abnegation Americanizes those it leaves behind. Mary can no longer return to England as she had wished, because, she explains, "'my boy would disgrace me, and I never will leave him; for love to him is the only way that I can now repay my debt of gratitude'" (*Hob*, 148). Instead, she must remain in the New World to reconstruct the American family both by reconciling with her Puritan father and by reconstituting Charles Hobomok.

The significance of Hobomok and his son inheres in the family's re-

---

20. Lydia Maria Child, *Hobomok and Other Writings on Indians* (New Brunswick: Rutgers University Press, 1986), 136. Subsequent references are cited in the text as *Hob*.

constitution according to the ideology of the early nineteenth century. Mary and Hobomok's amalgamation reconciles the austere Mr. Conant to Charles Brown, and her return re-forms her rigid father into an affectionate patriarch and, "partly from consciousness of blame, and partly from a mixed feeling of compassion and affection" (*Hob*, 149), a doting grandparent. Hobomok's erasure is signaled rhetorically through Charles Hobomok's assimilation: "He departed to finish his studies in England. His father was seldom spoken of; and by degrees his Indian appellation was silently omitted" (*Hob*, 150). The tacit agreement, denoted by passive voice, that whitewashes Mary's son attests to a faith in consensus and in the community's ability to absorb a dash of Indian blood. In fact, that blood seems to be just the seasoning necessary to de-anglicize, or nativize, the fledgling national culture. But Charles (Hobomok) Conant Brown's Indianness can metaphorically occasion his family's Americanization only if his father departs, a contingency that recalls the appropriating of tribal names, insignia, dress, customs, and even bastardized ceremonies as badges of Americanness. Hobomok occasions a transformation of the Conant family that symbolically links colonial and early nineteenth-century America as it distinguishes both from England. Hobomok's son can even be schooled in England precisely because he can never be anglicized, only further Americanized.

As an Indian, however, Charles Hobomok simply ceases to exist. And in the Supreme Court case of *Worcester v. Georgia* (1832), Justice John McLean similarly argues that their Americanization entitles the Cherokee to federal protection but, in turn, requires their complete acquiescence. "By entering into [these treaties]," asks McLean, "have we not admitted the power of this people to bind themselves, and to impose obligations on us?"[21] When their communalism is recast in nationalistic terms ("this [not these] people"), then the "obligations" are incurred. Moreover, McLean recognizes that the United States assimilation policies, such as the Indian Civilization Fund ("the means adopted by the general government to reclaim the savage from his erratic life, and induce him to assume the forms of civilization"), have analogously Americanized the tribal nations into certain entitlements: their "tendency to increase the attachment of the Cherokees to the country lands" (*WG*, 397). But it is precisely *as* Americans that the tribal nations must submit to the United States government's authority to define rights:

---

21. *Worcester v. Georgia, United States Reports*, vol. 31, 393. Subsequent references are cited in the text as *WG*.

> The exercise of the power of self-government by the Indians, within
> a state, is undoubtedly contemplated to be temporary. . . . [A] sound
> national policy does require, that the Indian tribes within our states
> should exchange their territories, upon equitable principles, or even-
> tually consent to become amalgamated in our political communities.
> (WG, 400)

The use of "amalgamated," especially in light of the anti-amalgamation
legislation, is startling here, although, like "domestic dependent nations," it
subtly articulates the subtext of the legislation. Just as women were disenfranchised by marriage, so the "Indians'" amalgamation would necessarily
entail a surrender of any property held in the name of a tribal affiliation.[22]
In light, moreover, of anti-amalgamation laws, even the most enlightened
official policies did no more than advocate a national forgetting, such as the
tacit agreement that allows Charles Hobomok to pass in the name of his
adopted father. Of course, the exception of an individual whose features
obscure his bloodline could certainly not hold true for an entire tribe. Hence,
the national fairy tale of *Hobomok* and the failure of Marshall's efforts at
peaceful resolution.

It is, then, as a *collective* entity that the tribe (and, by *extension*, each
of its members) must cease to exist. And it is *Worcester v. Georgia* that,
through the uncanny resemblance, most pointedly depicts the untold history
of the fate of the racialized other within American rhetoric as an extension of the fate of the American self within an American collective identity.
Significantly, the federal intervention called for by the plaintiff in *Cherokee
Nation* is conferred by the Court in *Worcester*, where the case now involves
"the personal liberty of a citizen" (WG, 364). The Court's *apparent* reversal, which is actually not quite a reversal, of the *Cherokee Nation* decision
attests to the national stake in maintaining the apparent priority of "the
personal liberty of a citizen." The case rules on the claim of the plaintiff,
Samuel A. Worcester, of rights violations—including wrongful detainment—
on the part of the state of Georgia, and it revolves around the constitu-
tionality of an act passed by the Georgia legislature on 22 December 1830

---

22. While social commentators noted the connection between married women and slaves
that helped fuel the ill-fated universal suffrage movement in the United States, the link
between tribespeople and married women seems less apparent. The phrase "domestic
dependent nations" is cited in the link between children and Indians, but the interesting
correlation between women and tribespeople exists mainly in the problematic use of Indians to articulate a displaced female sociolegal invisibility in works by such novelists as
Child and Catharine Maria Sedgwick (*Hope Leslie*).

claiming state jurisdiction over tribal territory. Georgia charges Worcester and a small group of fellow missionaries with residing in Cherokee territory without a permit and without taking "an oath to support and defend the constitution and laws of the state of Georgia" (WG, 350). Worcester's defense calls forth the federal treaties that uphold Cherokee sovereignty within established boundaries. Not only is there now a "plaintiff in this suit," but the case, which links the American citizen's "personal liberty" to tribal land rights, comes dangerously close to demonstrating a correlation between the legal representational invisibility of the racialized other and the necessary self-abridgment of even the most apparently representative Christian white male within a collective identity. Hence the ruling against Georgia, although in favor of Worcester rather than the Cherokee.

The threat of the Cherokee's mimicry, which largely inheres in the conceptual resonance between an American citizen's "personal liberty" and Cherokee land rights, is fully enacted in the Cherokee Constitution. Land distinguishes the Cherokee nation from the original Cherokee. The first section of Article 1 spells out the "boundaries of this nation," which do not encompass the Cherokee who had migrated West in accordance with United States government colonization programs—that is, those who had allowed themselves to be translated out of Georgia's boundaries. The second section defines the land as the nation's exclusive property:

> The sovereignty and Jurisdiction of this Government shall extend over the country within the boundaries above described, and the lands therein are, and shall remain, the common property of the Nation; but the improvements made thereon, and in the possession of the citizens of the Nation, are the exclusive and indefeasible property of the citizens respectively who made; or may rightfully be in possession of them; Provided, that the citizens of the Nation, possessing exclusive and indefeasible right to their respective improvements, as expressed in this article, shall possess no right nor power to dispose of their improvements in any manner whatever to the United States, individual states, nor individual citizens thereof; and that whenever any such citizen or citizens shall remove with their effects out of the limits of this Nation, and become citizens of any other Government, all their rights and privileges as citizens of this Nation shall cease.[23]

23. Emmet Starr, *Starr's History of the Cherokee Nation*, ed. Jack Gregory and Rennard Strickland (Fayetteville, Ark.: Indian Heritage Association, 1967), 55–56.

The passage articulates the distinctly Lockean concept of entitlement ("ownership") based on work ("improvements"). This proprietorship, however, is contingent upon membership in the collective national identity.[24] Since this land is explicitly indefeasible, it cannot, strictly speaking, be said to *belong* to any single proprietor.

In mimicking the de facto United States policy of contingent entitlement, the Cherokee Constitution exposes the conventionality of inalienable rights. First, it rearticulates (with significant slippage) the decision in *Johnson v. McIntosh*, which involves the dispute over the title to land that the plaintiffs had purchased from the Piankeshaw Indians and that the United States had granted to the defendants. Marshall's uncontested opinion upholds the defense counsel's appeal to "the uniform understanding and practice of European nations, and the settled law, as laid down by the tribunals of civilized states, [that] denie[s] the right of the Indians to be considered as independent communities, having a permanent property in the soil, *capable of alienation* to private individuals" (*JGL*, 565; my emphasis). The brief report of the defense repeats "alienation" two more times: "The extent of their right of alienation must depend upon the laws of the dominion under which they live" and "The Indian title to lands [is] a mere right of usufruct and habitation, without power of alienation" (*JGL*, 567). The defense counsel invokes Locke, among other sources, to naturalize the indigenous tribespeople's inalienable rights to their land: "By the law of nature, they had not acquired a fixed property, capable of being transfered [*sic*]" (*JGL*, 567).

The Cherokee Constitution signals the Cherokee's adopting the concept of provisional land rights, but in the service of Cherokee, rather than United States, nationalism. That constitution, however, makes apparent that these rights are the result of positive, rather than natural, law. A similar implication plays throughout Marshall's rhetoric:

> As the right of society to prescribe those rules by which property may be acquired and preserved is not, and *cannot, be drawn into question*; as the title to lands, especially, is, and must be, admitted, to depend entirely on the law of the nation in which they lie; it will be necessary, in pursuing this inquiry to examine, not simply those principles of abstract justice, which the Creator of all things has im-

---

24. It is interesting to note, in this context, that the Cherokee Constitution excludes descendants of Africans, including products of miscegenation, from "the rights and privileges of [the] nation."

pressed on the mind of his creature man, and which are admitted to regulate, in a great degree, the rights of civilized nations, whose perfect independence is acknowledged, but those principles also which our own government has adopted in the particular case, and given us as the rule for our decision. . . . [I]f the principle has been asserted in the first instance, and afterwards sustained; if a country has been acquired and held under it; if the property of the great mass of the community originates in it, it becomes the law of the land, and *cannot be questioned. (JGL,* 572, 590; my emphasis)

Marshall insists on the irrefutability of established laws, especially governing property. In the interest of the "categorical authority" of the law, he blurs the distinction between the "principles of abstract justice" and "those . . . which our own government has adopted," a distinction upon which he ostensibly insists.[25] By accepting the concept of provisional land rights but implicitly rejecting its genesis in natural law, the Cherokee Constitution restores the questioning agent that Marshall's passive voice would erase.

The effect of the mimicry extends, more importantly, to the concept of inalienable rights. In its strictest sense, as the *Johnson* decision makes apparent, inalienability countermands the agency of the subject itself as well as of the larger community. The Indians cannot "alienate"—that is, sell— their land because they do not own it. This context adds a new and troubling perspective to the politically fundamental concept of inalienable rights. Jefferson intends a natural law argument when he asserts the inalienability of certain individual rights in the Declaration. Nevertheless, rights that cannot be alienated are not, strictly speaking, *owned.* The individual rights protected by United States law are, technically, the *property* of American society conferred upon subjects recognized by United States law and who in turn (at least in theory) accept the terms of that law. Like the Indians' property, they are more accurately rights of proprietorship than (alienable) possessions. Hence Mary Conant's automatic forfeiture when she consents to join Hobomok's world. Natural rights are rights that inhere in a certain conception of personhood, but that conception—and those rights—extend only to certain persons. Personhood is itself conceptually constructed by

25. I have taken the phrase "categorical authority" used in this context from Jacques Derrida, who argues that the law's obscured origins serve to obfuscate the positivist sources of its categorical authority. See "Devant la loi," trans. Avital Ronell, in *Kafka and the Contemporary Critical Performance: Centenary Readings,* ed. Alan Udoff (Bloomington: Indiana University Press), 128–49.

convention. *Cherokee Nation* and *Dred Scott* demonstrate the contingency of inalienable rights upon a government that chooses to define and protect them as such; they also reveal persons within that government's borders to whom those rights do not extend.

The political complexity of these cases lies in the many ways in which they threaten to represent both the legal construction of identity in rights discourse and the shifting basis of the authority to confer and protect those rights. In his concurring opinion in *Worcester*, Justice McLean tries to cover up the justification for the claims, made by proponents of states' rights, "that the federal government is foreign to the state governments; and that it must, consequently, be hostile to them." McLean argues that "foreign" and "state governments . . . [proceed] from the same people," and that the people of the state are also "the people of the Union" (*WG*, 386). Yet, no amount of insistence on national unity can obscure the fundamental question of the case that McLean himself must finally ask: "Which shall stand, the laws of the United States, or the laws of Georgia?" (*WG*, 391). In the shifting field of inquiry, from the status of "the Cherokee Nation" (and hence, Cherokee's legal representability) to the "personal liberty" of white male United States citizens, the nature of citizenship—and, more fundamentally, personhood—in the Union emerges as the anxious inquiry of these cases. But the anxiety overtakes the inquiry, which is in turn displaced or suppressed. When, for example, the Nullification Crisis in South Carolina helps turn the *Worcester* decision into a threat to the Union, and to the authority of the Court, both the Court and the plaintiffs demonstrate a willingness to compromise.[26] Although the South balked at the economic nationalism signaled by the protective tariffs in the 1820s, and although John C. Calhoun emphasized an analogy between South Carolina's right to nullify federal tariff regulations and Georgia's right to supersede federal treaties with indigenous tribes, Indian legislation generally inspired more obvious divisions among partisan, rather than sectional, factions. What may at times have seemed to be an East/West division was complicated by an emerging nationalism. Between *Cherokee Nation* and *Dred Scott*, how-

26. Richard Ellis's *The Union at Risk* (New York: Oxford University Press, 1987) offers insight into how the Nullification Crisis influenced the resolution of *Worcester*. Jackson, already no friend to the Cherokee, was ironically supported in his position by Calhoun's skillful maneuvering to identify South Carolina's position with Georgia's. The fate of the Union prompted all parties except the Cherokee (the government, the Georgia legislature, the Marshall Court, and even Worcester himself) to modify their stances. This outcome ensured the Cherokee's subsequent removal from Georgia.

ever, these debates would more clearly reinscribe "We the People" into two distinctly competing sectional narratives.

Divergent national narratives, in other words, coalesce into two dominant narratives, as the related issues of slavery and state sovereignty inescapably force constitutional ambiguities to the fore in the antebellum United States. The Taney Court must therefore resolve what the Marshall Court can still try to obscure. Taney's opinion, which becomes the Court's official opinion, returns to the language of eighteenth-century political discussions to maintain Dred Scott's legal unrepresentability.[27] Excluding descendants of Africans from "We the People," Taney insists that the Constitution prohibits their holding federal citizenship while any state precludes them from holding state citizenship. Nor, however, are they eligible for alien status. Dred Scott consequently cannot sue for his freedom because he is not and cannot be a citizen of the state of Missouri. Because of the centrality of the issues raised in *Dred Scott* to the mounting political crisis, however, Taney rules on other controversies touched on by *Dred Scott* as the case had made its way, in several incarnations, through other courts. Taney's majority opinion describes a constitution that prevents the federal government from prohibiting slavery in a territory, and that gives a state, rather than the federal government, jurisdiction over the regulation of domestic institutions, including slavery. Even if Dred Scott could sue in state or federal court, his master's sojourns in the free state of Illinois and in the territory designated free under the Louisiana Purchase could not legitimate his suit for freedom in Missouri. Thus the Taney Court upholds the "squatter sovereignty" of the 1854 Kansas-Nebraska Act and (necessarily) affirms the unconstitutionality of the 1820 Missouri Compromise.

Taney carefully distinguishes between Indians and descendants of Africans. By the late 1850s, the government's aggressive policy had substantially diminished any significant physical or representational challenge

---

27. Don E. Fehrenbacher explains the context of this "official" opinion in *Slavery, Law and Politics* (New York: Oxford University Press, 1981). Taney offers a long, partisan, and sometimes inaccurate opinion on contradictory aspects of the case (for example, his jurisdictional and territorial rulings may be in conflict). As a result, several of the concurring opinions do not seem fully to concur; nevertheless, the Court's majority concurrence designates Taney's opinion as the "official opinion" of the Court. Fehrenbacher presents convincing evidence that Taney rewrote (and significantly augmented) his opinion in response to Curtis's lengthy and impressive dissenting opinion; the Court records are, therefore, not what was actually heard at the trial (and consented to by the concurring justices).

from the tribes. And by 1857, Taney could *contrast* the legal invisibility of "a negro, whose ancestors were imported into this country and sold as slaves" (*DS*, 700), with the status of "Indian governments [that] were regarded and treated as foreign governments, as much so as if an ocean had separated the red man from the white" (*DS*, 700). One must either question Taney's legal scholarship or interrogate his willful misconstrual of *Cherokee Nation*. His decision reveals a deliberative shift of emphasis that elucidates an important difference between these groups:

> It is true that *the course of events* has brought the Indian tribes within the limits of the United States under subjection to the white race; and it *has been found necessary*, for their sake as well as our own, to regard them as in a state of pupilage, and to legislate to a certain extent over them and the territory they occupy. But they may, without doubt, *like the subjects of any other foreign government*, be naturalized by the authority of Congress, and become citizens of a State and of the United States; and if an individual should leave his *nation or tribe*, and take up his abode among the white population, he would be entitled to *all the rights and privileges which would belong to an emigrant from any other foreign people*. (*DS*, 700; my emphasis)

No longer a threat, the "Indians" could now comprise an alien nation, and their lack of proximity to the white family permits suggestions of their assimilability.[28] In contrast, each side of the slavery debate invokes the mulatto to depict the gruesome consequences of the other side's institutions. Black subjectivity evidently presents the more serious danger in the antebellum United States. The descendant of Africans registers the uncanniness of the legally unrepresentable subject perhaps even more forcefully than the member of a tribal nation. "Indian governments" had represented the *collective* threat offered by the proximity of an alternative collectivity. A descendant

28. Walter Benn Michaels, in "The Vanishing American," *American Literary History* 2, no. 2 (Summer 1990): 220–41, traces the logical culmination of this process in the official policies through which, by the twentieth century, Indians were viewed as potential citizens and, with the Citizenship Act of 1924, were declared citizens. He convincingly reads the act as "at worst a cynical acknowledgment of the ultimate irrelevance of citizenship to the Indians' predicament" (222) and explains the symbolic process by which "Indians" were appropriated as "American" ancestors and had their identity reconceived as a cultural inheritance. I read Taney's contrast between tribal nations and descendants of Africans as an early indicator of the direction of this process.

of Africans, in Taney's narrative, embodies the *individual* threat of a human being deprived of choice and self-possession within (but not of) the Union.

Taney's reconstructed historical narrative seeks to legitimate—and moralize—slavery ("for their sake as well as our own"). At stake is the states' rights claim that the state, rather than the federal government, protects the liberties of *all* citizens. The majority opinion in *Dred Scott* must establish the priority of both the master's property rights over the slave's right to self-possession and the state's right to regulate slavery over federal legislation.

Taney's narrative must present a government dedicated to the preservation of individual liberty. Inconsistencies within that program must be rhetorically elided. Accordingly, Taney uses a rhetoric of inevitability to emplot Indian removal within the progressive movement, the "manifest destiny," of the American people. His loose echo of the Declaration of Independence ("course of human events"; "found necessary") ensures that the subjection of tribes remains within the terms of the American Revolution, although emigration of these "nations or tribes" (the distinction is no longer so crucial) has removed the immediate risk of an imperial analogy between the United States and England that, for example, the Cherokee resemblance to the revolutionary colonies had promoted.[29] The Union's prosperity inevitably results in the civilization or removal of the tribal nations (either way, the passing of tribal cultures). That same prosperity depends upon the extension of slavery, which, consequently, is as inevitable and beneficial to all concerned as Indian removal. Both are the outcome of civilization. Hence, the familiar paternalistic rhetoric that enslaves Africans and their descendants, as it removes tribal cultures, "for their sake as well as our own."

Whereas Indian removal makes it possible to emblematize (and thus Americanize) tribal culture, however, the slave remains within United States culture as a visible symbol of nonpersonhood: neither *potential* citizen nor alien. The rhetoric of two southern justices who concur with Taney's opinions evinces concern that *Dred Scott* somehow challenges the "*status* of [white] persons" in the United States. Justice John A. Campbell argues that the individual's inalienable rights curb Congress's power to "determine the condition and *status* of persons who inhabit the Territories" (*DS*, 744).

29. Taney goes on to cite directly the first two paragraphs of the Declaration of Independence both to contrast policy toward Native and African Americans and to preempt the abolitionist appeal to the language of the Declaration.

Campbell imagines "an American patriot" who contrasts the European and American systems by affirming

> that European sovereigns give lands to their colonists, but reserve to themselves a power to control their property, liberty and privileges; but the American Government sells the lands belonging to the people of the several States (i.e., United States) to their citizens, who are already in the possession of personal and political rights, which the government did not give, and cannot take away. (*DS*, 745)

Inalienable rights, here, restrict the United States *government's*, rather than the individual's, access, which was also Jefferson's intention. Largely on the basis of this distinction, the colonies declared their independence. Campbell, however, uses the "American Government" to conceptualize a transfer of rights that is regulated by a legal system. That system controls the distribution of those rights—not unlike the European sovereigns—by its power to decide exactly *who* is "already in the possession of personal and political rights, which the government did not give, and cannot take away." For Justice Peter V. Daniel, the slave's status as property makes citizenship unthinkable. Daniel insists that "the power of disposing of and regulating . . . vested in Congress . . . did not extend to the personal or political rights of citizens or settlers . . . inasmuch as citizens or persons could not be property, and especially were not property belonging to the United States" (*DS*, 735). Americans' self-ownership is evidently at issue in *Dred Scott*.

The counternarratives offered by the two dissenters, Justices McLean and Curtis, paradoxically maintain slavery's general legality and suggest the challenge that slavery poses to the law. Curtis's reluctance to contest the legality of slavery stems from the New Englander's conservatism. Justice John McLean, on the other hand, manifests a politician's fervency—and his own presidential ambitions. He summons the danger of the nation's dissolution, posed by slavery, in an effort to save the Union. McLean draws on precedent to "show that property in a human being does not arise from nature or from the common law, but, in the language of this court, it is a mere municipal regulation, founded upon and limited to the range of the territorial laws" (*DS*, 760). This precedent establishes Scott's right to freedom on the basis of his having lived in free territory. But he ambiguously (and ominously) evokes the crux of impending national crisis in labeling "this decision . . . the end of the law" (*DS*, 760). To enslave a person is to push the law to its extreme: If a law that turns a human being into property "does not arise from nature," then what, he wonders, stops a government from making "white men slaves?" (*DS*, 757). Moreover, the law that creates slaves also, by extension, creates the natural rights that constitute personhood. This is to envision the *end*, in both senses of the word, of the law.

In the debate over the power of the federal government, each side had to establish itself as safeguarding "the people's" liberty (individual rights). But the focus on individual liberty was, as many argued, inconsistent with the slave's status as a potential citizen. Accordingly, the slave had to be either excluded from the possibility of citizenship or emancipated. *Dred Scott* accordingly manifests the social and legal consequences of the black subject's rhetorical elision in the haunting possibility of a legally invisible subject.

• • • •

Within a decade of the *Dred Scott* decision, Abraham Lincoln would connect the white subject's similar rhetorical disappearance to the dissolution of the Union in his Second Inaugural Address. Lincoln ends the first paragraph of this brief speech, which concerns the Union's reconstruction, ambiguously: "With high hope for the future, no prediction in regard to it is ventured." The dangling modifier and passive voice defer a subjectivity apparently contingent upon the fate—the reconstitution—of the Union. Lincoln similarly constructs three of the four sentences that comprise this paragraph around the passive voice, and the first person—singular or plural—appears only embedded within a clause: "I trust." In the wake of a crisis concerning the collective identity, the subject, which certainly cannot act, can barely even exist—can only "trust." The deferred subject begs a central question of the conflict: Whom does "We the People" include, and, more pointedly, who speaks in their (its?) name? Is the United States itself a plural or singular subject? Lincoln's rhetoric announces his stand; the American subject cannot exist without the Union, in the name of which it is held *in trust*. The subject's contingency promotes a personal investment in the fate of the Union, now unobstructedly on the way to nationhood.

The questions raised in *Cherokee Nation* and *Dred Scott* motivate but are not finally resolved either by Lincoln's rhetoric or the reconstructive strategies it articulates. Instead, they resurface in the anxious efforts to legislate mimicry and difference out of official existence, and they emerge from, as they attest to, fundamental contradictions of United States subjectivity. These contradictions are not resolved in the Fourteenth Amendment, which establishes federal and state citizenship for all persons born in the

United States or in the postwar nation. Debates surrounding overseas expansion of the late nineteenth and early twentieth centuries evince renewed concerns for the nation's stability and the fate of Americans, as well as reinvigorated strategies of rhetorical erasure. In particular, the 1901 Supreme Court case of *Downes v. Bidwell* forcefully registers the return of the issues (and decisions) of *Cherokee Nation* and *Dred Scott*. The case, which explicitly sanctions the nation's right to own territory and to legislate over subjects that it does not incorporate, declares inhabitants of United States overseas territories neither citizens nor aliens; hence, they are, just as the Cherokee and Dred Scott were, legally unrepresentable. Although *Downes v. Bidwell* divides the Court, both sides show marked concern for national stability. Those favoring the decision—and thus legislating imperialism—imagine a territory that is necessary to "the peaceful evolution of national life" but inhabited by a "people utterly unfit for American citizenship." Dissenting justices are equally troubled by Congress's alleged power to turn such a territory into "a disembodied shade, in an intermediate state of ambiguous existence for an indefinite period." [30] In legislating the ambiguous status of (nonwhite) inhabitants of overseas territories, however, the Court creates disembodied subjects who bear witness to the fate most feared by both sides.

In *Downes v. Bidwell*, as in *Cherokee Nation* and *Dred Scott*, the perceived threat to national stability (actual or imagined) gives rise to an almost apocalyptic anxiety over the fate of American subjects. These cases do not interrogate the source of that concern—the rhetoric through which the nation constitutes its subjects—and that concern continues to motivate the creation of subjects who embody precisely that fate. From the judg-

---

30. *Downes v. Bidwell, United States Lawyer's Edition 179–182*, 1116, 1139. Even the 17 October 1899 platform of the American Anti-Imperialist League, while "regretting that the blood of the Filipinos is on American hands," is explicitly more troubled by "the betrayal of American institutions at home" (cited in Carl Schurz, *Papers, Correspondence and Political Speeches*, ed. Frederic Bancroft, vol. 6 [New York: G. P. Putnam's Sons, 1913], 77–79).

In an extraordinary discussion of the relationship between popular historical romances and American imperialism, Amy Kaplan shows how disembodied national power allows for an economic expansion that is not based on territorial expansion. See "Romancing the Empire: The Embodiment of American Masculinity in the Popular Historical Novel of the 1890s," *American Literary History* 2, no. 4 (Winter 1990): 659–90. The "disembodied shade" of a territory thus (un)incorporated threatens to bring such strategies to consciousness.

ments of *Cherokee Nation* and *Dred Scott* to Lincoln's Second Inaugural Address and into the twentieth century with *Downes v. Bidwell*, the disembodied subject continues to haunt the imperial nation. The history of these subjects is a "tale twice-told but seldom written": the story of subjectivity in the United States.[31]

31. The quoted phrase is from W. E. B. DuBois's *The Souls of Black Folk*, in the collection *Writings: The Suppression of the African Slave-Trade, The Souls of Black Folk, Dusk of Dawn, Essays and Articles* (New York: Library of America, 1986), 357–547, especially 359. He refers to cultural observations so (ominously) obvious that they must be repressed.

Plains Indian Native Literatures

Douglas R. Parks and Raymond J. DeMallie

Among scholars, as among the general public, there is a compelling desire today for authentic material documenting the experiences of the native peoples of the Americas. Yet, the only truly authentic voices that document the American Indian past come to us in native languages accessible solely through translation. Of the hundreds of distinct languages and dialects that existed throughout the five centuries of European presence in the Americas, only a handful are still vital today. More and more, we must face the inevitability of turning to native language texts preserved during the last hundred years through the efforts of American Indian people themselves, most frequently in collaboration with linguists and anthropologists, as the only authentic record of the American Indian cultural worlds now unrecoverable because of the effects of cultural change and language loss. Although they preserve the actual words of American Indian people from the past, such texts cannot speak to us directly. As historical documents, they require, in addition to translation, the careful evaluation given to any other type of historical document. Specifically, they call out for study using ethnohistorical methods: a combination of historical, anthropological, and linguistic approaches that can situate native language texts in the fullest possible historical and cultural context to allow the American Indian voices they preserve to speak through the generations and across the barriers of language and culture to become intelligible and articulate representations of the past.[1]

For peoples of the North American Plains, in particular, a very large body of native language texts—primarily composed from the 1880s to the 1940s—has been preserved that provides direct insight into the cultural world of the Plains tribes at the end of the buffalo days and through the trying decades of adapting to reservation life. These texts are of two types: those written by native people, and those dictated (and sometimes sound-recorded) by native people. The two types invite comparison: the former as representing native language literacy, the latter as representing oral style.

We are engaged in transcribing, translating, and editing for publication representative collections of these texts. Parks is working on a collection of narratives dictated by the Skiri Pawnee religious leader Roaming Scout and recorded on wax cylinders by James R. Murie and George A. Dorsey during the first decade of this century. DeMallie is working on a similar collection of Lakota (Western Sioux) texts written by George Sword on the Pine Ridge Reservation during the first decade of this century. Our project, entitled "In Their Own Words," is the preparation of editions of important collections of texts in Plains Indian languages that explicate historical lifeways of the Pawnee and Sioux from the perspectives of members of these cultures, in their own words. The goal is thus to bring into the published record of Plains Indian culture history some of the native component that has heretofore been lacking or neglected. At the same time, the project seeks to establish principles for the presentation of native language texts—to publish scholarly editions of these manuscripts that preserve their integrity as historical documents and that, through annotation and translation, make them accessible to a wide audience.[2]

In the following description of two components of the project, the first section, on the Roaming Scout texts, was written by Parks, and the second

---

1. Dennis Tedlock coined the term *ethnopaleography* to designate the dialogical process of reconstituting historical written texts, exemplified in his translation of the Popol Vuh in collaboration with contemporary Mayan speakers. See Tedlock, *The Spoken Word and the Work of Interpretation* (Philadelphia: University of Pennsylvania Press, 1983), 124–55.
2. This project has been supported by grants from the National Endowment for the Humanities and from Indiana University.

section, on the Sword texts, was written by DeMallie. In the final section of the paper, we again unite our voices to offer some general conclusions.

The Skiri Pawnee Texts of Roaming Scout

The Roaming Scout texts are part of an extensive collection of Paw- nee narratives compiled through the collaborative efforts of George A. Dorsey and James R. Murie at the turn of the century. In 1899, Dorsey, who was curator of anthropology at the Field Columbian Museum, under-took a systematic, extended study of the mythology and ceremonies of the Caddoan-speaking tribes—the Arikara, Pawnee, Wichita, and Caddo. Although the project involved all these tribes, in the end his work with the Pawnee was, by far, the most extensive because of the indispensable aid of Murie, a mixed-blood Skiri born in Nebraska in 1862 who had graduated in 1883 from Hampton Institute in Virginia and who, during the 1890s, had assisted Alice C. Fletcher when she was recording the Pawnee Hako cere-mony and was collecting other ethnographic material. For Fletcher, Murie had provided entrée to Pawnee religious leaders and had served as trans-lator, and later had written out and translated Pawnee linguistic material that Fletcher recorded on wax cylinders. Through his work with her, then, he had become acquainted with the goals and methods of contemporary ethnography.[3]

Dorsey met Murie soon after beginning his comparative mythology project and, because of Murie's previous experience and willingness to col-lect material in the field, he hired him as a full-time assistant in 1902. In this capacity, Murie began his anthropological career by recording the collec-tions of myths that comprise the two volumes of Pawnee and one volume of Arikara oral traditions published by Dorsey,[4] as well as by acting as a field liaison in the purchase of Pawnee material culture specimens for the Field Columbian Museum.

---

3. Alice C. Fletcher, *The Hako: A Pawnee Ceremony*, Smithsonian Institution, Bureau of American Ethnology 22d Annual Report, pt. 2 (Washington, D.C., 1904). For a descrip-tion of Murie's work with anthropologists, see his biography, *Ceremonies of the Pawnee*, ed. Douglas R. Parks (Smithsonian Contributions to Anthropology, no. 27, 1981; reprint, Lincoln: University of Nebraska Press, 1989), pt. 1, 21–28.

4. George A. Dorsey, *Traditions of the Skidi Pawnee*, Memoirs of the American Folk-Lore Society, no. 8 (Boston: Houghton, Mifflin, and Co., 1904); *Traditions of the Arikara*, Car-negie Institution Publications, no. 17 (Washington, D.C., 1904); *The Pawnee: Mythology*, Carnegie Institution Publications, no. 59 (Washington, D.C., 1906).

After the volumes of mythology were completed, Dorsey and Murie turned their attention to Pawnee ceremonialism and social life, and on these topics, too, Murie recorded a voluminous amount of material from the oldest, most knowledgeable Skiris, most of whom were related to him by blood or by marriage. Murie attended surviving ceremonies, at first as an observer and later as a participant, and subsequently wrote out descriptions of them, recorded their songs on wax cylinders, and then transcribed and translated the lyrics. Although most of Murie's work was accomplished in and around Pawnee, Oklahoma, he also lived for a year or more in Chicago, where he worked with Dorsey at the museum and served as a source of ethnographic information himself. In 1906, Dorsey and Murie's collaborative effort culminated in a 450-page manuscript entitled "The Pawnee: Society and Religion of the Skiri Pawnee," which is an idealized account of the structure of Skiri society and ceremonialism based on, but generally not including, the accounts of specific rituals and their myths that Murie had recorded.[5]

Complementing the preceding undertakings was yet another one, linguistic in nature, that was begun in Chicago in 1906. Whether Murie or Dorsey conceived the idea is unknown, but in order to document traditional Pawnee culture from an insider's perspective—to get at the emotion and intangible overtones as well as the facts of behavior and belief—and to make a record of an older form of Skiri speech, Murie enlisted the aid of Roaming Scout, one of his lifelong mentors and primary sources, a monolingual Skiri religious leader born in the 1840s, when traditional Pawnee culture still flourished on the plains of Nebraska. Murie brought Roaming Scout to Chicago, where the elderly man recorded approximately seven hours of narration about traditional Skiri life, covering subjects that range from religion and philosophy to daily social practices, with an emphasis on the ethical and moral foundations of Pawnee culture.

Murie recorded these accounts on wax cylinders. Later, he transcribed the Skiri speech in a practical alphabet, which, in the absence of any standardized system for writing Pawnee, he had apparently developed himself, perhaps in collaboration with Fletcher, for it is the same system he

5. It also does not contain the song lyrics that were recorded. The manuscript was supposed to have been published in 1907 by the Carnegie Institution under the joint authorship of Dorsey and Murie, but for some now unknown reason it was not; its fate was to languish in typescript. Alexander Spoehr edited and published parts of the first half under the title *Notes on Skidi Pawnee Society*, Field Museum of Natural History, Anthropological Series, vol. 27, no. 2 (Chicago, 1940). Parks is preparing a modern critical edition of the entire manuscript for publication.

used to record Pawnee names on censuses and allotments at the Pawnee agency beginning in the 1880s. Then, after transcribing the narratives in Skiri, he wrote out two English translations of them, one a literal, putatively etymological interpretation, and the other a very free rendition. (Most of the free translations, if they were in fact made, no longer exist.)

In September 1906, once the transcriptions had been completed, Dorsey wrote Franz Boas to make arrangements to go to New York City for a six- to eight-week period to, as Dorsey wrote, "take up the study of phonetics and linguistics in general, at any rate so far as relates to the Pawnee." Dorsey's intention was to learn basic linguistic techniques under Boas's tutelage so that he could refine the transcriptions of the Roaming Scout texts, hoping that the material itself would be of sufficient interest to Boas to compensate him for the time he would devote to the endeavor. Boas agreed to the proposition but told Dorsey frankly that it would be impossible for someone to learn linguistic methods in so short a period and that he himself had other projects which would not allow him much time to spare "unless I should want to take up the study of Pawnee myself."

Dorsey and Murie arrived in New York in early 1907. They remained there, working at Columbia University for ten weeks, but precisely what they did can only be inferred. Boas and Dorsey, using the written texts together with the cylinder recordings and Murie as a speaker, sought to establish the phonetic elements of Pawnee in order to create a systematic phonetic transcriptional orthography. The biggest problem for the two anthropologists, judging from their correspondence, was the Pawnee *r*, which often varies phonetically among four distinct sounds (*l*, *r*, *n*, and sometimes *d*), and which Boas later described in the introduction to the *Handbook of American Indian Languages*.[6] More significant problems, such as vowel and consonantal length, were seemingly less consequential to them, since Dorsey marked vowel length only sporadically and never indicated a recognition of the geminate consonants *tt* and *cc*.

After Dorsey returned home, he wrote Boas that he was continuing to study the variants of *r* and had found that they did not create meaning differences—that is, they were, as we would say today, variants of a single phoneme. Nevertheless, Boas urged him to continue to write *l*, *n*, and *r* just

6. Franz Boas, *Handbook of American Indian Languages*, Smithsonian Institution, Bureau of American Ethnology Bulletin no. 40 (Washington, D.C., 1911), vol. 1, 16–17. The letters between Dorsey and Boas are in the correspondence files of the Department of Anthropology, Field Museum of Natural History, Chicago, and the Boas Collection in the American Philosophical Society Library, Philadelphia.

as they were articulated rather than to use a single symbol *r* for the sound, as Dorsey was inclined to do. (Dorsey took the middle road and wrote *r* and *n*, but not *l*.)

At some point, presumably after returning to Chicago, Dorsey emended Murie's handwritten transcriptions and had them typed double-spaced on legal-size sheets. Then he proofread them, added diacritical marks, and made editorial notations, such as joining separate elements to make a single word or indicating a space where he thought a word boundary occurred. This work continued from March to at least October 1907, when Dorsey wrote Boas that he was continuing to devote every minute of his time to the Pawnee linguistic study and proposed writing a paper on the structure of the language. The October letters are the last time he mentioned the work, however.

Sometime in 1908, or soon thereafter, Dorsey's interests or priorities shifted, for he never did anything further with the Roaming Scout texts, and from 1912 to 1914 Dorsey wrote periodic letters to Murie, apologizing for not being able to continue their project. From that time until 1929, the texts remained shelved.

Although Boas never did take sufficient interest in Pawnee to study it himself, he assigned the project of recording Pawnee language and culture to his student Gene Weltfish, who engaged in fieldwork in Oklahoma between 1929 and 1931. Sometime during that period, she undertook the retranscription and retranslation of the Dorsey and Murie version of the narratives, after Dorsey had turned over all of the manuscripts to Boas. Weltfish worked on the project for at least two months and then either abandoned the effort or lost part of her work later, for the surviving results of her accomplishments are mixed: of the thirty-six texts, there are thirteen retranscriptions—about half of the collection, since three of these are the longest narratives. Only three of the thirteen texts were reelicited from a Skiri speaker, however; the other ten were reelicited from speakers of the South Band dialect, which differs significantly from Skiri speech. Weltfish's transcriptions are also phonetic and so, in most ways, do not differ significantly from Dorsey's, although she made more vocalic distinctions than he did. These vocalic distinctions are unnecessary, however, and, like Dorsey and Boas, she failed to realize that both vowel length and consonantal length are critical to an accurate, phonemic writing system.

After Weltfish ended her work with them, the Roaming Scout texts went into a period of dormancy for fifty years, until 1982, when I located the original handwritten versions in the archives of the Department of Anthropology in the American Museum of Natural History and copied them. Three years later, I found Dorsey's original typed versions together with Weltfish's surviving handwritten reelicitations among Weltfish's papers, which were deposited posthumously in the archives of Fairleigh Dickinson University. Together, copies of these three sets of documents provided each of the historical, written versions of the collection.

Meanwhile, in 1940, the original 215 wax cylinder recordings made by Dorsey and Murie were sent from the Field Museum to Ralph Linton at Columbia University. In 1948, George Herzog brought them to Indiana University, where they are now preserved in the Archives of Traditional Music. In 1972, the surviving 212 cylinders were copied onto tape, making them accessible for study. Unfortunately, however, the ravages of repeated playing, as well as later storage and neglect—the latter resulting in mildew on most of the cylinders, cracks in many, and the shattering of others—reduced their sound quality to the point that many of the recordings are now inaudible or of only marginal utility. Nevertheless, the sound quality of over half of the recordings is sufficient that they can be used to compare Roaming Scout's speech with that of contemporary Skiri speakers.

Once copies of all extant written and sound-recorded versions were obtained, the primary task of the project was to establish a definitive linguistic text that would preserve the integrity of the original document by replicating it exactly as it was written, and then to emend or revise that version so that a new, linguistically accurate version would exist. At the same time, it was necessary to create a new literal English translation, since Murie's original one, which was intended to be etymological, assigned a translation to each syllable of every word and resulted in an overly complicated, unwieldy translation that was sometimes incorrect and frequently unfathomable.

The procedure for obtaining an emended or revised version of the original Murie-Dorsey version was to reelicit the Skiri text word by word, which in original typescript was 160 doubled-spaced legal-size pages, using the original as the basis for the reelicitation, and in the process to develop a new translation. Although I was initially concerned whether it would still be possible to accomplish the task, since today there are no more than a half-dozen speakers of Skiri, the work has now been completed for the entire collection. Also, contrary to initial fears that there might be too much archaic vocabulary and grammatical usage that would present overwhelming translation problems for a contemporary speaker, it proved possible to edit the collection thoroughly, generally with no more than one or two enigmatic forms per text.

My collaborator in this work has been Nora Pratt, an elderly full-blood Skiri speaker who is the niece of Murie's mother-in-law. The last truly fluent Skiri speaker with a sufficient knowledge of ritual vocabulary and older grammatical usages, she is a social leader among the conservative members of the tribe, is the keeper of the Morning Star bundle, a historically important religious shrine, and is the daughter of a hereditary chief—facts I mention because they account, in part, for the conservatism of the family and the tenaciousness with which the family has retained its Skiri identity. For most of her life, moreover, Mrs. Pratt lived with her monolingual mother, who as a child came to Oklahoma from Nebraska and lived to be over one hundred years old. Nevertheless, throughout the project Mrs. Pratt has expressed surprise that, since the recordings represent Skiri speech of the nineteenth century, she has been able to understand and translate the texts with no more problems than we have encountered. At the same time, much of the content of the texts has been new to her, and she has expressed amazement at how much she, too, has learned about historical Pawnee culture, especially religion, from Roaming Scout's narratives.

The endeavor has resulted in a two-part presentation of the texts, as illustrated in Appendix 1. There, in the first part, the original transcription of the Murie-Dorsey version appears as the first line, reproduced exactly as it was written, with errors retained and explained, when necessary, in footnotes. The second line, in italics, is a phonemic retranscription, and on the third line, under each Pawnee word, is a literal English translation. After this interlinear presentation is a free translation that closely follows the original, preserving, insofar as it is possible, in a comprehensible English rendition, the structure and stylistic features of Roaming Scout's Skiri.

Initially, it was questionable which version of the Murie-Dorsey transcriptions—Murie's first handwritten version or the copy after it that was emended by Dorsey—was to be considered the original document. Arguments could be made for each one, but since the project was a collaborative one between the two men, with Dorsey making his emendations on Murie's handwritten copy, I decided to treat the emended version as the original. It should also be noted that all of the reelicitation was done from the original typed version, checking the retranscriptions when possible against the sound recordings. Only occasionally did I have recourse to the Weltfish retranscriptions and translations, since Weltfish (or her consultant) frequently reinterpreted forms—and in virtually all instances I learned that the original transcriptions and translations by Murie were correct.

Roaming Scout and the Textual Content

The narrator, Roaming Scout, was born into a chief's family about 1845, a time when the semisedentary Skiri lifestyle, which for centuries had alternated between horticulture and hunting, had already for several decades been experiencing gradual—and soon to be profound—changes brought about by the incorporation of the Plains region into the new United States and by an ever-expanding Euro-American population in the eastern part of the country. Although desultory at first, missionary activity among the Skiri and the closely related Pawnee bands began as early as 1835; and in the years immediately preceding Roaming Scout's birth, the United States government was trying to settle the Skiri and Pawnee in agricultural communities during the first attempts to acculturate them. By 1857, little more than a decade after Roaming Scout's birth, his people had signed a treaty at Table Creek in which they relinquished their freedom to rove throughout their old hunting territory and ceded most of their lands; in exchange for the concessions, they were to live as dependents of the government on a small reservation.

Throughout the three decades preceding the Table Creek Treaty, and intensifying over the two decades succeeding it, the Skiri and Pawnee in Nebraska were plagued by a combination of pressures and adversities that ultimately shattered their life there. White immigrants, at first passing through Skiri country on their way west and later settling in the territory surrounding them, made traditional Skiri life progressively more untenable. But affecting their life even more drastically were unremitting epidemic diseases and the relentless attacks of the Sioux and Cheyenne, who continued to engage in intertribal warfare long after the Skiri and Pawnee acceded to government efforts to settle Plains Indians on reservations and to induce them to give up fighting. These two interrelated afflictions—disease and enemy raids, which not infrequently were massacres—took drastic tolls on the Skiri and Pawnee populations, reducing tribes that had numbered some ten thousand people at the turn of the century to a mere two thousand in the 1870s. Finally, in 1874, these formerly independent peoples, who now formed a single tribal entity designated Pawnee, agreed to their removal to Indian Territory. Two years later, in 1876, the tribe was settled on a reservation south of the Arkansas River, and their new agency was established on a site just outside the present town of Pawnee, Oklahoma.

It was into this cultural context that Roaming Scout was born, when Skiri life was first beginning to experience drastic changes. His childhood and youth, to judge from his autobiography, were typical of the traditional lifestyle, but as he grew older, he lived through the years of upheaval that ultimately resulted in that lifestyle succumbing to an alien one—one, in fact, to which he never adapted. Although the cultural changes that the Skiri experienced were profound, Roaming Scout rarely mentioned them in his recordings for Murie, except for occasional incidental references to white people in his reminiscenses and acknowledgments that the old Indian ways had been permanently replaced by new ones. According to his autobiographical account, he evinced a strong interest in religion and ritual activity while he was young—interests that are, in fact, the themes dominating his autobiography, which unfortunately ends immediately after his first war expedition while he was still a teenager. Other information about his religious life and thought, however, occurs throughout the narratives and suggests that religion was, indeed, the dominating force throughout his life and apparently created for him a world in which he insulated himself against the changes engulfing him and his people.

Beyond what can be gleaned from the texts, little is remembered or recorded about Roaming Scout today. Although married twice, he had only one surviving child, a daughter, and she had no offspring. At the turn of the century, he was, nevertheless, the foremost religious leader of the Skiri by virtue of his being priest of the Evening Star bundle, the leading shrine in Skiri ritualism. All Dorsey wrote of him was: "This interesting priest of the Skidi . . . is one of the most influential, and perhaps the most learned, of the Skidi today."[7] Roaming Scout died in 1914.

The contents of Roaming Scout's narratives vary dramatically. Representing one genre is his autobiography, presented in a long text that reveals much about boyhood in Pawnee society, particularly about the thinking and behavior of a male child who is born into a leading family and who has religious inclinations. Roaming Scout's earliest memories are of his grandfather—the things he and his grandfather did together and the advice the older man gave him. Later, after his grandfather's death, his reminiscences turn to the deeds he performed while still young, deeds that he thought would gain the approval or admiration of others, particularly of adults: how he consecrated the first birds he killed to a sacred bundle; how on one occasion he led back to the village a mule with consecrated meat for an older hunter; and how he brought back to his family's lodge the first game animals he killed.

More revealing, however, are the descriptions of his first religious deeds and the instructions in ritual behavior that he received. While still a

---

7. Dorsey, *Traditions of the Skidi Pawnee*, 329.

boy, for example, he consecrated a buffalo to one of the leading Skiri sacred bundles, and in minute detail he recounts the procedure for taking the meat to the priest's lodge and what occurred when they ceremonially received his offering. Immediately following that deed, which gave him the right to make a smoke offering to the deities himself, he again describes in step-by-step detail the instruction he received from a priest in his family's lodge who was the keeper of the Calf, or Evening Star, bundle. Sometime later, he was motivated to make a ritual meat offering to the council of chiefs—a secular act—and again he recounts the details of his experience, which in this instance was initially marred by the inappropriate behavior of one chief, who postponed the ritual. He then relates a subsequent visionary experience in which the Heavens called down to him in his sleep to tell him that the powers in the Heavens had motivated him to do what he had done for the chiefs, that he had acted properly, but that the one chief who postponed the event had wronged him and had thereby ruined his good deed. The experience, Roaming Scout recounts, left a lasting impression on him, suggesting that it would somehow affect his fortune: "And after I woke up I thought about the dream all the time. 'Now let's see what will happen. I wonder what's going to happen in my life?'"

After these experiences, Roaming Scout finishes his autobiographical narrative with a long account of his first war party—when he sneaked away from home to join it; when his father, thinking the boy too young, pursued the party to bring him back home; and when, on their way home, the boy slipped away from his father to rejoin the party. The account, although rich in ethnographic detail, is even more poignant for its personal perspective on this archetypical male activity, and particularly for its description of interpersonal relations among members of the party, as well as among the leaders of this and another war party that is encountered during the expedition.

Representing another narrative genre in the collection is a set of texts explaining the Skiri concept of *waaruksti* 'holy, mysterious, powerful, awesome.' Some of these tell of Roaming Scout's own experiences and so flesh out the story of his life after his autobiography ends. In one account, for example, he tells Murie at the outset, "Brother, the Heavens is the one who gave me my mysterious power. And, brother, I was holy when I went around while I was young. The Heavens was the reason I was powerful, and this Sun was the cause." Then he describes an event that simultaneously exemplifies his powers and an error in his judgment. Once, during the doctors' late summer performances in the Medicine Lodge, Scabby Bull, a doctor who was Roaming Scout's brother, wanted to perform a public demonstration of his power by slitting open his nephew's belly. Rather than subject the nephew to the ordeal, however, Roaming Scout insisted that Scabby Bull use him instead. After Roaming Scout began the performance in the lodge by imitating a deer, another doctor, not Scabby Bull, came out of his booth and shot Roaming Scout with an arrow that rendered him unconscious and caused him to hemorrhage. From that dramatic moment, when Roaming Scout lay near death, the narrative becomes an extended description of his recuperation, of how, over an eight-day period, he was saved by a combination of various doctors' ministrations and the intercession of his own supernatural benefactors, Sun and a certain small animal.

In a related text entitled "Animal Spirits," Roaming Scout describes how, through the intention of the Heavens, the Skiri and all animal kind were created to live impermanently on this earth and how power, through animals on earth and celestial bodies above, was conveyed in dreams to favored Skiri, enabling them to perform miraculously in healing, war, and hunting. The account, which ends with several examples of individuals who had had power bestowed on them, is a document unparalleled in the Plains ethnographic literature as a comprehensive, conceptually cohesive, native description of an American Indian worldview.

In addition to the preceding two texts, six other narratives recount individual visions and exemplify the powers of men who had been blessed by Sun and various animals. Among them is the story of Pahukatawa, a nineteenth-century legendary Skiri who was killed and dismembered by the Sioux but was restored to life by the animals so that he could return to his people as a spirit to forewarn them of impending enemy attacks. Pahukatawa's story is instructive, too, Roaming Scout explains, because it illustrates how people all too frequently are skeptical of individuals with supernatural powers and how that skepticism and the disrespect it represents ultimately deprive people of benefits intended for them. And so, when people scoffed at his existence as a spirit after death, Pahukatawa forsook his tribe and went up into the northern Heavens, where he continues to live as a star.

Expanding Roaming Scout's portrayal of the Skiri conception of human life and humankind's place in the universe are two other important texts. The longer one, entitled "Life, Death, and Burial," comprises a philosophical discussion of life and death, with descriptions of mourning customs and the burials accorded individuals from the various strata of Skiri society. Included in it is a long, verbatim recounting of a priest's oration delivered during Roaming Scout's youth to the relatives of a group of young men who had been killed while on a war party. In it, Roaming Scout repeats in detail the priest's words describing how life is impermanent for humans at every stage of their existence on earth and how death may come for anyone at any moment and for whatever reason when the Heavens wishes it. Equally instructive is Roaming Scout's descriptions of the interrelations between the living and the spirits of the dead, especially where he repeats at length what surviving relatives used to say when speaking to the dead before burial. Moreover, nowhere in the ethnographic literature is class distinction more vividly illustrated for the Pawnee than in Roaming Scout's account of the differences in the treatment of the dead, which ranged from elaborate funerals for members of wealthy families to mere abandonment of the body for poor individuals with no relatives.

The other, related text, which Murie entitled "Spirit Land," is a description of the afterlife. In it, Roaming Scout recounts the story of a man who once seemed to have died and who, after his body had been wrapped up in buffalo robes for burial and had lain there for some time, suddenly began to move. After the man was unwrapped, he returned to lead a normal life and later told people how he had gone to the land of departed spirits after his apparent death. It was a land, he told them, like this one, and the spirits there lived in a village like theirs on earth. His family, like all others, had its own lodge, and when he went to it his deceased relatives told him that it was not yet his time to join them—that he was too anxious to come to their world and that there still were things on earth that he must learn and do. When the spirits became angry with him, the man revived. Once he came back to life, he was able, as the spirits had instructed him, to affirm that people do indeed live after death. Later, he was made a chief, and then the Heavens gave him power, and he became a noted warrior who brought prosperity to his band.

Comprising yet another genre complementing the preceding groups of narratives is a set of cosmogonic texts that derive at least in part from Roaming Scout's transfer of his Wolf Was Fooled bundle to Murie, to whom he entrusted this village religious shrine so that Murie, in turn, could place it in the Field Columbian Museum.[8] In the process of transferring the bundle to him, Roaming Scout told Murie what he knew of the bundle's history and rituals in a text entitled "The Wolf Was Fooled Bundle." In it, he summa-

8. Roaming Scout, who was keeper of several sacred bundles, including the Evening Star bundle that his family owned, entrusted them to the Field Museum.

rizes the Heavens' creation and arrangement of the world—of the natural elements and living beings on earth, and of the stars and other bodies in the Heavens, the latter represented on a star map drawn on a buffalo scalp that is among the contents of the bundle. In memorized recitative form, Roaming Scout repeats the teachings given by the Heavens to the original visionary who was instructed to make the map and was told what humans were to call each of the stars and constellations in the Heavens.

Following this cosmogonic account, the narrative content turns to Wolf, the primary power of the bundle, a mythological star deity represented by wolves on earth and represented in the bundle by a wolf skin that lay over it. In one section, Roaming Scout explains that he does not know all the bundle's ritual songs, but he recites one of the fundamental ones, the lyrics of the song of Wolf, which is a step-by-step account of the creation of everything in the world and which was sung when the bundle was opened during ceremonies. After this recitation, Roaming Scout recounts the origin myth of the bundle. The story tells how Holy Being came down from the Heavens to earth carrying a bag containing the first people, how Wolf stole the bag, how the people escaped while Wolf was sleeping, and how Wolf later tried unsuccessfully to deceive the people by pretending to be Holy Being and imitating Holy Being's buffalo calling rites. After Holy Being exposes him, the people kill Wolf, and Holy Being instructs them to make the Wolf Was Fooled bundle and to have Wolf as the leading power in it.

Other narratives in this genre include numerous descriptions of individual stars and constellations, most of which were recorded when Roaming Scout and Murie were examining the star map in Chicago. In these narratives, Roaming Scout names the major celestial bodies known to the Skiri and tells whatever he knows about their lore. For some—such as the constellations the Skiri called the Chiefs, the Bow, and the Big and Little Stretcher—he remembers their explanatory stories, but for many others he can provide little more than their names and perhaps only a fragment of what was once told about them. The short text describing the Chiefs constellation, illustrating this genre as well as the entire collection of narratives, is presented in Appendix 1.

Finally, representative of another genre are several texts that are more specifically ethnographic in content. The longest is one Murie entitled "Ethics," which is actually a concatenation of many stories of people and incidents, each designed to illustrate Pawnee attitudes and behavior toward such ethical issues as stealing, murder, lying, infidelity, and other forms of socially incorrect behavior. Also included among these stories are descriptions of the hunt and its regulation, childhood activities and games, and marriage. There are anecdotes, as well, often humorous, of individuals whose behavior was abnormal and of older peoples' foibles. Concluding this collection is a long story about a boy, a chief's son, whose speech and behavior were socially inappropriate, to the exasperation of his family, but who ultimately revealed himself to be endowed with supernatural power and achieved great war deeds, instituted the Children's Iruska Society, and in the end became the head chief of his people. An exceptionally well-told story, it is an account of deviant behavior masking supernatural power, a theme typical of the Pawnee and Arikara oral traditions.[9]

Another long text is one Murie entitled "Women's Work," again a composite of ethnographic description and an illustrative story. Roaming Scout begins by declaring a religious sanction for the division of labor between the sexes in Skiri society:

> Now, brother, I am going to tell you what He planned for our tribe while it was living here on earth—about the ways that the women had. When the Heavens gave them their ways, the things the women did were good. I am going to tell you about them.
>
> Our Father Above did not intend that men among us should work the way they do among your people, but that is the way He gave to women.

After this explanation, he proceeds with a detailed description of women's activities organized around the seasons, beginning with their work in the fall, as well as descriptions of the manufacture of such women's crafts as bulrush mats, mortars and pestles, and beds. Also integrated into the narrative are related discussions of gender roles, gender relations, and kin relations. He discusses berdaches, for example, and explains why there were males "who had a woman's ways":

> Brother, long ago it was that way. There would be a male among the people who had a woman's ways and he would grow up. Sometimes after She made a man that way, so that he would act that way, She gave him power so that he would not be poor. He was given the power to be successful as a warrior and yet he was a man who acted like a woman. And this Moon—this Moon was the cause of it, brother, when She put the mind of a woman in a man; and this Moon

9. Douglas R. Parks, *Traditional Narratives of the Arikara Indians* (Lincoln: University of Nebraska Press, 1991), volume 3, 55–56.

was the cause of it. "I'll put the mind of a woman in this man! I'll put the mind of a woman in him even though he is a man!"

In this, as in every other description he gives of Skiri behavior and custom, Roaming Scout explains how things were the way they were because the Heavens created them that way:

> Brother, what I am telling you about is the way He made it for us Indians to do. But, brother, the customs of your white people now living here are different. Your custom is different, and our Indian custom is different. These things I am talking about are the way the Heavens made it for my tribe to do while it was here on earth. We are no longer that way, brother. It is no longer that way among our tribe.

Even though many of his people continued to speak their language and to observe traditional behavior and customs at the time when Roaming Scout recorded his narratives for Murie, for him the old Skiri way of life had disappeared. As he told Murie in the conclusion to the narrative about the Wolf Was Fooled bundle:

> I have lost all my ways—all the ways. We do not have any of our ways any more, brother. But now, brother, the Heavens desired that I should find you and that you should find me. [The Heavens said,] **"Then you will be the one to be his companion after you meet each other."** [10]

For Roaming Scout, the loss of his and his people's ways was embodied not only in the loss of Skiri territory and independence but, more fundamentally, in the loss of religious and doctoring powers that they formerly had possessed and that had come to selected individuals in dreams through the medium of animals and other powers of the universe, but ultimately from the Heavens. This was a loss that he himself had experienced when he was younger and had had power—power that he no longer possessed but only remembered. When Murie came to Roaming Scout to record what the old priest knew of the tribal past, Roaming Scout interpreted their collaboration, as he interpreted every object and event in the world, as motivated by the Heavens. Thus, he believed that their work and what he was recording were divinely inspired, motivating him to tell his brother, as he addressed Murie, all that he knew in order to preserve an accurate, authentic record of

10. In free translations of Roaming Scout's narratives, the words of the Heavens are set in bold type.

his people's past. As a result of this unique collaboration, Roaming Scout's narratives are not only exceptionally rich in hitherto undocumented ethnographic description but, even more significantly, they are invaluable for their wealth of self-expressed native attitudes and perceptions, which are unparalleled in the literature on the Pawnee and are certainly rare for North America as a whole.

The Sword Lakota Texts

Unlike most American Indian languages, a practical orthography for writing Sioux was developed during the mid-nineteenth century and was widely used by Sioux people for record keeping and letter writing. Thus, during the early reservation years, native language literacy was one means available to the Sioux to aid them in the transition to reservation life. On the Pine Ridge Reservation, no one made more effective use of native language literacy than George Sword, an Oglala born about 1847, whose life truly spanned the dramatic transition in Plains Indian societies. Although he was unique among his contemporaries for preserving a record of traditional culture written in the native language, his writings are not well known, and most have not yet been published either in the original or in translation.[11]

• • • •

The first systematic orthography for writing Dakota, representing the eastern dialects of the Sioux language, was devised in 1834 by Samuel W. Pond and Gideon H. Pond, Congregational missionaries to the Sioux in Minnesota. The Pond brothers soon began to publish material in the Dakota language to aid in their teaching and missionizing efforts. With the arrival of a group of missionaries from the American Board of Commissioners for Foreign Missions, work in promoting Dakota literacy escalated rapidly. Some alterations in the original orthography were made, and the publication of Bible translations and pedagogical materials proliferated. The Dakota grammar and dictionary begun by the Ponds was completed by Stephen R. Riggs and his missionary associates and was published in 1851 by the

11. See Sword's own autobiographical statement in James R. Walker, *Lakota Belief and Ritual*, ed. Raymond J. DeMallie and Elaine A. Jahner (Lincoln: University of Nebraska Press, 1980), 74–75. Sword's manuscript writings are in the Department of Anthropology archives, American Museum of Natural History, New York, and in the Colorado Historical Society, Denver.

Smithsonian Institution. As a government document, this work was widely distributed; for example, copies were sent to army posts on the frontier. In 1880, the Bible translation was completed, was published in its entirety by the American Bible Society, and was also widely distributed.[12]

In addition to religious publications, of major significance were the newspapers published in the Sioux language. The first was short-lived, the *Dakota Tawaxitku Kin* (*The Dakota Friend*), edited by Gideon Pond and published in St. Paul from 1850 to 1852. Following the military conflicts of the 1860s, which led to the dispersal of most of the Minnesota Sioux, the *Iapi Oaye* (*The Word Carrier*) was founded in 1871 by missionaries of the Congregational and Presbyterian churches. First printed in 1877 at the Yankton Agency at Greenwood, Dakota Territory, it moved to the mission school at Santee, Nebraska, where it continued to be published until the 1930s. This widely circulated monthly paper—which developed into separate native language and English editions, whose contents, in most cases, were entirely different—published material written by individuals from all of the widely scattered Sioux communities. Editorials and letters were printed in the dialect in which they were written, making the *Iapi Oaye* a historical archive representing the diversity of spoken Sioux dialects. In 1878, the Episcopals launched a similar paper called *Anpao Kin* (*The Daybreak*), and in 1893 the Catholics followed with *Sinasapa Wocekiye Taeyapaha* (*The Catholic Herald*); both of these also continued publication until the 1930s.

It was in this atmosphere of developing native language literacy that the Sioux people made their accommodations to reservation life. These newspapers served as bulletin boards to transmit information and to voice opinions. The material they contain is of endless interest to anthropologists and historians: They provide a record of births, marriages, and deaths; community news; political commentaries; articles on traditional beliefs and customs; and abundant material for the study of the Sioux accommodation to Christianity.

In addition to these published sources of Sioux literacy, a substantial amount of unpublished material has been preserved. Much of it represents personal documents, but there are also bodies of material recorded for explicitly historical purposes: to memorialize specific events and to preserve a record of traditional culture for the future. Among these unpublished docu-

12. Bibliographic data on these nineteenth-century Dakota publications is found in James Constantine Pilling, *Bibliography of the Siouan Languages*, Smithsonian Institution, Bureau of American Ethnology Bulletin no. 5 (Washington, D.C., 1887).

ments is one archived in the Colorado Historical Society, a ledgerbook written entirely in Lakota (the dialect of the Western Sioux), which has, pasted to the front, a small paper label that reads, simply, *George Sword lena owa* (George Sword wrote these). The volume is penned in a strong, sprawling hand, in heavy ink; the words have obviously been committed slowly and meticulously to the paper, syllable by syllable, with rarely a correction.

• • • •

Born during the buffalo hunting days, before Lakota lifeways began to change under the pressures of American settlement on the frontier, Sword had been raised to be a warrior and fought with honor in many conflicts against the Pawnee, the Crow, the Shoshone, and other tribes. In the early 1870s, he came to the Red Cloud Agency, where he decided that the best hope for the Indians was to ally with, rather than to fight, the whites. He enlisted as a scout with General George Crook and served in Colonel Ranald S. Mackenzie's raid on the Cheyenne village in the Big Horn Mountains in 1876. During that winter, he visited Crazy Horse's camp of Oglala as an emissary from the army to ask that Crazy Horse and his people return to the agency and live in peace. Appointed first captain of the Indian Police at the new Pine Ridge Agency in 1879, Sword soon joined the Episcopal church. In time, he became a deacon in the church and, after leaving the police force with the rank of major, was appointed one of the first tribal judges of the Court of Indian Offenses. He visited Washington on several occasions as a member of delegations to negotiate with government officials. He was a representative to the tribal council and served for a term as its president. By the time of his death in 1910, he was among the most important leaders of the Oglala people—and literacy was the vehicle of his success.

When Sword settled at the agency, he traded in his weapons for pen and paper and became record keeper for his people. He learned to read and to write in the alphabet used in the native language newspapers, although exactly how he learned is unknown; perhaps he received instruction from a missionary or an army officer. In 1882, he published his first letter in the *Anpao Kin*. Subsequently, he kept police and court records, as well as church attendance records, and served as amanuensis for his people. Then, in 1896, he met James R. Walker, the medical doctor at Pine Ridge, who began anthropological studies under the direction of Clark Wissler, curator of anthropology at the American Museum of Natural History in New

York. About 1905, Sword wrote for Walker a record of Lakota culture, as well as the story of his own life. Unfortunately, Walker himself was unable to decipher the Sword texts fully, nor was he satisfied with the translations he paid others to make of them. First, he hired Clarence Three Stars, an Oglala who had attended Carlisle Indian School in Pennsylvania. Three Stars, however, rewrote Sword's texts after his own ideas and translated them in modern reservation-English idiom so that their cultural content was obscured. (Walker declared Three Stars's translations worthless, claiming they totally destroyed the ethnological value of Sword's writings.) Next, Walker hired Charles Nines, a non-Lakota Indian trader's son who was a fluent speaker of the language. His translations were overly literal, and he found the work tedious and frustrating, eventually giving up on it. Afterward, Walker labored on alone, until his death in 1926.

• • • •

About 1937, Franz Boas, professor of anthropology at Columbia University, apparently received the Sword ledgerbook from Clark Wissler and hired Ella Deloria, a native Sioux whom he had trained as a linguist, to retranscribe the texts phonemically and to translate them into English. Deloria, however, took a somewhat adversarial attitude toward Sword's writing. From the outset, she objected to his writing style because it differed from normal speech. For example, as a result of his careful syllable-by-syllable writing, Sword did not generally anticipate morphophonemic changes; thus, the texts are written without the usual elisions that occur in actual speech. Moreover, perhaps because writing was a slow and painstaking process for him, the texts do not embody the repetition that characterizes oral style. In addition, Sword frequently omitted the definite article $kį$, the use of which is normally pervasive in Lakota speech. These, and other stylistic idiosyncracies, make Sword's writings unique.

Deloria also protested that since the subject matter of many of Sword's texts was unknown to her—for example, the description of ritual games; the prayers of medicine men; the details of ceremonies; the terms for warfare—it was impossible for her to make a complete and accurate translation. Sword obviously assumed that readers would be familiar with these matters and rarely provided explicit description. Although she discussed the texts with Lakota elders, Deloria inadvertently introduced errors based on historical misunderstanding. For example, after discussing the Sun Dance text with her consultant Fire Thunder, Deloria dismissed Sword's statement that a woman's work bag was attached to the center pole of the ritual lodge, asserting instead that Sword had miswritten and should have used the term for a warrior's bag. Deloria so "corrected" the text in the edited version she published.[13] Comparative ethnographic study of the symbols of the Sun Dance, however, convincingly demonstrates that Sword knew whereof he wrote: The Sun Dance pole sheltered the symbols of both women's and men's work. Thus, by failing to accept the integrity of the text as a historical document, Deloria was led into error.

Sword himself told Walker that when he spoke, the younger Oglala ridiculed his style. He spoke in the old way, he proudly told the physician, as people did before their language was contaminated by the missionaries and by the act of writing.[14] Sword conceptualized the Lakota language syllabically, assuming that each syllable was a discrete unit of meaning, and he considered word boundaries to be an artifact of writing. Moreover, many of the topics about which he wrote were esoteric and outside the experience of those who had been born after the people settled at Pine Ridge. It is, therefore, understandable why the work of translation has seemed so daunting.

After establishing a corpus of Sword's writings—probably not all that actually exist, but about one-third more than were known to Ella Deloria—I began the process of translation by studying the work of my predecessors. Having sorted out some of the problems, I then worked with an elderly Lakota speaker long renowned for his oratorical abilities—Vine Deloria, Sr., the brother of Ella Deloria. That he would work on the project was fortuitous, for it allowed me access to essentially the same linguistic forms that were familiar to Ella Deloria. In short, we were able to pick up the project exactly where she had left off. Here was an intellectual adventure that took us sometimes far afield from Sword himself, digressing to discuss subdialectal differences and perceived changes in the Lakota language over time. Nevertheless, despite minor confusions caused by occasional uncertainty about context or grammatical forms, we found the texts, though idiosyncratic, clearly intelligible.

Ethnographically, Sword's writings center on warfare and religion; historical context is provided by Sword's autobiography. The texts represent Sword's own literary genre; although they include standardized song lyrics,

13. Ella Cara Deloria, "The Sun Dance of the Oglala Sioux," *Journal of American Folk-Lore* 42 (1929):354–413.
14. Walker, *Lakota Belief and Ritual*, 75.

prayers, and ritual speeches, they are not, on the whole, simply written versions of oral narratives but are instead a new type of written narrative. They are invaluable for presenting the perspectives of late nineteenth-century Lakota on their rapidly changing world, and they also provide new perspectives on even well-known ethnographic topics. A discussion of some of what can be learned about Lakota warfare from Sword's writings will serve to exemplify their importance anthropologically and historically.

One text relates the familiar story of the bringing of the sacred pipe to the Lakota people by White Buffalo Woman; this is the instrument of prayer and of peace, a covenant between *Wak'ą T'ąka* 'Great Spirit' and the Sioux. But this peace, as Sword told the story, was not understood to be a universal one:

> Then she [White Buffalo Woman] told them that those who fought each other within the tribe must be friends instead. But those who were tribal enemies were not to be friends, but enemies; and then as enemies they would remain.
>
> And she said everything done in warfare was to be accounted as a good deed.

Thus, Sword offers a religious justification for intertribal warfare— war with the enemy. *T'óka* 'enemy' is the key concept, the term implying 'nontribal member, stranger, enemy'. It is the opposite of *Lak'ota*, implying 'ally, tribal member, friend'. From this Lakota cultural perspective, the very existence of the enemy fuels warfare.

This enemy, however, is a faceless other, and when individual enemies were dealt with in a friendly manner, they ceased to be *t'óka*. In this way, for example, the Lakota had allied with the Cheyenne, sometimes referring to them as *Lak'ota Šahiyela* 'Cheyenne Sioux'. And so it was with enemies adopted into the tribe; they became full tribal members, just as if they had been born Lakota. According to Walker, women captives who were taken as wives by Lakota men—the most numerous class of adoptees— were considered to be full tribal members when they learned to converse in the Lakota language.[15] It seems, therefore, that the alien status of enemy was most fundamentally symbolized by language.

The enemy status had another aspect, as well. Like the Lakota themselves, enemies were *ikce wic'aša* 'common men'—that is, 'Indians'; white

15. James R. Walker, *Lakota Society*, ed. Raymond J. DeMallie (Lincoln: University of Nebraska Press, 1982), 54–55.

people had no place in this classification. In fact, the first whites with whom the Sioux came in contact were considered to be not human in the same way as the Sioux. The Sioux called them *wasicu*, using the name of a type of powerful spirit; when whites proved their all-too-human qualities, the term tended to be restricted exclusively to designate whites, and the older usage to indicate spirits largely died out. By the twentieth century, the Lakota began to search for explanations for the origin of the term, creating—as all languages do—folk etymologies to make cultural sense out of a word whose origin was no longer remembered. One of the most frequently repeated today is *wasj icu* 'takes the fat', reflecting Lakota perception of the white people's greed, investing an old term with new relevance.

In the mid-nineteenth century, fighting the enemy was the most honorable duty of a man's life. In telling about the roles of men and women, Sword began: "The work of men is: they take part in fighting the enemy; that is a great honor." Everything else was secondary. The Lakota word *okic'ize* designates 'fighting' or a 'fight'; warfare is called *ozuye* 'going to war'. Both are activities; neither is a state of being. In contrast, *wólak'ota* designates 'peace', but no parallel construction was used to indicate the state of war; between *Lakota* and *t'óka*—that is, between Sioux and enemy—war was an undeviating relationship.

If warfare against enemy tribes was a natural state of affairs for the Lakota, what about fighting the whites? They were not *t'óka*; therefore, there was no honor in fighting them, and the scalps of white people were not valued as trophies. If the Lakota were to be successful in resisting the white advance on their territory, then in cultural terms they needed to transform white people into enemies. In his autobiography, Sword records how this was accomplished.

When Sword was about sixteen years old (about 1864), during the winter, the Hunkpapa and Minneconjou met together in council to consider the problem of the white people and came to the decision to fight them. Then a man named Red Dog visited the Oglala at their camp on the Yellowstone River and told them that he had been appointed to go around to the Lakota camps to forge a general agreement. After discussion, Sword's father, a chief named Shot in the Eye, along with others, voiced opposition to treating the whites as enemies. Sword wrote:

> But Red Cloud himself wanted to make war on the whites and many
> people supported him. And now that year they fought the whites determinedly. For what the Sioux principally resented was this: "The
> white men have come to take over the entire land," they said, "so

in this manner they press on and they will completely annihilate the Sioux people!" That is what they said, therefore they were frightened. So they planned a great war.

And there at a big council they publicly announced it and thus they spoke: "All young men, hear this! The white men will take our entire land from us and we will no longer comprise a people! Therefore we will make war on them, so whoever strikes a white man, that shall be a coup against the enemy! Whoever is wounded by a white man, that one shall be wounded by an enemy!" it was announced. "And if you take his horses and perform any other deeds, they shall be counted as honors!" it was said.

The decision-making process obviously operated by majority opinion, not consensus, but those such as Sword's father, who disagreed with the proposition, nonetheless remained in the Oglala camp.

The effect of this transformation of whites into enemies is reflected in Sword's autobiography, which begins with a chronological account of his brave deeds. He joined his first war party at age fifteen—an unsuccessful trip, since they failed to find the Crow, yet because he went out with the intention of fighting the enemy, this act was counted as a brave deed. During the next year, Sword went on five more expeditions against enemy Crow and Shoshone. Then, in the spring, following the council's decision to fight the whites as enemies, Sword accompanied a war party up the Yellowstone River to the mountains. There the scouts located a group of three white men, all armed. The war party charged on them, and Sword, using his quirt, whipped one of the white men across the chest; this was his first coup. The autobiography then records ten more war parties and fights, the last of which was fought against white soldiers; he was brave in this fight, Sword wrote, even though the soldiers' bullets tore his headdress to shreds. His eighteenth war party was the first that Sword himself led, and, again, the enemies were white soldiers; this time, his horse was shot out from under him. Sword went on thirty-four more war parties, many against the soldiers. Finally, he ends his record of war deeds with this disclaimer, "Surely at least one war party was overlooked . . ."

At this point, there is a major transition in Sword's autobiography; he says simply that he made friends with the whites and lived with them (at Red Cloud Agency, Nebraska, near the military post of Camp Robinson); it was 1876, the year, Sword wrote, when Custer and his troops were annihilated by the nonagency Indians, whom he now designates *wat'ogla* 'wild, untamed', the Lakota equivalent for what the army called "hostiles."

Importantly, Sword's autobiography preserves a Lakota perspective on those troubling days and a sense of the fear that if peace were not made with the whites, the agency Sioux would be sent to live in Oklahoma. The conditions of life were changing for the Lakota people; new routes for proving one's bravery and for providing for one's family were being opened up as old ones disappeared. The distinctions between white man and Indian, and between Lakota and enemy, were becoming blurred. It was a period of confusion, in which the very ways the Lakota understood the world were in flux.

Exemplifying his account of those times is Sword's report of his visit with other Indian scouts to the camp of Crazy Horse's people in Montana in January 1877. Serving as an emissary (*akic'ita* 'soldier') for the U.S. Army, Sword was charged with persuading these holdouts to make peace with the government and to come to the Red Cloud Agency. A dangerous and dramatic diplomatic mission, Sword recounts how he dealt not with Crazy Horse himself, but with the chief's spokesman, Iron Hawk. The latter was no stranger to Sword, for he had, in the past, accompanied war expeditions led by Iron Hawk. At this time, Sword's name was *Tok'ic'uwa*, which Ella Deloria translated as 'Enemy Bait'. Only after returning from this expedition was he given the name *Miwak'ą Yuhala* 'Sword Owner', the name of one of his older brothers, a chief, who had died. Sword's account is as follows (for the interlinear Lakota text, see Appendix 2):

> So an Indian soldier from the great council stood up and said: "Well, Enemy Bait, now tell what you have to say! What have you come here seeking?" So Enemy Bait himself spoke.
> "My friends, I consider myself to be one of you people so I gladly came over here on your behalf.
> "And this day gladly I join you in making this great council.
> "And I am filled with happiness," he said. "A soldier called Three Stars [General George Crook] sent me to you."
> And he said: "From this day on the President wishes the Indians not to fight, so throughout the land there will be no more fighting and all, no matter who they are, will be at peace. All my friends will return together in peace.
> "And as for them, many Sioux live here [at the agency] in peace; you will live the same as they," he said, and "although my friends return, nothing bad will happen," he said.
> And again that Indian soldier stood and: "Listen!"
> Iron Hawk stood.

And: "You reply to Enemy Bait's speech, but the way in which we told you to speak, speak in that manner," he said.

Iron Hawk spoke: "Well, Enemy Bait, sit and listen carefully! This is my country and in this manner the Great Spirit raised me so in this manner I live, but, my friend, the white men from where the sun rises came stealing my land and now the country is small so I do not permit him in my country, yet he comes in and when he sees me, then he shoots at me, and then I too shoot at him and I kill some of them and while I stand looking at them, I am sorrowful. 'These, I have beaten their relatives!' I think, and so I bring grief upon myself.

"So he who acts for the President: 'He wishes peace,' you all say.[16]

"Well, it shall be a great peace! As for me, when anyone brings good to me, he will not outdo me. I will come moving camp but I have much food; I am heavy; there is much snow; all the rivers lie across the way; they are deep. So I will come slowly moving camp.

"Enemy Bait, before I have arrived you will come to me again, or perhaps you will send your young man," he said. Then the soldier said this: "That speech alone is good, so only that he will relate," he said.

Iron Hawk said this: "The Oglalas and Cheyennes, these two together are the principal inhabitants of the land here, but I am alone![17] Now there will be peace, I have said. In this way the Minneconjous, Hunkpapas, those are living below me,"[18] he said.

And all the people returned in peace.

Sword's is the only participant's account of this important moment in Lakota history. Ethnographically, it presents a glimpse of the formal dynamics of the council, where a representative—in this case, Iron Hawk— is empowered by the akic'ita (representing the consensus of the chiefs in council) to speak for the people. In his ritualized speech, Iron Hawk repeats only the words he had been instructed to speak, and he speaks in the first person, representing the collective will of the people. Brief as it is, Sword's recounting of this important council richly informs our understanding of the Lakota political process and serves as an illustrative example of

16. That is, Sword and his companions have reported that General Crook, who represents the President, has announced the government's desire to make peace in the aftermath of the Battle of the Little Big Horn.

17. The collective "I" here stands for the united Cheyenne and Oglala.

18. That is, farther downstream on the tributaries of the Missouri River.

the value of his writings for cultural and historical understanding of the late nineteenth-century Lakota.

Conclusion

Although American Indian native language texts have received increasing scholarly attention in recent years, most studies have been of mythology and folklore and have focused on the structure and style of oral literature. Following the lead of Dell Hymes and Dennis Tedlock, many scholars have sought to discover the narrative structure of native language texts.[19] Important as their work is, it does not exhaust the possibilities for the study of Native American literatures. The Roaming Scout and Sword collections illustrate another type of Native American literature that developed out of the contact between Indians and anthropologists. Quite explicitly, Roaming Scout, in collaboration with Murie, as well as Sword, used the opportunities presented by the requests of anthropologists to record accounts of their respective cultures as they existed in the mid-nineteenth century. Both perceived their tribal cultures to be disappearing and wished to preserve some record of those older ways for the benefit of the future. In the process, they developed a new genre of native literature.

Though their underlying purposes were the same, the medium differed. Roaming Scout was not literate in the Pawnee language, so his texts were sound-recorded and therefore represent traditional Pawnee modes of transmitting religious and cultural knowledge from one generation to the next. Sword, on the other hand, had the ability to compose his record in writing, in the process deviating more radically from traditional Lakota narrative genres and devising specifically literary forms. Thus, although the content of the Roaming Scout and Sword narratives closely parallel one another, there are differences that reflect oral versus written style and that invite future study.

In discussing these two important bodies of texts, we have endeavored to underscore the importance of approaching all such collections in their historical context. They cannot be legitimately understood apart from the time and place of their composition. Ethnohistorical methods provide important means for placing text collections in the fullest possible cultural and historical contexts. In the absence of such context, analysis of native language texts is reduced to the timeless ethnographic present that has

19. See, for example, Joel Sherzer and Anthony C. Woodbury, eds., *Native American Discourse: Poetics and Rhetoric* (Cambridge: Cambridge University Press, 1987).

so hampered past studies of Native American peoples. The constant flux of change requires the specification of a time dimension for cultural description to be meaningful. Yet, only rarely have scholars appreciated native language texts as historical documents.

In fact, despite their significance for understanding the past, the historical collections of texts written or dictated in native languages and preserved in archives have long been ignored by anthropologists, historians, and linguists. Most scholars have been content, instead, to rely entirely on sources in European languages, assuming that native language documents are solely the preserve of linguists. And yet linguists themselves generally have not been interested in texts as historical or cultural documents but have utilized them narrowly as sources of lexical and grammatical data to be reelicited from contemporary speakers.[20]

For students of the American Indian past, it is essential to recognize native language documents as integral sources for the writing of truly *Indian* history. Understanding the past in native terms is the only way to escape the repetition of old interpretations based on outsiders' perceptions. Important to this endeavor is the realization and insistence that work with American Indian languages is essential to the proper training of scholars, so that native language documents can be edited and studied as similar documents are treated in other parts of the world.

Admonitions, however, are empty without exemplary studies to demonstrate the value of the method. This article is, therefore, a progress report on our project with Pawnee and Lakota texts. The translation, editing, and publication of large bodies of native language texts such as those of Roaming Scout and Sword is a time-consuming process, but it is only from the insights that such translation projects generate that meaningful ethnohistorical reconstructions, embodying native perspectives from the nineteenth century, can be written.

Translation projects based on historical text collections are depen-

20. Among students of American Indian literature, Tedlock has shown the greatest appreciation for historical context (see *The Spoken Word and the Work of Interpretation*). Recent publications of important collections of historical texts suggest that this is a developing trend. See, for example, Blair A. Rudes and Dorothy Crouse, *The Tuscarora Legacy of J. N. B. Hewitt*, 2 vols., Canadian Museum of Civilization, Mercury Series, Canadian Ethnology Service Paper no. 108 (Ottawa, 1987); Ives Goddard and Kathleen J. Bragdon, *Native Writings in Massachusetts*, 2 vols., American Philosophical Society Memoirs, vol. 185 (Philadelphia, 1988); John D. Nichols, ed., *The Dog's Children: Anishinaabe Texts Told By Angeline Williams*, ed. and trans. Leonard Bloomfield, Publications of the Algonquian Text Society (Winnipeg: University of Manitoba Press, 1991).

dent on close cooperation between scholars and native language collaborators. Both must be equally committed to the project and to interpreting the texts in their own terms. Simply being a speaker of the language is not sufficient; capable collaborators almost without exception today are elders who possess the requisite knowledge of older vocabulary and grammatical forms to translate the texts and who understand the cultural system that informs them. No translation based on mechanical reference to dictionaries and grammars will suffice, for the text is more than the sum of the meanings of the words that comprise it; cultural understanding is essential to provide the meaningful context required for translation. The anthropologist brings to the project a knowledge of the published and unpublished literature on the culture, as well as a comparative knowledge of geographically contiguous or historically related tribes, while the Indian collaborator brings the linguistic intuition of a native speaker, as well as a lifetime's reflection on cultural tradition. The dialogue between them, motivated by the desire to unlock the meanings of the text, determines the quality of the translation.

While the goal of our project is to produce authoritative reference editions of these text collections, we are not so presumptuous as to assume that our translations are the final word. Rather, the publication of the texts in their historical form, with modern linguistic retranscriptions and English glosses, bolstered by extensive editorial commentary, is intended to make them accessible to specialists and nonspecialists alike as resources for further study and reinterpretation. Each potential reader of the texts brings to them individual interests and perspectives; successful reference editions will guide readers with widely varying concerns to an understanding of the texts and encourage a broad spectrum of study. As editors and translators, we claim no monopoly over the texts, no matter how much time and work we invest in them, and we realize, in any case, that no one translation can do justice to the complexity and nuances of any text. Some scholars, for example, will want to rework the Roaming Scout and Sword texts from an ethnopoetic point of view and explore their structure. Other readers, Pawnee and Sioux people, for example, will read the texts as repositories of traditional knowledge, just as their authors originally intended, and the texts may serve to develop cultural links from the past to the future.

The documentary record of American Indian native language texts is a vast and barely explored cultural resource. These texts provide a level of information about historical cultures that qualitatively transcends outsiders' records written in English. As texts, they reflect their authors' personalities and the affective aspects of culture that so frequently elude both anthropological and historical studies. They are primary sources that can speak to us directly, but they require careful interpretation and coordination with other types of historical and anthropological documents, and in many cases alternative translations may support differing perspectives on the past. Used judiciously, native language documents can provide the data and the insights that allow us to transcend the normal Western bias of historical documents and can maximize the potential of the ethnohistorical method to write culturally sensitive history that truly represents Native American conceptions from the past.

Appendix 1: The Constellation of Chiefs

Roaming Scout

Náw[a],	irár[i],	irár[i],	šiksúrakut[a]	tirawa[21]
Ráwa	*iraári'*	*iraári'*	*cĭksu' rakuúta*	*Tiráwaahat*
Now,	brother,	brother,	be prayerful to Him	the Heavens,

irár[i],	hirurikutarúhkita	tirʌtaríraiwat[i]
iraári'.	*Hiru rikutarúhkita*	*tiratariíraa'iiwaati*
brother.	There that one is the cause	my telling you stories

a	nikurarúhkit[a]	tirʌspari	ariku-
a	*rikurarúhkita*	*tiráspari*	*a riku-*
and	that one is the cause	your going around here	and that

rarúhkit[a]	atí[ʌ]s	tirakítak[u]	tirʌtpari,
rarúhkita	*Atí'as*	*tirakítaku*	*tirátpari.*
one is the cause	our Father	the one above	my going around here.

nikutuhá[a]	tiwiwitirʌšihúras	irár[i].
Rikutuuhá'a	*tiwiwitiracíhuras*	*iraári'.*
That one is the reason	our finding one another,	brother.

---

21. Dorsey erroneously emended Murie's transcription by crossing out the final syllable of this word.

Náw^a,   irárⁱ,   tirasuhaíriku   tiráwah^Atⁿ   úrarisitⁿ
Ráwa   *iraári'*   *tirasuuhaa'iíriku*   *Tiráwaahat*   *uúrariisit*
Now,   brother,   these that you see   the Heavens   straight

tirawáh^Atⁿ   tiruhašákaku   hupíritⁿ   nikuwití-
Tiráwaahat   *tiruuhacaákaku*   *huupírit*   *rikuwitií-*
the Heavens   these sitting in a circle   stars,   they were the

r_Akt^u   atí^As   tirakítak^u,   irárⁱ,   nisaru-
raktu'   *Atí'as*   *tirakítaku*   *iraári'.*   *Riísaaru'*
ones He made   our Father   the one above,   brother.   Chiefs

wítiitⁿ,   nisaruwítiitⁿ.   Kúrahus   rikutihwáki-
wíti'it.   *Riísaaru' wíti'it.*   *Kúrahus*   *rikutihwakí-*
they are.   Chiefs   they are.   The priests   those are the ones

ah^u   tirikur_Asah^Atⁿ,   "Harirahkawíkitaku
'aahu'   *tirikurásahat*   *"Haariiraahkaawíkitaku*
they called   when I grew up: "There they sit in a circle above

nísaru   tiráwah^Atⁿ."   I,   háwirisuhišis   tíraku
riísaaru'   *Tiráwaahat."*   *I*   *haawiirísuuhiicis*   *tíraaku*[22]
chiefs   (in) the Heavens."   And,   now you do know   this one

nárihur^u   háru_Atⁿ   haríwawaritⁿ
rárihuuru.   *Haáruu'at.*   *Haaríwaawaarit*
the large one.[23]   There it flies.   There they stand all around

hupíritⁿ,   nikúwitiitⁿ   tiráwa[24]   atí^As
huupírit.   *Rikúwiti'it*   *Tiráwaahat*   *Atí'as*
the stars.   They are the ones   the Heavens   our Father

---

22. A star is usually classified as standing, referred to by the demonstrative *tiraáku* 'this one standing.' Here the verb *ku* 'to sit' is used because the reference is to stars conceived to be chiefs sitting in council in the Heavens.

23. Murie translated this form as 'marked thing,' which is *ruúrariiru*. What he wrote is 'the large one,' given in the retranscription here.

24. See note 21.

áhira^u	nisáru.	Irár^i,	kuháraru
áhira'u	*riisaáru'.*	*Iraári'*	*kuuháraaru'*[25]
His having made him	the Chief.	Brother,	He made a way

atí^^s	tiráwa	asuhawíriku	itirasuha-
Atí'as	*Tiráwaahat*	*asuuhaawiíriku*	*i tirasuuhaa-*
our Father	the Heavens	that you see them	and when you see

wíriku	hírikuruʌt^n.	Irár^i,	tirʌstíwãt^u
wiíriku	*hi ríkuruu'ut.*	*Iraári'*	*tirastiíwaatu*
these things	and it is that way.	Brother	what you see

witúharu	tiráwih^ʌt^n	ihi	nisaruwitúharu
wituuháru'	*tiráwihat*	*ihi*	*riísaaru' wituuháru'*
there are	these (sitting),	uh,	chiefs there are

tiráwihʌt^n	ihi	núksiri ápitk^u.
tiráwihat	*ihi*	*rúksiri' a pítku.*[26]
these (sitting),	uh,	twelve.

Náw^a,	irár^i,	nikuwitú^^t^n	tirawawáriki	iká-
Ráwa	*iraári'*	*rikuwituú'ut*	*tirawaawaáriki*	*iká-*
Now,	brother,	it is that way	these various ones	in the

rik^ʌt^n	ikárikʌt^n	irawawáriki	niku-
rikat	*ikárikat*	*irawaawaáriki*	*riku-*
center,	in the center	those standing here and there	they are

witíit^n	tárušúhusiriruk^i.	Irár^i	tirasá-
wití'it	*táruucuhus iriiruúki.*	*Iraári'*	*tirasaá-*
the ones	errand men those who are.	Brother,	where the sun

kaku	tirasákaku	irutpitáwiku	húpirit
kaku	*tirasaákaku*	*irutpitáwiku*	*huúpirit*
passes,	where the sun passes	that one on the end	star,

---

25. Also *kuhiíhaaru'* [NP].
26. The usual term for *twelve* is *pítkusuusiri'*. What the narrator has used is literally 'ten and two.'

irutpitáwiku nikuwitiraríku nahápakihu
irutpitáwiku *rikuwitiraríku* *rahápakihu*
that one on the end that one sits holding them what we call

náwis[u] nataráwis[u]. Nisarúwitirihkukarúku.
raáwiisu' *rataraáwiisu* *riísaaru' witirihkukarúku.*
paints, paints chiefs when they painted themselves

Kítuwitírariku kiskukáwi[u] a,
Kítuu'u' witiírariku *kiskuhkáwi'u'.* *A*
All he sits there holding them the white downy plumes. And,

irár[i], tiharakahuráhkatituh[ʌ]t[n] irutpitáwiku niku-
iraári' *tihaarakaahuraáhkatiituhat* *irutpitáwiku* *riku-*
brother, this black world (*ie* north) that one on the end that

ahakitáw[i] nísar[u], nikuwitiháktariku-
'ahakítawi' *riísaaru'.* *Rikuwitihaáktariku*
is the leading one chief. That one sits there holding them

rʌktáwiskaru. Irár[i], nikutiwakiáh[u] tirʌtarira-
raktaáwiskaaru'. *Iraári'* *rikuwitihwakí'aahu'* *tiratariíraa-*
the pipes. Brother, that is what they say this that I

iwãt[i] ihi nísaru nʌtkurákʌtkuk[u] háw[a],
'iiwaati *ihi* *riísaaru'* *ratkuraákatkuku* *haáwa'.*
tell you, uh, the chiefs when I listened to them, too.

nisarurʌtkurákʌtkuku sirakukuhárikahu
Riísaaru' ratkuraákatkuku *sirakukuuhaárikaahu*
The chiefs when I listened to them when they were telling me,

irár[i], nikuwitúʌt[n]. Irasákaku irakahuráh-
iraári' *rikuwituú'ut.* *Irasaákaku* *irakaahuraáh-*
brother, that is how it is. Where the sun passes that red

pahat[u] tirawahákspahat[u], hirikuaharuhú[u] tíra-
pahaatu *tirawaahákspahaatu* *hi riku'aharuuhú'u* *tíraa-*
world this red Heavens and that is the way it is this one

hu	háwitⁿ	tírahu	nikuwítira	iráruru-
hu	*haáwit*	*tíraahu*	*rikuwitirá'*	*iráruuruu-*
coming	east	this one coming	that is the way	those of his

ši	náwisᵘ,	tirasákaku.	Atirakahurá-
ci	*raáwiisu'*	*tirasaákaku.*	*A tírakaahuraah-*
(lying)	paints	where the sun passes.	And this black

katituhʌtⁿ	nikuaharuhúᵘ	tírakᵘ	nísaru	nikuastiká-
katiituhat	*riku'aharuuhú'u*	*tíraaku*	*riísaaru'*	*riku'aastikaá-*
world	that was the plan	this	chief	'that you be

wari	nakukitáwiᵘ	nisarúʌskᵘ
wari	*rakukitáwi'u*	*riísaaru' ásku*
the one to care for it'	to be the leading one	chief one

kurakukitáwiᵘ	hirikuahúʌtⁿ	ákitarᵘ
kurakukitáwi'u	*hi riku'ahuú'ut*	*ákitaaru'*
to seemingly be the leader	and that is how it was	the tribe

nikukstúwari	nísaru	ʌskuakuturaku-
rikukstuúwari	*riísaaru'*	*ásku a kutuú raku-*
his having cared for it	chief	one and it seems to be the

kitáwiᵘ,	hi	nurisararirúhšⁱ.	Awititiruhuh-
kitáwi'u.	*Hi*	*ruuriisaraaríruhci'.*	*A wititiiruhuh-*
leader.	And	there were many chiefs.	And they would (try to)

kitúwu	nísarᵘ.	Akihirikuahúta
kitáwu'	*riísaaru'.*	*Aki hi riku'ahuúta*
outdo one another	the chiefs.	And here and this what He did

tiráwah,[27]	"Tiwirʌstúwari	ákitarᵘ	tásasa-
Tiráwaahat	*"Tiwirastuúwari*	*ákitaaru'*	*taásasaa-*
the Heavens:	"Since you are caring for it[28]	the tribe,	you are

27. Dorsey erroneously emended Murie's transcription by first crossing out the final syllable of this word and then restoring a final *h*.
28. Literally, 'since you are carrying it around'.

rukst[a]	nísar[u]	hitiwirʌstuwarihús-
ruksta	*riísaaru'*	*hi tiwirastuuwariihús-*
going to be named	chief	and since you are going to care for

tarit[n]	ákitar[u],	kasirurapírihu[u]	ákitar[u].	Kási-
tarit	*ákitaaru'*	*kaasiruuraapírihu'u*	*ákitaaru'.*	*Kásii-*
it	the tribe	you must love it	the tribe.	You must

šikst[a]	nikutírʌšt[a]	šikstit[n]	nʌspari-
ciksta.	*Rikutíraacta*	*cíkstit*	*rasparii-*
watch over it.	That is the way it is going to be	well	your

hústarit[n]	ákitar[u]."	I,	irár[i],
hústarit	*ákitaaru'."*	*I*	*iraári'*
going to be going around (*ie* living)	the tribe."	And,	brother,

nikúahušuks	nísaru	nahkukstiká-
riku'áhucuks	*riísaaru'*	*raahkukstikaá-*
that is how he was	the chief	when he used to care for it in this

wari	ákitar[u].
wari	*ákitaaru'.*
world[29]	the tribe.

Recorded while Roaming Scout and Murie were examining the star map in the Wolf Was Fooled bundle, this narrative accounts for a constellation known to the Skiris as the Chiefs. Roaming Scout's commentary, like his explanations for other constellations and stars, illustrates the Skiri belief that the arrangements of social groups on earth reflect celestial phenomena. Here Roaming Scout describes a constellation of stars forming a circle that is conceived of as a group of chiefs, organized in the manner replicated by Skiri chiefs seated in council. He explains how the Heavens, when creating the first Skiris and their social order, instituted the office of chief (riisaáru') and at the same time

29. Literally, 'when he used to carry it around inside', *i.e.*, inside the world covered by the vault of the Heavens.

established the form of their meetings in council, on the model of
the Chiefs constellation in the Heavens.

Now, brother—brother, you must be prayerful in your thoughts toward
the Heavens, brother. That one is the cause of my telling you stories, and
that one is the cause of your living here on earth, and our Father Above is
the cause of my living here on earth. That one is the reason we have found
each another, brother.[30]

Now, brother, these objects that you see in the Heavens—these stars
sitting in a circle straight above in the Heavens—were ones our Father
Above created, brother. They are chiefs. They are chiefs. The priests are
the ones who used to say that when I was growing up: "There the chiefs sit
in a circle up above in the Heavens."

And now you know this large star. There it flies. There the other ones
stand all around it.[31] They are the ones in the Heavens that our Father
created to be chiefs. Brother, our Father created it this way so that you
should see them in the Heavens, and that is the way it is when you see
these things. Brother, these that you see here are there in the Heavens—
uh, they are the twelve chiefs in the Heavens.

Now, brother, it is this way with these various stars in the center—
those standing here and there in the center are the ones who are errand
men.[32]

Brother, here on the south side—that star on the south(east) end—
that one on the end is the one who sits holding what we call paints, the
paints that the chiefs use when they paint themselves. He also sits there
holding all the white downy plumes.

And, brother, that last star on the north(west) end is the leading chief.
That one sits there holding the pipes.[33]

Brother, what I am telling you is, uh, what the chiefs used to say when
I listened to them, too. When I listened to the chiefs when they told me

30. A reference to Roaming Scout and Murie's collaboration and companionship.
31. The narrator is pointing to these stars on the star map.
32. They are inside the circle of Chiefs.
33. The council of Chiefs in the Heavens is, like councils in earth lodges, divided into two
groups: those sitting on the south side and those on the north. The keeper of the paints
and white downy plumes is the star on the end, near the doorway, of the south side; while
the keeper of the pipes, who is the leading chief, is the star on the west end of the north
side, where the leader always sits.

things, brother, that is the way it was. That red world in the southeast—
this red Heavens is the way it is when the Sun rises in the east. It is that
way because of the paints the keeper has there where the Sun rises in the
southeast.[34]

And it was the plan that this chief in the northern sky be the one to
care for it—that he be the one leading chief, to be the leading chief. And
that is the reason that one chief cares for the tribe and, it seems, is to be
the leader. There used to be many chiefs. And the chiefs would try to outdo
one another.

And so that is what the Heavens did when He told the chief: "Since
you are to care for the tribe, you are going to be named chief; and since you
are to care for the tribe, you must love it. You must watch over it. That is
the way it is going to be, and your tribe is going to live prosperously."

And, brother, that is how it used to be with the chief when he cared for
the tribe in this world.

Appendix 2: The Great Council in Crazy Horse's Camp

George Sword

hecel	ikce	wicasa	Akicita	wanji	ominiciye	tanka
Héc'el	*ikcéwic'asa*		*akíc'ita*	*wąží*	*omníciye*	*t'ąka*
So	Indian		soldier	a	council	big

etan	Najin	na	heya[35]	iho	Toqicuwa	wanna
etą	*náži*	*na*	*heyé:*	*"Ihó*	*T'ok'íc'uwa*	*waná*
from	he stood	and	he said this:	"Well	Enemy Bait	now

34. The Sun reflects the red color of the paints held by the keeper of the paints, who is
the one on the end in the south, that is, in the southeast.
35. In this form, as frequently throughout his texts, Sword did not write the ablauted form
of the final vowel.

woglaka yo	taku	owe	lel	ya u he	cinhan	hecel
wóglaka yo.	*Táku*	*owé*	*lél*	*yaú he"*	*cįhą.*	*Héc'el*
tell yours!	What	seeking	here	you come?"	then.	So

toqicuwa	iye	woglaka
T'ok'íc'uwa	*iyé*	*wóglake.*
Enemy Bait	himself	he spoke.

Mitakolapi	oniyatepi	kin	lematahan
"Mit'ák'olapi	*oníyatepi*	*kį*	*lemátąhą*
"My friends	you are a people	the	I am from here

micila		kin	on	liciya	niyepi	on
mic'íla		*kį*	*ų́*	*léc'iya*	*niyépi*	*ų́*
I consider myself		the	so	over here	you all	on account of

iyuskiya	wau
iyúskįyą	*waú.*
gladly	I came.

Na	anpetu	kin	le	oiyokipiya	omniciye	tanka
"Na	*ąpétu*	*kį*	*lé*	*oíyokip'iya*	*omníciye*	*t'ą́ka*
"And	day	the	this	pleasantly	council	big

yakagapi	el	owapa
yakáǧapi	*él*	*ówap'a.*
you make	in	I join.

Na	woiyuskin	omajula		eya	Akicita	wan
"Na	*wóiyuskį*	*omáżula,"*		*eyé.*	*"Akíc'ita*	*wą*
"And	happiness	I am filled with,"		he said.	"Soldier	a

wicarpi	yamini	eciyapi	ca	he	Niyepi	ekta
Wic'áħpi	*Yámni*	*ecíyapi*	*c'a*	*hé*	*niyépi*	*ektá*
Stars	Three	they call him	such	that one	you all	to

umasi
umási."
he sent me."

Na   heya   ikce wicaṡa   tunkaṡilayapi   kin   wanna
Na   *heyé:*   *"Ikcéwic'aṡa* *t'ukáṡilayapi* *kị*   *waná*
And   he said: "Indians   President[36]   the   now

lehanyan   Anpetu   kin   okicize   cin ṡni   ca   maka
leháya   *apétu*   *kị*   *okíc'ize* *c'íṡni*   *c'a* *mak'á*
so long   day   the   fighting   he wishes not   so   earth

sitomniya   okicize   henala   na   tuweceṡa   oyasin
sitómniya *okíc'ize*   *henála*   *na* *tuwéceṡá*   *oyás'ị*
throughout   fighting   no more   and   no matter who   all

olakota kta   ca   Mitakola   oyasin   witaya
olák'otakta   *c'a* *mit'ák'ola* *oyás'ị* *wítaya*
there will be peace so   my friends   all   together

olakota   kupi kte
olák'ota *kúpikte.*
in peace   they will return.

Na   iṡiya   lakota   ota   lel   olakota   onpi
"Na   *íṡ'iyá*   *Lak'óta*   *óta*   *lél* *olák'ota*   *úpi*
"And   as for them   Sioux   many   here   in peace   they live

kin   lena   iyececaya   yaonpi kte   eya   na
kị   *lená*   *iyéc'ecaya*   *yaúpikte,"*   *eyị,*   *na:*
the   these   in the same way   you will live,"   he said,   and:

mitakolapi   glipi   eyaṡ   taku   ṡica   wanicin kte
"mit'ák'olapi *glípi*   *éyaṡ* *táku*   *ṡíca* *wanícịkte,"*
"my friends   they return but   something   bad   none will be,"

eya
eyé.
he said.

36. Literally, 'they regard him as grandfather'.

Na	ake	ikce	wicaśa	Akicita	he		inajin	na
Na	*ak'é*	*ikcéwic'aśa*		*akíc'ita*	*hé*		*ináżį*	*na:*
And	again	Indian		soldier	that one		he stood	and:

iho	wo
"Ihó	*wo."*
"Well!"	

Ceta	maza	inajin
C'etą́	*Máza*	*ináżį.*
Hawk	Iron	he stood.

Na	toqicuwa	woglake	cin	niś	Ayupta	yo	tka
Na:	*"T'ok'íc'uwa*	*wóglake*	*cį*	*níś*	*ayúpta*	*yo,*	*tk'á*
And:	"Enemy Bait	speech	the	you	reply!		but

tokel	woglaka	uniśipi		kin	hena	iyecel
tók'el	*wóglaka*	*uníśipi*		*kį*	*hená*	*iyéc'el*
how	to speak	we told you		the	those	likewise

iwoglaka	yo	Eya
iwóglaka	*yo,"*	*eyé.*
speak!"		he said.

Ceta	maza	woglake	iho	toqicuwa	waśteya
C'etą́	*Máza*	*wóglake:*	*"Ihó,*	*T'ok'íc'uwa*	*waśtéya*
Hawk	Iron	he spoke:	"Well,	Enemy Bait	carefully

Nonogopta[37]	yanka	yo
nų́goptą	*yąká*	*yo.*
listening	sit!	

Makoce	kin	le	Mitawa	na	lecel	wakantanka
"Mak'óc'e	*kį*	*lé*	*mit'áwa*	*na*	*léc'el*	*Wak'ą́t'ąka*
"Country	the	this	it is mine	and	thus	Great Spirit

37. The second *o* is apparently a scriptographic error.

icagemaya   ca   ecel   waon   tka   kola   wasicunla
ic'áhmaya   *c'a*   *ec'él*   *waų́*   *tk'á*   *k'olá*   *wasícųla*
he raised me   so   thus   I live   but   my friend   white men

wi   ohinape   kin   heciyatanhan   Maka   mitawa
wí   *ohínap'e*   *kį*   *héc'iyatạhạ*   *mak'á*   *mit'áwa*
sun   where it rises   the   from there   land   mine

manon   Au   na   wanna   Makoce   kin   ciqala
manų́   *aú*   *na*   *wanạ́*   *mak'óc'e*   *kį*   *cík'ala*
stealing   they came   and   now   country   the   it is small

heon   mitamaka   el   iyowin wakiye sni   kes   Mahel
heų́   *mit'á mak'á*   *él*   *iyówįwak'iyesni*   *k'es*   *mahél*
so   my country   in   I do not permit him   yet   into

u   na   wanmayaka   canna   makute   canna
ú   *na*   *wạmáyaka*   *c'ạ́na*   *mak'úte*   *c'ạ́na*
he comes   and   he sees me   then   he shoots me   then

misiya   wakute   na   wica wakte   na   wan wicayag
mis'íya   *wak'úte*   *na*   *wic'áwakte*   *na*   *wạwíc'ayak*
I too   I shoot him   and   I kill them   and   looking at them

nawajin   iconhan   cante masice   lena   titakuye
nawáži   *ic'úhạ*   *c'ạtémasice.*   *'Lená*   *t'ítakuye*
I stand   during   my heart is bad.   'These   their relatives

wicawakastake lo   epca   na   o   iyokisica   miciya
wic'áwakastake lo,'   *epcá*   *na*   *ų́*   *iyókisil*   *mic'íye.*
I have beaten them!'   I think   and   so   grieved   I make myself.

hecel   tuwe   tunkasilayapi   skan   wan
"Héc'el   *tuwé*   *t'ųkásilayapi*   *skạ́*   *wạ*
"So   someone   President   he acts   a

wolakota   cin   kehapi
'Wólak'ota   *c'į,'*   *kehápi.*
'Peace   he wishes,'   you all say.

iho   olakota   tanka kte lo   miyeṡ   tuwa   waṡte
Ihó   *olák'ota* *t'ạkakte lo.*   *Miyéṡ*   *tuwá*   *waṡté*
Well   peace   it shall be great!   As for me   whoever   good

amaon[38]   eyaṡ   Makte ṡni   ca   le
amáu   *eyáṡ*   *maktéṡni*   *c'a*   *lé*
they bring to me   but   he will not best me   such   this

iglaka   wau kta   eyaṡ   woyute   ota   bluha
igláka   *waúkta*   *eyáṡ*   *wóyute*   *óta*   *bluhá;*
moving camp   I will come   but   food   much   I have;

Matke   wa   ota   wakpa   iyuha   glakiya   rpaya
matké;   *wá*   *óta;*   *wakpá*   *iyúha*   *glakíyạ*   *ḣpáya*
I am heavy;   snow   much;   rivers   all   across   lying

mniṡma   ranhiya   iglaka   wau kta   ca
mniṡmáṡma.[39]   *Ḣạhíya*   *igláka*   *waúkta*   *c'a*
deep waters.   Slowly   moving camp   I will come   so

    Toqicuwa   iwahuni ṡni han   ake   ekta
    "T'ok'íc'uwa   *iwáhụnihạsni*   *ak'é*   *ektá*
    "Enemy Bait   I have not yet arrived   again   to

mayahi kta   iṡ   nitahokṡila   eṡa   hiyaṡi kte
mayáhikta   *iṡ*   *nit'áhokṡila*   *eṡá*   *hiyáṡikte,"*
you shall come to me   or   your boy   perhaps   you shall send,"

eya   hehala   Akicita   kin   heya   hecela
eyé.   *Hehạl*   *akíc'ita*   *kị*   *heyé:*   *"Hec'éla*
he said.   Then   soldier   the   he said this: "Only that

wooglake   waṡte   ca   hecela   woglakin kte   eya
wóoglake   *waṡté*   .   *c'a*   *hec'éla*   *wóglakịkte,"*   *eyé.*
speech   it is good   so   only that   he will relate,"   he said.

38. The final *n* is apparently a scriptographic error.
39. Ella Deloria noted that since the reference is to more than one river, this form should
be reduplicated to indicate plurality.

Ceta	maza	heya		oglala	na	śahiyela
C'etą́	Máza	heyé:		"Oglála	na	Śahíyela
Hawk	Iron	he said this:		"Oglalas	and	Cheyennes

heniyos	maka	kin	lel	aitancanya	waon	tka
heníyos	mak'á	kį	lél	aít'ąc'ąyą	waų́	tk'á
these two	land	the	here	chiefly	I live	but

Miśnala ye	wanna	olakota kta		kepa		hecel
miśnála ye.	Waná	olák'otakta		kep'é.		Héc'el
I am alone!	Now	there will be peace		I have said.		Thus

Minikowoju	Honkpapaya	hena	mihukuya	onpi
Mnik'ówożu,	Hų́kpap'aya,[40]	hená	mihúk'uya	ų́pi,"
Minneconjous,	Hunkpapas,	those	below me	they live,"

eya
eyé.
he said.

Na	oyate	oyasin	wolakota	ahi
Na	oyáte	oyás'į	wólak'ota	ahí.
And	people	all	in peace	they arrived.

---

40. This name is usually Hų́kpap'a, but Sword consistently wrote it with a final -ya, which Ella and Vine Deloria considered to be the correct form.

Transitional Narratives and Cultural Continuity

Elaine A. Jahner

Fiction that emerges from the immediate and consciously negotiated experience of radical cultural change constitutes a category of world literature with exemplary pragmatic value for contemporary criticism. American Indian writing provides some notable examples of transitional texts, in which the act of writing is simultaneously a development of an imaginative tradition and an attempted entry into a new cultural order without known precedent and beyond any anticipation implied by the cultural past. Such writing lets us glimpse the challenge of the unimaginable as it provokes experiments with form and content in order to increase the range of a society's imaginative resources. Of course, these general assertions have value only in relation to specific texts.

One largely unpublished body of writing that promises to be a significant stimulus to thoughtful analysis of transitional texts when it is finally published was written by George Sword, an Oglala Sioux political leader, tribal court judge, and spiritual leader, who was born in 1846 and died in

1910.[1] At his funeral, orators called him the Abraham Lincoln of the Sioux nation.[2] In Sword's case, that comparison was more than just occasional rhetoric. The political conflicts that he had to negotiate and the threats to the future of Lakota cultural identity that he understood as clearly as anyone else gave enough legitimacy to the reference so that its repetition affirms its justice.

Sword lived through fundamental social and cultural changes. During his lifetime, the United States forced the Oglala to move from their traditional, seminomadic culture to reservation living, and Sword's continuing leadership role was, in large part, a result of his ability to understand and communicate the terms of necessary adaptations.[3] He learned to be an effective leader within dual political structures, the traditional Lakota ones and the imposed reservation institutions of governance. His responsible determination to understand the spiritual dimensions of his own experience even prompted him to seek grounds common to two different belief systems—Episcopalian Christianity and the visionary Lakota approach to relations between humans and other cosmic powers. He wanted others to benefit from his knowledge, so he cooperated with scholars documenting Lakota history and culture and, in the process, he learned how anthropologists framed their questions about Lakota culture. Finally, his fascination with the effects of transitions from orality to literacy and his desire to en-

1. Raymond J. DeMallie is currently editing and preparing a new translation of Sword's writing for publication by the University of Nebraska Press. It will be the fourth volume in a series presenting all the manuscripts that James R. Walker acquired while at Pine Ridge Oglala Sioux Reservation. The first volume, edited by DeMallie and Elaine A. Jahner, is *Lakota Belief and Ritual* (1980); the second, edited by DeMallie, is *Lakota Society* (1982); and the third, edited by Elaine A. Jahner, is *Lakota Myth* (1984). All are published by the University of Nebraska Press, Lincoln. Quotations from these works are cited in my text by title and page number.
2. A. F. Johnson of the Pine Ridge Presbyterian Church first used the phrase in his funeral oration. He added, "Perhaps the next generation may appreciate his worth" (see the Pine Ridge Reservation publication *Oglala Light*, November 1910, 21–23, available through the Nebraska Historical Society).
3. For general historical accounts that include mention of Sword's role, see James C. Olson, *Red Cloud and the Sioux Problem* (Lincoln: University of Nebraska Press, 1965). Also useful is Robert Utely, *The Last Days of the Sioux Nation* (New Haven: Yale University Press, 1951). A revealing, if slanted and prejudiced, source is Julia B. McGillycuddy, *McGillycuddy* (Palo Alto: Stanford University Press, 1946). The daughter of the agent who worked closely with Sword, Julia McGillycuddy gives revealing vignettes of Sword's activities as understood from the perspective of a government agent.

sure remembrance of his role in major historical events motivated him to write extensively about his personal experiences and even to record some of his thoughts about what happens to language when people first learn to write it.[4]

Sword gave most of his writing to James R. Walker, the physician and amateur ethnologist who became his friend at Pine Ridge. Partly in response to Walker's questions, Sword spoke and wrote about Lakota beliefs, rituals, and folklore. Some of the resulting texts are direct transcriptions of speech. Other texts, though, show significant evidence of the reflective reconsiderations and aesthetic structuring that occurs when writing provokes awareness of text as artifact. Sword developed a highly idiosyncratic writing style, and he engaged in similarly unique theorizing about etymological sources for Lakota words (see "Plains Indian Native Literatures," by Douglas R. Parks and Raymond J. DeMallie, in this issue). Of particular importance and interest is a ledgerbook in Sword's own Lakota handwriting. Initially translated by Ella Deloria, that collection of writing on various topics is currently being retranslated by Raymond J. DeMallie and will be published bilingually.[5] The Walker manuscript collection also contains imaginative narratives in a mythic mode, for which attribution is still uncertain,

---

4. Currently published Sword texts can be found in *Lakota Belief and Ritual* and in *Lakota Myth*. These books also contain some analysis of the Sword corpus of writing and of our efforts to find information that allows us to attribute the texts and judge their status. For other references, see Raymond J. DeMallie and Douglas R. Parks, *Sioux Indian Religion* (Norman: University of Oklahoma Press, 1987). My article in that volume, entitled "Lakota Genesis: The Oral Tradition," addresses some of the same issues as this one, but it gives only passing attention to George Sword and his texts because I concentrate on more traditional precedents for what Sword has done.

5. The ledgerbook has 245 pages in Sword's Lakota handwriting. Inside the front cover is pasted a small piece of paper, on which is written, in Lakota, "George Sword, these he wrote." There are thirteen separate sections and topics: (1) Thunder; (2) Killed by Thunder; (3) Warpath; (4) Singing while Fire Gazing; (5) Sword's Autobiography; (6) Indian Ways Explained; (7) Calf Pipe; (8) Men's and Boys' Games; (9) The Sun Dance; (10) The Fox Society; (11) The Beloved Ceremony; (12) About Questing; and (13) Winter Quarters. The ledgerbook is in the Archives of the Colorado Historical Society, in Denver. Microfilm copies of the ledgerbook and of Ella Deloria's translations are in the Boas Collection, Archives of the American Philosophical Society, in Philadelphia; see the files "Dakota Ethnography; Linguistics" and "Dakota Texts from the Sword Manuscript."

In this article, all references, except Iron Hawk's speech, are to Ella Deloria's translation and are cited in my text by manuscript page number only. The Iron Hawk speech is from Raymond J. DeMallie's translation published in this issue of *boundary 2*.

and on that uncertainty hangs much of the tale that this article recounts. Archival research has turned up enough information for us to favor strongly the hypothesis that these texts are the written fictions of George Sword rather than the myths from oral tradition that people long assumed them to be. Slightly reworked English versions of these texts were first published in 1917 as anonymous Lakota myths, and they soon achieved international status as textbook examples illustrating how myth charts worldview.[6] We know from Walker's correspondence with Clark Wissler that they were originally written in Lakota, but the Lakota texts have not yet been found and may well have been inadvertently destroyed. Translations that are as close to the original texts as we have been able to find were published in *Lakota Myth* in 1984. The present essay concentrates on these texts, their relationship to Sword's other writing, their history, and their significance today as exemplary writing that should be compared to transitional texts from other cultures.

With all the possibilities suggested by Sword's other work, why concentrate on texts that might not even be Sword's, that appear to be fictions written to teach about myth rather than orally transmitted communal narratives, that may or may not be an effort to save sacred knowledge for future generations? Why try to second-guess a mystery? My primary reason is that the mythic texts have already had definitive influence on the way people think about American Indian traditions and about the nature and function of myth, in general. The Lakota people themselves and non-Indian scholars have invested these texts with active social and intellectual significance, although for the Lakota this process has been significantly different from the non-Indian developments. For the Lakota, the narratives have proved a bridge to older ways of thinking and interpreting, while scholarly uses of them have been instrumental in shaping theories about relationships between myth and culture. The history of these texts is really a study of what different interest groups want to find in mythic narrative and of how social need informs literary interpretation. Furthermore, it is a history that could be recast with all the fascination of a suspense novel, replete with visions, secrets and vows, discoveries and cover-ups. Having become part of that history by publishing the mythic texts in 1984, however, I resist the easy switch to a sensationalizing tone as inappropriate, even exploitative. My

6. James R. Walker, "The Sundance and Other Ceremonies of the Oglala Division of the Teton Dakota," American Museum of Natural History, *Anthropological Papers*, vol. 16, pt. 2 (1917).

efforts to find the original versions of the texts and my relationships with different people for whom these texts validated spiritual beliefs incline me to treat them as a revered and threatened cultural resource.

The history of these narratives is a dauntingly complex tale that can easily dominate the story that the texts themselves tell. The possible relationship between the two stories is, finally, the theme linking all others in this essay. My speculative interpretation of the mythic narratives, occurring as the last section of this essay, depends upon historical research that reveals facets of Sword's accomplishments and personality. The significance of the mythic texts is, I believe, bound to Sword's personal sense of mission and destiny as enacted in his political life, friendships, and the various kinds of writing that were a direct response to both. The historical record does not give definitive answers to very many of the questions we have about Sword's life and work. Nevertheless, it is rich and complex enough so that pursuing our questions yields a variety of insights about Lakota culture and, more generally, about narrative in relation to radical cultural change. Whatever position people finally choose to take on the unanswered questions surrounding Sword's texts, no one can deny that they continue to have extraordinary influence, and, I believe, they deserve to have an even larger audience. Therefore, Sword's risks paid off. Walker wrote that Sword had a hard time convincing the elders to allow their knowledge to be written down, so he "argued to the holy men . . . that the Gods of the Oglalas would be more pleased if the holy men told of them so that they might be kept in remembrance and that all the world might know of them" (*Lakota Belief and Ritual*, 47). The fear of being forgotten proved great enough to justify the risks of breaking taboos against telling privileged information to outsiders.

Sword's Life and Writing

Recorded Oglala history gives us regular glimpses of George Sword as an important supporting actor in dramas that starred Red Cloud and Crazy Horse, Charles Eastman and James R. Walker. Historical accounts of events occurring between the 1867 Wagon Box Fight and the early reservation years mention Sword as an advisor who occasionally stepped out of his background role to do what other leaders seemed unwilling or unable to do. Standard historiographic narrative conventions, however, distort the roles of people, such as Sword, who remained at the sidelines of the most public exchanges between the United States government and the Lakota nation even though their knowledge and understanding of what was at stake may well have been central to the outcome of political negotiations.

One event that allows us to compare Sword's account with published historical versions was his January 1877 visit to the Crazy Horse camp, a journey made in order to urge the charismatic and still-resistant Crazy Horse to bring his people to the reservation because it was their only chance for survival. Crazy Horse finally agreed and led his people to the agency, but soon after his surrender, he was murdered.[7] Then, as now, the mediator risks setting up the conditions of betrayal, a basic human fact that seems to have worried Sword, because he took every chance he could get to set the record straight, not just in reference to his active role but in regard to his motives, as well. He wrote about the Crazy Horse episode in two sections of his autobiographical statement, and, judging from notes, it was the first issue he addressed in his interview with Eli Ricker, even though Ricker himself seems to have been more interested in events such as the Fetterman Massacre and the Wagon Box Fight.[8] It is as though Sword knew that he was caught in a vortex of historical currents and countercurrents, and he wanted to leave no doubt that his consistent goal as a leader was to establish the social conditions under which his people could "grow and thrive without fear."[9]

7. See Mari Sandoz, *Crazy Horse: The Strange Man of the Oglalas* (New York: Alfred A. Knopf, 1942).

8. Eli Ricker, interview with George Sword, 1907, MS tablet 16, Ricker Collection, Nebraska State Historical Society, Lincoln. Donald F. Danker, in *The Wounded Knee Interviews of Eli S. Ricker* (Lincoln: Nebraska State Historical Society, 1981), describes Ricker's methods: "Eli Ricker spent about a quarter of a century gathering material for the history that would be fair to the Indian. Participants in the final twenty to fifty years of the Indian-white struggle lived in the area. Ricker sought them out. He interviewed the Indians, the ranchers, the scouts. . . . He used interpreters if necessary and collected innumerable photographs. . . . However, the interview was his main research method. In the pre–tape recorder days he utilized the nickel tablet commonly used by school children. He filled tablet after tablet with interviews, others with notes from books and journals, documents, correspondence, and his own thoughts" (153).

The Sword interview in Tablet 16 is fourteen pages in length. The pages are not numbered.

9. In his autobiography, Sword wrote: "They [Crazy Horse's people] were a great people and the chiefest of all who repudiated peace, but to them Sword went to make peace and he did it. And brought them back to join the people friendly with the government and from this came the killing of Crazy Horse. All over the land, in all places whatever, wars ceased and since then there are no big fights. It was Sword who made the peace for all which men enjoy everywhere now; and now people grow and thrive without fear. He has made

On the question of motives, Sword's autobiographical statement gives information that alters what we can learn through other sources. Sword, more than anyone else, allows us to see clearly that neither he nor Crazy Horse was acting from a position of defeat or from motives of currying favor with the military. Sword gives the detail that allows us to reinterpret what appears to be a defeated people's concession to United States policies as being, in fact, a response that also enacts freely determined decisions about how to prepare for a new stage in their historical development. If, to outsiders, this seems impossible in the light of the military force brought against the Sioux after the Custer Battle, that perception only increases the need for information about how people such as Sword and Crazy Horse judged their own historical situation. In support of the resistance hypothesis, we have the recorded response of a soldier who watched Crazy Horse's surrender: " 'By God,' he said to those around him, 'this is a triumphal march, not a surrender.' " [10]

For Sword, whose role was far less dramatic, maintaining the position of freedom meant dissociating his own motives from General George Crook's orders without denying that he was privy to the general's plans. Eli Ricker's interview reveals Sword's careful and characteristic distinctions that allow us to judge the man at the same time as we gain some insight into historical events: "Sword says that none of this delegation went as scouts, but as volunteer Indians carrying the olive branch of peace and good will. He states that the Commissioner of Indian Affairs wrote General Crook to dispatch these Indians on this peace mission. He adds that besides the thirty men and himself three or four women went in the party."

Sword's autobiographical statement emphasizes that he was choosing and deciding on his own, for reasons that went beyond anything the military was telling him. As his version of events progresses, we find in it several clues that reveal a style of resistance based on doing what had to be done, but doing it for reasons that turn military defeat to moral victory. He tells about all the difficulties his group faced on their journey to Crazy Horse. Twice they wanted to turn back, "but Enemy Bait [George Sword] insisted on going on and challenged them to go with him; so they had a night meeting and agreed to continue on" (94).

---

a great success and given the people a thankworthy gift" (sections 197, 198, and 199 of the autobiographical statement).
10. Sandoz, *Crazy Horse*, 361.

By far, the most significant evidence for the attitudes that I am describing is Sword's transcription of a speech that Iron Hawk, speaking for Crazy Horse, gave in response to Sword's message of peace and safety for the Crazy Horse band. By including it in his autobiographical statement, Sword made it, by implication at least, a commentary on his own life:

> "Well, Enemy Bait, sit and listen carefully! This is my country and in this manner the Great Spirit raised me so in this manner I live, but, my friend, the white men from where the sun rises came stealing my land and now the country is small so I do not permit him in my country, yet he comes in and when he sees me, then he shoots at me, and then I too shoot at him and I kill some of them and while I stand looking at them, I am sorrowful. 'These, I have beaten their relatives!' I think, and so I bring grief upon myself.
> "So he who acts for the President: 'He wishes peace,' you all say.
> "Well, it shall be a great peace! As for me, when anyone brings good to me, he will not outdo me."

This speech turns concession into a victory. It stays one step ahead of the colonizers. It represents a form of resistance through belief in the traditional motivational foundations, and it transforms them into a way of living in the reservation environment. In Sword's other writing, we find regular evidence of this judgment style, which is really an ascription of Lakota evaluations to actions that could appear to be accommodations to the will of the conqueror. Even the mythic texts can be read as codes for using older beliefs as a basis from which to outdo the Americans in establishing a new way of life under reservation political structures. In support of such judgments about his actions and his writings, we have the facts of Sword's life history, which prove that he had the experience needed to understand the bicultural pressures that the Lakota nation had to face during those crucial turn-of-the-century years; and he had the literary ability to give narrative expression to the cognitive strategies that could help the people through the transitions.

Tracing all the historical references to Sword gives enough information to justify the belief that he walked the tightrope strung between competing loyalties with agility, integrity, and unfailing dignity. He certainly had to do it often enough under circumstances that even privileged historical judgment cannot lightly decide because the faces of human hunger, fear, and sickness have to be remembered and taken into account along with ideological positions. Sword did not even have the advantage of getting along with Red Cloud. His conviction that Red Cloud was not the rightful leader is recorded in a letter he wrote to the Commissioner of Indian Affairs. The conflict between the two men complicated an already tense and factionalized political scene that Sword had to negotiate in order to advance causes he believed in.[11] He was a complex man working amidst volatile and dangerous social tensions. Although I emphasize evidence of Sword's resistance to complete cultural assimilation as expressed through his determination to build a reservation way of life based on Lakota values, I also recognize that, from our current perspective at least, many of his actions seem to be inconsistent with an attitude of resistance to the domination of United States rule. He was captain of the Indian Police, tribal court judge, and a catechist in the Episcopal church. None of this fits with popular stereotypes of how to resist Euro-American influences. My arguments depend on what I can learn of his motivations and on his consistent efforts to preserve information about pre-reservation life and beliefs.

Before turning to Sword's own writing for evidence of awareness that maintaining the Lakota way of life demanded new expressive forms for old beliefs and values, we can note one more historical confirmation of Sword's conviction that traditional motivations could coexist with "a new order of things." Charles Alexander Eastman includes a telling episode in his autobiography that describes the "dignified and intelligent," but deeply worried, Sword, warning Eastman about the misunderstandings that eventually culminated in the massacre at Wounded Knee. At the time, Eastman was the newly posted Sioux Indian physician at Pine Ridge, having studied medicine at Boston University upon completion of his undergraduate work at Dartmouth College. Sword welcomed Eastman to the reservation and gave him a short speech to impress him with the fact that the presence of an eastern-educated Sioux at Pine Ridge was proof of "a new order of things." Sword hoped that Eastman's bicultural knowledge could reveal ways to avert the danger posed by the military's misunderstandings of the Ghost Dancers' intentions. When Eastman questioned Sword about why the people were dancing, Sword replied in a manner that showed him in his typical position of someone who had spoken to people on both sides of a conflict. He understood the grief that motivated the Ghost Dance just as he knew that the military leaders would not relent in their determination to stop the dancing with force if need be:

11. See Olson, *Red Cloud and the Sioux Problem*, 278–79.

All they ask is to be let alone. They say the white man is not dis-
turbed when he goes to his church. . . . But I must tell you, however,
that the agent has just ordered the police to call in all Government
employees with their families to the agency. This means that something is going to happen. I have heard that he will send for soldiers
to come here to stop the Ghost dance. If so, there will be trouble.[12]

Sword's own ability to recognize and to work within the "new order
of things" that was thrust upon the Sioux can be traced to his own first
visit to the East Coast as a member of the delegation that negotiated treaty
rights. In a document prepared for Walker, he lets us sense how the alien
sights and sounds combined to forge his conviction that the Lakota could
neither ignore nor escape the determined and aggressive permanence that
was symbolized by the architecture of cities like Washington, D.C. and New
York. "I went to Washington and to other large cities and that showed me
that the white people dug in the ground and built houses that could not be
moved. Then I knew that when they came they could not be driven away"
(*Lakota Belief and Ritual*, 74).

The intelligent young warrior who went to Washington proud of his
brave role in many battles returned to Dakota territory determined to understand more about the people whose very buildings symbolized the intent
behind the terrifying guns they had demonstrated for the visiting Sioux
delegation. Since his own spiritual beliefs taught him that all human accomplishments were concrete evidence of spiritual powers, Sword decided that
the white man's God must have some exceptional powers, and he decided
to find out more about the deity who had inspired all that he saw in the
urbanized East. This quest eventually led him all the way to positions of
leadership in the Episcopalian church. His formative experience in Washington, D.C. even inspired a new name—Sword. He explains that he took
that name "because the leaders of the white soldiers wore swords" (*Lakota
Belief and Ritual*, 74). That it also happened to be the name of his recently
deceased brother is another of the many examples of how Sword managed
to carry forward Lakota traditions, while investing them with a significance
that operated as evidence of change.

The matter of his name is pivotal in every sense. As we attempt to
judge how much of his writing is direct commentary and how much repre-

12. See Charles Alexander Eastman, *From the Deep Woods to Civilization* (Boston: Little,
Brown and Company, 1925), 82–88.

sents aesthetic restructuring, we can follow references to his name like a lure leading us into imaginative terrain. Sword's autobiographical statement in the ledgerbook appears to give a slightly different explanation of how he acquired his name: It links the name change to his visit to Crazy Horse's camp. That linkage is more a matter of narrative juxtaposition than implied cause and effect, so the one reference does not necessarily cancel out the other. The juxtaposition simply lets us know that the significance of the name derives from both sets of experience, each giving meaning to the proper name that can stand as its explanation and source. Nevertheless, to one reading with Euro-American narrative expectations, the different references seem to involve a contradiction, and they trigger a questioning response to an apparent contradiction. This kind of response alerts us to the fact that we are outside our usual narrative and aesthetic territories.

The problem of moving back and forth between Lakota and Euro-American interpretive narrative conventions is less difficult in Sword's work than in monocultural texts because of Sword's ability to understand so many non-Indian narrative expectations. We can trace references to two sets of cultural presuppositions, and that guidance is what gives particular value to Sword's writing. It is boundary writing and transitional writing that can be placed with other works functioning as literary thresholds between cultures. In Sword's case, the transitional nature of the texts is far more than the surface marking of a few concessions to another culture. A proper study of transitional features in Sword's writing would involve specifying the cognitive qualities of narrative as cultural form with meaning beyond its explicit content.

Sword's autobiographical writing provides several easily presented examples of the process. Its primary structure and content clearly follow the traditional Lakota conventions guiding formal, public oral presentations of personal experiences, and it has to be judged first in relation to these conventions. Of all the formalized modes of Sioux narrative, the recounting of one's accomplishments was perhaps the most central—it was the narrative performance for which all other types were prelude and preparation. The telling of one's own story was the occasion to prove that one had learned the lessons of the other tales and could add one's own deeds to the store of tales that marked the community's passage through time and space. Sitting Bull's earliest authoritative biographer noted that the stories of one's deeds formed "the invariable credentials for a man performing any public action." A man who could not show these credentials was "automatically banned from participation in tribal or ceremonial affairs. He was, in effect, disenfranchised and disqualified. He could not even name his own child." [13]

The Bushotter manuscripts tell us about the traditional content for such narrations and suggest the wide range of content accepted as appropriate to personal narrations. "They will recount brave deeds, say in what year they did them; what their thoughts were; how many women they seduced; how many divorced by public proclamation; how they treated their father-in-law or father. Furthermore, they will describe the kinds of country they have moved about in during their nomadic days; and altogether they will speak of the past with sad wistfulness." [14]

Sword's autobiography begins with content that seems in complete accord with what we know of traditional oral performances. He names his parents, brothers, and sisters, telling us that his mother was a Hunka (ceremonially honored child) and that his father was a brave warrior, whose several names all commemorated specific acts of bravery. Sword was the fourth and last-born son of his father's first wife. His childhood name was *Iciblebleca* (Shakes Himself). In the notes she appended to her translation of the autobiography, Ella Deloria comments on the name: "It means to shake one's self by inner force like a horse after rolling or a dog after swimming" (103).

Sword assures his readers that he was a docile child who grew up "without giving undue anxiety, for which his father and mother loved him" (84). This beloved child, however, apparently provoked plenty of anxiety when he reached the age of fifteen and began to chafe under his mother's watchful protectiveness. He ran away to join a war party. At this point in the autobiography, Sword's literary skill becomes evident. With deft timing and descriptive economy, he sketches a bit of humorous and gentle self-mockery. Referring to himself in the third person, as he does throughout his autobiography, he writes: "Here was his appearance. He rode a horse, two years old, awfully tame, with a big belly. He wore a robe of calf-skin, carried a quiver with three arrows and a bow. The party put up for the night; but he feared being scolded so he kept at a distance" (85).

Ella Deloria notes how Sword's Lakota style includes a suffix for the word *horse*, which "indicates amusement at the boy who thinks he can

13. Stanley Vestal, *Sitting Bull: Champion of the Sioux* (Norman: University of Oklahoma Press, 1932), 11.
14. George Bushotter, Lakota texts, MS 4800, section 6, National Anthropological Archives, Smithsonian Institution, Washington, D.C.

fight on such an unwieldy animal" (105). Sword could easily poke fun at his youthful self because his later exploits earned him enduring respect as a warrior. The next sections of the autobiography, in true oral conventional style, narrate how he got the physical battle scars that he could show as bodily marks that proved his narrative claims. He details the battles that earned him the name Enemy Bait. One wonders why he does not include mention of how he received the most impressive credentials of all, the Sun Dance scars; this kind of questioning takes us beyond the conventions of the oral account to awareness of writing as a medium that obviates the necessity for constant repetition. Sword wrote about his visions and the Sun Dance elsewhere and did not, perhaps, feel that this information needed to be repeated in the autobiographical section.

The principles that organize the narrative structure of the separate parts of the autobiography combine chronology with selective topicality. First, he presents his acts of military bravery, then he recounts details of his marital life, and, finally, he gives examples of his work as a negotiator of peace. The examples are apparently meant to show a typical pattern, a kind of paradigm for character development, because Sword certainly did not aim for a complete account of his life. (There is no mention, for example, of his role in such momentous historical events as the Wounded Knee Massacre.) The purpose of the narrative is not to tell the entire story of his life; instead, he is narrating examples of how he earned the right and authority to exercise leadership and to make judgments about the welfare of others. That is the primary presentational feature that distinguishes accounts such as Sword's from Euro-American autobiographical narrative. It leads to a sharply contrasting form of self-presentation. And Sword, perhaps as a gesture toward his non-Indian readers, explicitly notes the purpose of his particular narrative: "It is unseemly for one who can not accomplish such things to occupy a position of leadership. For himself, he never did any evil thing, but wisely and moderate in action, he lived. And he was not one to maintain a spirit of jealousy and all men were his friends. And he often gave feasts in his home" (102).

One definite formal adaptation necessitated by writing to and for an audience in distant places and cultures is his description of his own physical features. Sword concluded his autobiography with details that would have been obvious to anyone attending a proper oral performance.

> George Sword was nice-looking; very long hair, reaching down to
> the rounding points of his buttocks; and his body was neither long

nor short, in between; and neither too big nor too little, but in between. He was light skinned; kind of light complexion, as it were; his eyes were black. And his powers of perception were exceptional; so that he was skillful and could make anything; and he drew (or wrote or painted) well. He was gifted in writing the language of the Dakotas; and nobody was as learned in that among the Oglalas as he. Moreover, he could read words here and there in English. (102)

In 1896, the Lakota man who had run away from home to join a war party met another man from another way of life who had also run away from home to join an army.[15] James R. Walker came to Pine Ridge Reservation in 1896, and the friendship between Sword and Walker meant that the unusual conjunction of talents and obsessions driving each man resulted in exchanges with enduring cultural, as well as personal, importance. James R. Walker was a physician who found himself in charge of caring for more than seven thousand people at a time when disease was rampant. Tuberculosis had reached the epidemic stage. All efforts to check diseases were hampered by the general conditions of malnutrition. Knowing he could do little, Walker consulted the traditional healers, asked their help, and offered to exchange medical information with them. To gain the trade secrets of the traditional healers, he had to undergo a process of learning that involved his step-by-step initiation into the religious mysteries of the Lakota, an initiation that Sword supervised in the capacity of close friend and mentor and the one who had sought spiritual guidance for the entire project.

As time passed, Walker seemed to realize that he had found a spiritual home after a lifetime of a peculiar homelessness. He had run away from his family to join the army during the Civil War. Chronic dysentery weakened him, and, by war's end, he knew that he wanted to become a physician. He attended Northwestern University Medical School, where he did well academically, although his advisors told him that the physical rigors of practicing medicine in a city were too much for him. They gave him the outrageous advice that practicing on an Indian reservation would be less demanding. The idea appealed to Walker. His wife refused to live on reservations, so Walker finally left his family behind and went alone to the work that has had such an impact on Lakota culture and on the way the world perceives it.

The anthropologist Clark Wissler went to Pine Ridge in 1902 to do

15. For a biographical account of James R. Walker, see *Lakota Belief and Ritual*, 3–54.

fieldwork. There, he met Walker and recognized an exceptional opportunity. Walker was far better situated to get the information that Wissler sought than any ordinary fieldworker could ever be. During the next ten years, Walker and Wissler carried on a regular correspondence that enables us to follow the development of Walker's thinking about what he was learning at Pine Ridge. Wissler supervised the preparation of the monograph, published in 1917.

Sword seems to have been a consistent Lakota mentor and friend. Pine Ridge residents remember the long nights of conversation Walker enjoyed with Sword and other distinguished elders, such as Thomas Tyon and American Horse, because Walker's automobile was so conspicuous that people noted his comings and goings. As the friendship between Sword and Walker grew, so apparently did Sword's determination to tell Walker what otherwise would have been privileged sacred knowledge. Walker, for his part, promised not to tell anyone else but to record it for the benefit of future generations of Oglala. Insofar as we can judge, he kept his promises, and we assume that much of what he learned was woven into his retelling of the narratives Sword wrote for him. We do not know much about the circumstances of Sword's writing, although we can see from Walker's correspondence with Wissler that Walker was seeking mythic explanations for rituals, like the Sun Dance, and was unable to find them. Surely he questioned Sword, who finally must have decided to write just such an explanation, but he did it without telling Walker.

Walker left Pine Ridge in 1914, taking into his retirement all the manuscripts gathered during eighteen years. Among them were many that Sword had written in Lakota, covering aspects of belief, myth, and ritual. In addition, Walker had the ledgerbook in which Sword had written his autobiography. Sword died before Walker found time to translate most of this writing, so important questions about Sword's work will probably never be answered.

Reading Walker's letters to Wissler, we learn that Walker finally translated Sword's mythic stories while he was completing his Sun Dance manuscript for Clark Wissler. We can also deduce that the tales were a complete surprise to him, and he recognized them as a gift and an end to a long search. He immediately wrote to Wissler, expressing relief that he had finally found "myths" that explain all the others and that link mythic to ritual action. From that letter, we know that during all his years at Pine Ridge Walker had never heard anything like the stories he found among his manuscripts. He told Wissler that the stories answered all his questions about the relationships among supernatural beings and that he planned to publish them along with other myths to be appended to the Sun Dance study.

Parts of that letter are so crucial to the way we judge the mythic texts today that its rather inconclusive language requires quotation:

> In translating the legends of "When the People Laughed at the Sun" and "When the Directions Were Made on the World," as written by Sword, I came upon what appears to me to be valuable information relative to the relation of the supernatural beings. . . . There is also in these legends information relative to the establishment of the time, a moon and a year with its seasons. The mythology as I have written it leaves much to be explained and the information above mentioned explains some of this. . . . The legends are quite long; they, in fact, being of the kind told by the professional story tellers of the Lakota who tell their stories at the winter camp usually prolonging the story during the entire occupance of the camp. It appears to me that this information received in this way is sufficient for accepting it relative to the mythology of the Lakotas for it harmonizes with much that was only alluded to in other information I had received regarding the matters referred to. (*Lakota Myth, 12*)

Today, Walker's ambiguous phrase "relative to the mythology of the Lakotas" seems to conceal more about the lost original manuscript than it reveals. Whether it was deliberate evasion or simple stylistic clumsiness, Walker, guided by Wissler, chose to publish the tales as examples of Lakota mythology without attribution to Sword. The narratives evoked considerable interest globally among scholars analyzing relationships between myth and culture. During the early part of this century, anthropologists and folklorists were following the lead of Scandinavian folklore scholars as they traced the distribution of plots and examined local variations as evidence of distinctive features in the social life of specific cultures. Franz Boas's statement in his essay "Development of Folk-Tales and Myths" summarizes general anthropological beliefs of the time, and it lets us judge preferred methods of oral narrative study. By implication, Boas's statement shows why anthropologists at the time were so reluctant to give up their stakes in Sword's narratives as examples of orally transmitted mythic plots:

> From a study of the distribution and composition of tales we must then infer that the imagination of the natives has played with a few plots, which were expanded by means of a number of motives that

have wide distribution, and that there is comparatively little material that seems to belong to any one region exclusively, so that it might be considered as of autochthonous origin. The character of the folktales of each region lies rather in the selection of preponderant themes, in the style of plots, and in their literary development.

. . . everywhere tales attach themselves to phenomena of nature. . . . The distribution of these tales demonstrates clearly that the more thought is bestowed upon them by individuals deeply interested in these matters—by chiefs, priests, or poets—the more complex do they become and the more definite are the local characteristics that they develop.[16]

Walker's 1917 publication became a standard, worldwide source for information about the Oglala Sioux, their rituals and myths, and the relationships between the two. Scholars consistently mentioned the systematic, rational nature of Sword's tales and noted their consonance with the even more systematic explanations of symbolism and ritual that also came from Sword. But the mythic texts acquired other, quite different spheres of popular influence, as well, and their current vitality has as much to do with their general popular readership as it does with the way scholars used them to illustrate methods and theories.

Walker was so taken with the literary possibilities of what he had discovered that he decided to use the plot as the basis for a cycle of narratives incorporating all that he knew about Lakota belief, ritual, and culture. He continued to revise this magnum opus until his death, after which the many drafts were given to the Colorado Historical Society, where his unfinished compendium remained until the cultural revivals at Pine Ridge began to take place following the 1972 American Indian Movement's occupation at Wounded Knee.

Educators at Pine Ridge wanted to use traditional Lakota myth as a foundation for study of Lakota culture. Available mythic sources, oral and written, seemed fragmentary, however, and their connections with ritual action and symbolism were difficult to discern. The confusion that Walker had known in his earlier studies was also experienced by Lakota people after the traditional rituals and myths had been suppressed and their connections to details of daily life began to fade from collective memory. Then, after decades of underground existence, the old Lakota rituals were revital-

16. Franz Boas, *Race, Language, and Culture* (New York: Collier, Macmillan Limited, 1940), 404, 406.

ized, and they became, again, the openly acknowledged core of the nation's life. Much had been lost, however. Not surprisingly, Walker's unpublished narrative cycle had the emotional force and the clear intellectual scope that the Lakota sought as they returned to the older traditions. So, the least fragmentary of the drafts of Walker's long narrative cycle were returned to the Oglala people, who, for many years, used mimeographed copies of the 185 typescript pages in the reservation's schools. The situation changed when the founding committee of the Center for Great Plains Studies at the University of Nebraska in Lincoln asked the Oglala people what such a center could do to help them. Their answer was: Publish the Walker manuscripts. Some months later, I began that task and was soon joined by Raymond J. DeMallie.

In *Lakota Myth*, I publish both Walker's reworked narrative cycle and the versions of Sword's stories that were as close as I could come to Sword's own writing. I present what information we have been able to gather about the history and provenance of the texts. In its mimeographed format, however, both Walker's literary cycle and the summaries of Sword's stories published in 1917 had taken on a life of their own, and many people found that information about the texts got in the way of their responses to the texts.

In 1987, Dorothy Dooling published a slightly retold version of Walker's narrative cycle as a book for "lovers of myth." Her commentary is proof that when it comes to transitional texts with mythic roots, information about the creativity of specific individuals is easily set aside in favor of evidence of communal elements, even in the copyright-obsessed world of contemporary American publishing:

> My contribution seems to me to have been only in trying to carry to completion Dr. Walker's intention, letting the stories find their way into a connected whole and editing and smoothing over certain inconsistencies of detail and style. Nevertheless, I am sure that willy-nilly something that is personal to my own appreciation and understanding has crept in to shape my retelling, and so added another shading of interpretation to those of each of the others who have told these tales before me. It is an inevitable part of the process of myth's transmission that all its lovers leave in it something of their own substance.[17]

17. Dorothy Dooling, *The Sons of the Wind* (New York: Parabola Books, 1987), vii–ix.

The determination to view as legitimate myth not just Sword's narratives but Walker's, too, is far stronger than any willingness to see them as carefully constructed narrative codes that teach about myth and belief. Part of the difficulty derives from the fact that Sword's tales represent a form of creativity that does not fit any of our complex categories for describing narrative. If, as close study of the texts suggests, they are a kind of metamyth that facilitates understanding among different mythic and cultural systems, then all the different uses of them are fulfilling the grandest hopes of Sword and Walker, and debate about authorship quickly turns to questions about the impact of religious belief on narrative. On that point, Vivian Arviso One Feather, writing an introduction for Dooling's volume, made the comments that account for the position of many Lakota:

> My personal perspective is to stress the urgency of sharing this knowledge. My children, being of Lakota descent, were raised within the social traditions of their father's tiospaye (community). This particular tiospaye is proud of its history of having produced strong leaders among the Oglala Lakota on the Pine Ridge Indian Reservation in South Dakota. Like other concerned parents, I desire that my children understand and develop a deeper appreciation of their human existence and mature with the knowledge that the Lakota Nation began, not with the arrival of Columbus, but with the creation of this universe. And more importantly, they comprehend that as a people the Lakota Nation will endure indefinitely.[18]

Sword's Mythic Texts

Using whatever historical information we can find about George Sword, we can build a case for reading his fictional narrative as a showpiece of resistance and transitional literature that highlights features of traditional beliefs in order to reveal their significance within the changed circumstances of reservation life. The details of such a reading are, of course, speculative and inconclusive, but, as his life history and his other writing shows, Sword undoubtedly possessed the quality of mind and experience that prompted him to think about the connections between the traditional Lakota culture and the new, imposed reservation culture. All of his writing indicates that he had a powerful rationalizing and systematizing intelligence able to abstract cultural principles that could help people function within a new environ-

---

18. Vivian Arviso One Feather, introduction to Dooling, *The Sons of the Wind*, viii–ix.

ment. This talent was accompanied by an exceptional capacity to adapt to changed circumstances. Scholars from Clark Wissler to Paul Radin, to Clifford Geertz, to William Powers have all been impressed with Sword's "reasoned articulateness," even though they did not necessarily connect what they read in Walker's 1917 publication with the actual historical contributions of Sword and his closest friends. Clark Wissler wrote, "Among the Teton there were philosophers of no mean order who reflected upon things as experienced, sought explanations in terms of causes and looked for the signs of a unified system embracing the universe. They gave numbers a place in the mysteries, placing all powers in a hierarchy of fours."[19]

Wissler based his general comments largely on what he had learned from Walker, and Sword was preeminent among the philosophers Wissler admired. I quote these observations because it is precisely Sword's frequently noted ability to abstract the patterns guiding ritual and narrative imagery and then to use them to show connections with other facets of the culture that I want to use as the basis of my reading of his fictional texts. First, though, a summary of the actual narrative content is in order.

The first tale begins in a world below the current one, where a chief and his wife have a daughter who is "the most beautiful of women." She marries Tate (the Wind) and gives birth to quadruplets, a sign that these children are gods. Her father, Wazi, is not content to be the mere grandfather of gods. He wants to have godlike powers for himself. That excessive desire provides the entrance cue for Trickster, who in this tale is a tempter bearing a definite resemblance to Satan in Genesis. He tells Wazi that he can have what he wants only if he will scheme to make the other gods look ridiculous. Wazi is nervous and consults his wife. She turns out to be a truly devious strategist who comes up with the altogether logical idea that they can trick the Trickster, believing that once they become gods they will be more powerful than he is, and they can simply ignore him. Wazi falls for this specious logic and agrees to help Trickster in exchange for godlike powers.

The logic of power, however, does not cover all contingencies. Wazi's wife can see into the future, so she already knows that their daughter will some day be seated with the most powerful gods. Therefore, when her beautiful daughter claims that she wants to become even more beautiful just in order to achieve what has, after all, been preordained, her parents

---

19. Clark Wissler, *Indians of the United States* (New York: Doubleday and Company, Inc., 1954), 163. See also Clifford Geertz, *The Interpretation of Cultures* (New York: Basic Books, 1973), 128; and William Powers, *Oglala Religion* (Lincoln: University of Nebraska Press, 1977).

test their new divine powers by letting her use a charm they have made. It works. The daughter is soon so beautiful that one look at her makes Wi (the Sun) forget everything else, including his wife, Hanwi (the Moon). Contrary to all the dictates of law and order, he gives Hanwi's symbolic place to Wazi's daughter. The Moon is displaced. She is deeply insulted and goes to Skan, the supreme judge and arbiter, to protest her injured pride, grief, and anger. Skan acts like the wise judge that Sword surely tried to be during his years as judge at Pine Ridge. He questions all participants in this event and renders the series of judgments that exile Tate and his motherless sons to the next world, where there are no directions, no spatial or temporal markings. The only existing order is that which reigns in Tate's tipi, where each inhabitant has his rightful place in relation to all the others.

The next narrative tells about creating order in the New World. One day a woman arrives. She introduces herself as the daughter of Skan and says that she has come to help the sons mark directions on the world so that each can know where he belongs in space and in time. The oldest son, a surly, discourteous fellow, is to have the first direction. The Wizard, another exile from the previous world, tricks the elder brother and arranges to have his birthright given to the next brother, a far more worthy type. The duped brother complains, but it is too late—he has lost his birthright. Jealousy and resentment become part of the order of creation. Eventually, after a series of adventures, each brother establishes his direction and with it the possibilities of temporal and spatial divisions in this world that can be marked on the circular picture of the cosmos that Wohpe keeps. Therefore, their actions become the means of "drawing" the basic Lakota symbolic form, namely, the circle divided into four quadrants.

By giving explicit narrative references that corresponded with the visual details of the basic circular imagery, Sword could show how mythic signifiers summed up by the circle image might be systematically translated and expanded into easily updated social, political, and psychological references. Sword's obvious theme of exile and beginning anew after the collapse of a previous way of life is set in relation to a plot episode that, in its general outline, owes more to the biblical story of Adam and Eve than it does to plots that were part of the Lakota oral tradition. If Sword was inspired by biblical episodes, however, he was equally alert to the tropological resources of the most frequently narrated Lakota tales. As noted above, the basic symbolism, the working of circular imagery, in his tales is definitely Lakota. It owes little or nothing to biblical sources. The same is true for the conventional opening motifs in Lakota hero tales that often begin by mentioning four brothers who live together. The action of the tale gets under way when an unknown woman comes to the tipi. Sword's tale uses the same motif, except that he explicitly identifies the brothers with the four winds and the woman with Wohpe, the mediator. He gives the brothers a task and a quest that allows him to use the story about the winds as a way to explain and to dramatize the range and functions of the primary Lakota symbolic structures, all of which were traditionally subsumed under references to circle imagery. Within this symbolic construct, spatial references to the four directions coincide with temporal references to four phases of human life, and these, in turn, involve seasonal, vegetal, and zoological divisions. Traditional Lakota belief taught all these connections, and people used that knowledge in reference to rituals and to oral narratives. In traditional storytelling, narrators could count on people understanding brief references that subsumed many traditional cognitive domains. A directional reference to the West, for example, could evoke a whole series of associated concepts that the storyteller could use without making them explicit. Sword, however, knew that his audience would include non-Indians, so he had to be clear in his references to all the major associations, and he had to explain them in one tale. The tropological resources he was employing were undoubtedly traditional, but many other features of Sword's tale were far from traditional, and, thanks to Franz Boas and Ella Deloria, we know how the Lakota reacted to Sword's tales during the early part of this century.

When Franz Boas read Sword's tales, he was definitely interested in them, and he sent them for verification to his former student Ella Deloria, who was sending him fieldwork data from several Sioux reservations.[20] Deloria herself was a member of a leading Sioux family, and she was a native Dakota speaker. Her professional anthropological training, combined with her personal experience of the traditions, made her the most qualified person to verify Sword's work by trying to find other oral versions. Using her knowledge of Lakota traditions and applying the standard criteria of the time, namely, the existence of variants and alternative versions for plots and motifs, Deloria concluded that Sword's texts were not examples of oral literature. Nevertheless, always willing to try to accommodate Boas, she interviewed several Lakota people, including Edgar Fire Thunder, one of Sword's friends who was living in a retirement home. Deloria transcribed and translated what he said about the tales, and, in an unusual and possibly

20. For more information on Ella Deloria's research on the Sword texts, see *Lakota Myth*, 17–27.

even unprecedented detail of ethnographic interviewing, she asked him to sign his name officially to the statement. Deloria apparently knew that the statement would be met with skepticism in New York.

Fire Thunder's testimony tells us much about how the Lakota viewed their traditions of storytelling, and it remains the single most important critical statement about Sword's texts. Fire Thunder left no doubt about his belief that the tales were examples of individual, not communal, creativity and that they differed significantly from any tales he had ever heard before:

> In former times, the Dakotas had legends and beliefs, here and there, in a reasonable sort of way; and to this day, we live with them, more or less in our midst. There never was anybody telling such fantastic things in such infinite detail as this; if narrators had known any such tales as these they would have come out with them, for when they were commissioned to entertain with legends, and were given handsome rewards, they always went at it with the attitude, "Oh, for something new to tell"; or "I could tell anything." . . . The Dakota race lived on, with screens only the thickness of animal hide for protection; how is it that a big matter like these tales, however secretly discussed, could not have been overheard at sometime or other by some eavesdropper through thin walls?[21]

In spite of the testimony of Deloria and Fire Thunder, Franz Boas would not give up his hopes of finding validating evidence in oral traditions that would allow him to use the tales as examples of myth. He urged Deloria to continue to search. She did, even going so far as to ask her many friends and relatives to help her, but everyone apparently gave her the same kinds of response that she summarized in another letter to Boas: " 'That must be from another tribe'—'That may be from the Bible'—'Somebody made that up according to his fancy'—'That's not Dakota!' Not once so far has anybody said of this part that maybe it was so believed in the past."[22]

In another letter to Boas, Deloria included a paragraph in which she astutely distinguished between folklore and oral fictional composition. That letter is another of her significant, but largely unnoted, contributions to our understanding of oral traditions. In it, she describes a process of individual oral creativity that other scholars and fieldworkers generally ignored be-

---

21. The complete transcript of this interview is in the Archives of the American Philosophical Society, Philadelphia. It is entitled "Dakota Commentary on Walker's Texts."
22. Deloria to Boas, 28 June 1938.

cause it fit none of their expectations. Perhaps they simply did not pay attention to phenomena that they were not looking for, whereas Deloria knew the entire spectrum of Lakota narrative art:

> [Sword's tales] might have been the creation of one mind. I am sure there were such cases of persons with superior imagination inventing tales which were their very own—not folklore. They might have been the beginnings of fiction writers. One woman used to weave such tales for us. Some of those I wrote out last spring are that kind; and others took, for instance, the Buffalo Wife story and embellished it so it sounded entirely different from the usual versions.[23]

I choose to accept Deloria's judgment, and I find Deloria's recognition of the original forms of fiction to be of extraordinary literary historical importance because she documents an expanded range of creative expression in communities where narrative continuity and development depended entirely on oral resources. I see Deloria's comment as evidence that the Sioux people did not always use traditional motifs and plots as building blocks for their tales. Those so inclined apparently allowed their imaginations to find new expressive and interpretive range that went far beyond the patterns set by the traditional tales. We can only regret that we have so few recorded examples of such fictional creation. I assume Sword's tales represent one example. Obviously, I assume that Sword's exceptional (and bicultural) imagination created tales that comment on ways in which traditional values and beliefs could continue to function in a reservation and a Christian environment.

In her statements about Lakota narrative genres, Deloria has also indicated that many Sioux people understood the tropological instrumentality afforded by the rich imagery of the traditional tales. Deloria describes the attitudinal frames used to interpret the *ohunkakan* (the oldest and most complex genre of tales):

> To our minds, they are a sort of hang-over, so to speak, from a very, very remote past, from a different age, even from an order of beings different from ourselves. These tales, in which generally some mythological character like Iktomi, Iya, the Crazy Bull, the Witch, or Waziya (the Cold), takes part together with human beings, are part of the common literary stock of the people. Constant allusion is made

---

23. Deloria to Boas, 14 Feb. 1938.

to them; similes are drawn from them which every intelligent adult is sure to understand.[24]

Viewed from within this literary context, we can see that Sword's narrative speculations were true to the spirit and the function of the folktale even if they were much more than usually original in their development. As the people's experiences changed, so did their needs for an expanded body of common literary allusions that could encompass features of the new way of life. That new way included non-Indians. Sword had goals that most traditional tellers did not have to consider—he had to make sure that his tales would explain features of Lakota worldview to cultural outsiders. He had, after all, taken upon himself Walker's instruction. Sword had given Walker an exceptionally complete Lakota education, but even Walker could not see the relationships between ritual actions and the traditional tales. Sword seemed to create a plot that dramatized just how the traditional metaphors worked. Or, to state his accomplishments in more academic terms, he managed to show how audiences with native textual competence understood the bonds between features of the texts and basic cognitive themes in the culture. Sword certainly did not know how to state what he understood in theoretical language, but he did know how to tell good stories, and he had a highly developed analogical imagination that was enhanced by his philosophical speculation on the meaning of Lakota stories, as well as the biblical stories that he told in his role as an Episcopalian catechist. So, he made up a story of his own that would explain some of the meaning that an intelligent pre-reservation Lakota took for granted as part of the knowledge everyone had about how "the powers of the world live and move."[25]

Tate and his sons, living in their tipi in a world in which there is no direction, no marking for space and time, and hence no structure for social life, are personified symbols that function as condensed, but easily comprehensible, cultural references. Their retained vestiges of traditional roles are definite enough, so that, with a little bit of concentration and research, anyone from any culture can see how all of social structure is implicit and suspended in this family unit with its own spatial image, the tipi, which visually defines the place of each individual inhabitant in relation to all the others. Before this symbol can become operative, though, the woman who

---

24. Ella Deloria, *Dakota Texts* (New York: AMS Press, 1932), ix.
25. The phrase comes from John Neihardt, *Black Elk Speaks* (New York: William Morrow and Company, 1932), 208. Its usefulness derives from the way its dynamic emphasis captures the force of the ethnical imperatives within the Lakota worldview.

will guide each of the men in working out his destiny has to come. As soon as she introduces change, the static, familial symbol is catalyzed into a dynamic model for action, which each of the four brothers dramatizes in his journey to create temporal and spatial divisions in the world. What was implicit in the image of the tipi gets played out on the historical stage of the New World, revealed in Sword's tale as an unsocialized macrocosm. Once its significance is enacted, the kinship image with its implicit reference to structure becomes a cultural grammar—in other words, a means of connecting details that would otherwise seem unrelated. Sword's story can remind the Sioux that their traditions prepare them to socialize (civilize) worlds. If the Americans thought they were civilizing the Sioux, men such as Sword could turn that belief on its head. Sword's tale seems to say that the Sioux needed to civilize the American influences that had their advantages if used properly but that were dangerous, too. Sword's narrative clearly points out that the way to civilize and to socialize is to follow the old patterns of kinship obligations in order to create new worlds.

To make explicit the ethical and emotional presuppositions that were implicit in the style and the structure of oral narratives, Sword chose to employ some of the conventions of literary realism. He dramatized motivations, fears, lusts, and loves, so that no one, no matter what his or her cultural background and training, could fail to grasp what was happening. Or, to return to the comments of the people that Ella Deloria interviewed, he had to make the spirits "act like people," so much like people that he exceeded what the conventions of oral literature could accommodate. His sympathetic characters step beyond the condensed form of myth into the grand, expansive, and more psychologically realistic schemes of epic. They cross over into interpretive frames that are bound to history, but they maintain definite ties with myth; they bring mythic symbolism into the workings of historical thought.

The best illustration of this dimension of the tales involves the characterization of Wohpe, the woman whose mythic role sums up most of the major features of woman's role in Lakota ritual and, therefore, in Lakota culture. We can glimpse the significance of Sword's changes by contrasting his psychologically realistic text with another one that has all the earmarks of a genuine, orally transmitted myth. This closely related tale tells about the Four Winds' dispute over which one will be Wohpe's husband. She chooses the South Wind, but the North Wind refuses to recognize her choice and tries to rape her. As one extant translation of the tale states,

When she found what the North Wind was trying to do, she took off her dress and spread it out and got under it to hide. So when the North Wind came to the dress, he thought he had found the beautiful being and he embraced it but everything on it grew hard and cold and icy. The South Wind found only a cold hard thing like his woman's dress but he could not find the woman so he went back to look for her. When he had gone, the North Wind came again and said to the woman, "I know you are under this dress and I am coming under there also." So he went to the edge of the dress but the woman spread it out farther that way. Then he went to the edge at another place and she spread it that way. He kept going from place to place and she kept spreading her dress wider and wider until it became so wide that there was no end or side left. Then he heard the South Wind coming again and he ran away to his tipi and when the South Wind came again he examined the dress and found that it was truly his woman's dress and then he knew that the North Wind had embraced it. He called loudly for his woman and she answered him that she was under the dress but that she had stretched it so wide to keep away from the North Wind, that there was neither a side nor an end to it and she could not get out from under it. (*Lakota Myth*, 184–85)

Sword retells the tale so that the powerful cosmological linkage between sexuality and the earth's fertility is retained, but he gives us a far more realistically portrayed woman. Gone is Wohpe's phenomenological identification with the earth, and the North Wind's attempted rape is gone, too. Instead we have a love story, in which Wohpe chooses the South Wind, while the North Wind stubbornly ignores her choice. He goes off on his journey to found his direction, still refusing to listen to her: " 'When I come, I will take you for my wife.' 'I will always be your sister,' said Wohpe. 'You will be my wife,' said Yata" (*Lakota Myth*, 77).

Later, after the North Wind has lost the first direction to his younger brother, he learns from the wizard, who is guiding the brothers in their journey, that when he gets back home he will experience Wohpe's pity, "as a sister should pity a brother" (*Lakota Myth*, 85). Then, in disappointed rage, the North Wind weeps, but Wohpe herself has no cause for fear. She is safely at home with Tate, dreaming of the brother she really loves. The story of the brothers and Wohpe is a romance complete with daydreams and conversations about the attributes of the beloved. It is a long way from the stark, ontological consequences of the other myth.

As Sword gives us the narrative detail that sometimes reveals and sometimes alters the cognitive significance that was implicit in oral narratives, he also helps us understand a narrative logic that depends on traditional and recognized mythic oppositional categories. His own narrative goals, though, have the practical effect of subverting the oppositions and establishing still higher-level structures of inclusion. He avoids the kind of thinking that requires one to choose either one or the other interpretation. As he struggled with the new bicultural conditions of life at Pine Ridge, he used mythic narrative as a means of charting changes in a way of thinking. I do not mean to imply that he did this consciously. I believe that he instinctively used the analogical resources available to him within his tradition to show more than one cognitive domain operating in relation to basic Lakota symbolism. This highlighting of narrative's potential to create polyvalent forms may be the most brilliant aspect of his creativity and the finest evidence of his rationalizing intelligence. He sets forth a narrative logic governed at every level by both/and propositions that work as a kind of narrative circuit breaker, allowing each term to achieve its maximum semantic range in order to include apparent contradictions within that range. The dynamic is implicit in traditional Lakota stories, but when Sword reveals its explicit narrative structure in his tales, he also changes the nature of its impact from the imagistic, analogical, and ontological impact of myths to a more realistic and historical scheme.

Throughout the development of Sword's plot, we can watch various kinds of dual logic unfold. One striking, and easily explicable, feature of it is revealed through the way characters become dualistic representations. Plot action evolves so that characters' actions have the effect of making an individual stand for different, even contrary, facets of Lakota symbolism. For example, plot establishes conditions under which the Moon is always both near and far from the Sun. When she is literally near her husband, the Sun, she must hide her face, thus becoming figuratively distant. The situation is reversed when she is physically distant. Then, her face is clear for all to see, and her visibility functions as a mode of proximity. Ite, the woman who takes the place of the Moon, is a figure who can take on several functions of duality. The temporal progression shows her first as a wife, then as a desired, but inaccessible, woman. She even acquires two faces and two distinct identities; hence, she gains the name Double Face, she is celestial in origin but terrestrial in destiny, she is the mother of sons who inherit both divinity and humanity, and she can, therefore, understand both but finally possesses neither. Likewise, Wohpe, the woman who guides the creation of the directions, achieves a relationship that alternates between sister and desired lover to the winds, and this composite identity has meteorological, as well as cosmological, significance. When they view her as a sister, the weather is good; when they imagine her as a potential lover, the weather is stormy. In every way, these manifestations of dualism reflect narrative participation in and departure from the traditional mythic system, functioning as a narrative that is finally both Lakota and Christian.

As the Lakota people stated so definitely to Ella Deloria, certain of Sword's stylistic and content features have unmistakable resemblances to Genesis. The Bible was translated into Dakota by 1880, and it became primary reading material for the literate Lakota.[26] Certainly Sword knew it well, and his narratives show direct evidence of his imaginative reworkings of his catechistic reading and teaching. A comparison between the biblical text and the section of Sword's narrative in which Skan gives his judgment on all who participated in the unseating of Hanwi shows obvious similarities:

Sword	Genesis
Skan said to Wi, "Why have you permitted a woman to sit on the seat of Hanwi?	The Lord God called to the man . . . "Have you eaten of the tree of which I commanded you not to eat?"
Wi replied, "This woman is the wife of a God and the mother of Gods and should be honored above all other women. As chief of the Gods, I would honor her as she deserves so that others would do so. I bid her to the feast. She sat on the seat of Hanwi and I looked on her beauty and it caused me to forget my companion. (*Lakota Myth*, 54)	The man said, "The woman whom thou gavest to be with me, she gave me the fruit of the tree, and I ate." (Gen. 3: 9–12)

26. We have documented evidence of Black Elk's use of biblical references. He even took the Bible with him to England when he traveled with Buffalo Bill's Wild West Show. See DeMallie, *The Sixth Grandfather* (Lincoln: University of Nebraska Press, 1985), 10–11. For a Lakota translation of the Bible, see Thomas S. Williamson and Stephen R. Riggs, trans., *Dakota Wowapi Wakan: The Holy Bible, in the Language of the Dakotas* (New York: American Bible Society, 1880).

The deities question each participant in the event; the shamed ones answer, and each interaction has the length of a biblical verse and the ontological impact of a biblical judgment. Perhaps the most significant parallel between Sword's narrative and the Bible occurs at the level of plot adaptations, because the story of the lost Garden of Eden had so many potential resonances among Lakota audiences. Sword's story differs from the biblical Genesis primarily on the matter of the level of social organization in the idyllic lost world. Sword places a whole Lakota band in his lost Edenic world, where life is lived much as it was in pre-reservation times. What is more, his character analogue to Eve gets mixed up in rather more devious problems than Eve, who is faced with a single tempter. Sword's character makes her mistake because she fails to understand just how weak a leader can be. Her seeking after power might have worked if the Sun had not neglected his wife in favor of the beautiful Ite. Similarly, Sword's tempter has a more developed narrative complexity than we find in Genesis. In the Lakota translation of Genesis, the tempter is called the "wise serpent" (*ksapa*). The particular combination of wisdom and cunning that the tempter represents gets transferred easily to the whole tradition of the Lakota Trickster figure even if the moral characteristics undergo some significant changes in the process, and manuscript evidence from the Walker collection suggests that Sword was inclined to make that potentially controversial character transfer.

Sword found a second plot in the Bible and adapted it to fit his Lakota purposes in the story of how the North Wind loses his birthright to the West Wind on the journey to create directions on this world. In the Lakota Bible, the word for *birthright* is *watokahe*. It is a nominalized extension of the term for *first born*, making that state into an abstract condition. What came first is displaced in Lakota culture, just as it was with Abraham's sons. The Lakota people undoubtedly experienced their historical displacements as an end to life as they knew it. Sword's narrative, though, suggests that displacement can be a beginning. Such displacement is a beginning in the Bible, as well as in the stories Sword is telling.

Thus, Sword's Lakota characters retain their own value and their specific determinations within the Lakota worldview at the same time as they show their ability to play some of the mythic roles found in biblical narratives. He seems to be saying that each people has its own ways. Sword's story, however, allows Christian Lakota to see that one way does not necessarily have to cancel out the other. At every level then, Sword's texts can be seen to articulate the same message. Out of the long night of military defeat, the people can create anew, and they can do it in their own way; there need not be a complete break with the cultural past, and Sword creates narrative transitions that bridge the ideological breaks. His narratives show the possibility of a sovereign ethos that avoids the colonial mentality and that motivates people to keep alive the political sovereignty guaranteed them by treaties. Political sovereignty is founded in historical continuity. Helping people perceive continuity amidst the changes of the reservation era appears to have been Sword's goal. He reveals the cognitive presuppositions that sustained myths, reaffirming interpretive strategies that are bound to the pragmatics of language use. In cultural contexts where people fear that their indigenous cognitive models are no longer workable, many experience that loss as the imposition of a crushing silence, a response that literature from many cultures dramatizes. Sword showed a way beyond the silence that descends when all language seems to have been shifted to another interpretive realm without leaving behind the new code for current use. Technically, according to the criteria that narrative scholars use, Sword's tales are fictions, but they fulfill all the functions of myth because they show the conditions for fundamental cultural creation. Sword was using the resources of his own imagination to establish dramatic examples of how to maintain endangered values and beliefs.

Some of the scholarly commentary on Sword's work supports the reading that I have been proposing. Clifford Geertz uses the statements of Sword and Tyon as examples of "the fusion of the existential and the normative . . . a subtle formulation of the relation between good and evil, and of their grounding in the very nature of reality. Circle and eccentric form, sun and stone, shelter and war are segregated into pairs of disjunct classes whose significance is aesthetic, moral, and ontological." In the same context, Geertz notes that "the tendency to synthesize worldview and ethos at some level if not logically necessary, is at least empirically coercive; if it is not philosophically justified, it is at least pragmatically universal."[27]

Sword's life history is strong evidence that his mythic narratives are indeed metaphorical realizations of an empirically coercive synthesis, with the coercive force deriving from the pervasive insecurity of the initial phases of reservation life. The insecurities have not gone away. The renewed interest in Sword's narratives testifies to the fact that their messages of self-determination continue to engage Lakota people. I give the last word in this essay to Vivian Arviso One Feather, who articulated some contemporary Lakota reasons for valuing Sword's narratives:

27. See Geertz, *The Interpretation of Cultures*, 127–28.

In a very simplified and yet profound manner, the basic guiding principles of Lakota culture are portrayed through the lives of these
Sacred Beings. Unashamed of their surly and pouting behavior,
these Sacred Beings continually tested the limits of their own powers.
They coped with inner family quarrels, had strained relations in their
marriages, and had to contend with those among themselves who
desired greater powers. Ironically, even as they resolved their conflicts, they discovered newer conflicts within the solution.[28]

28. In Dooling, *The Sons of the Wind*, vii.

Francis LaFlesche's "The Song of Flying Crow" and the Limits of Ethnography

Jarold Ramsey

> long ago her mother
> had to sing this song and so
> she had to grind along with it
> the corn people have a song too
> it is very good
> I refuse to tell it
> —Armand Schwerner, "What the Informant Said to Franz Boas in 1920," *Shaking the Pumpkin*

1

The unpublished writings of "the first professional American Indian anthropologist,"[1] Francis LaFlesche (1857–1932) of the Omaha tribe, include a file of handwritten and typed manuscripts in the National Anthro-

---

1. Margot Liberty, "Francis LaFlesche," in *American Indian Intellectuals*, ed. Margot Liberty (St. Paul: West Publishing Co., 1978), 99.

pological Archives of the Smithsonian Institution in Washington, D.C.[2] The bulk of these manuscripts reflect LaFlesche's literary inclinations; more specifically, they seem to represent his ongoing interest in finding new ways of "doing" ethnography, beyond the standard forms of discourse established in the Boas era of American anthropology and followed by LaFlesche himself in his monumental collaboration with Alice Fletcher on the culture of his own people, *The Omaha Tribe*, and other scholarly writings.[3]

Thus, the "LaFlesche File" includes a fascinating range of pieces, all centered on Omaha culture and history but written in a variety of forms, from the personal essay, to the short story, to what appears to be the beginnings of a novel, to the outline of a grand opera, *Da-o-ma* (eventually completed by LaFlesche and Nellie Eberhart in 1912, with music by Charles Wakefield Cadman, but never performed), to poetry. Clearly, LaFlesche had literary aspirations (on the occasion of receiving an Honorary Doctorate of Letters from the University of Nebraska in 1926, he remarked that "as a lad he had planned to be a great buffalo hunter, but the white people came and ate up the buffalo, so he turned to writing"[4]), and he did publish two short stories in his lifetime,[5] but the manuscript material in the Smithsonian file indicates

2. Alice Fletcher and Francis LaFlesche, Papers, #4558/48, National Anthropological Archives of the Smithsonian Institution, Washington, D.C. I am grateful to the National Anthropological Archives, and, specifically, to Kathleen T. Baxter, Reference Archivist, for help with this project and for granting permission to publish the text of "The Song of Flying Crow" for the first time.

3. In *The Omaha Tribe*, Annual Report of the Bureau of American Ethnology, vol. 27 (1911), LaFlesche is allowed to break into the standard scholarly format (presumably laid down by Fletcher and the BAE) from time to time with short personalized accounts of Omaha rituals, anecdotes about the difficulties of collecting material, and so on—but in agate type! This is his account—relevant to the present text—of recording the songs of the Sacred Pole from an Omaha elder, Yellow Smoke, having been at first refused: "As I listened to the old priest, his voice seemed as full and resonant as when I had heard him years ago, in the days when the singing of these very songs in the Holy Tent meant so much to each gens and to every man, woman, and child in the tribe. Now the old man sang with his eyes closed, and watching him there was like watching the last embers of the religious rites of a vanishing people" (251). Hardly conventional ethnography!

4. In Norma Kidd Green, *Iron Eye's Family: The Children of Joseph LaFlesche* (Lincoln: Johnson Publishing Co., 1969), 196.

5. Both pieces appeared in *The Southern Workman*: "The Story of a Vision" (February 1901), 106–9, and "One Touch of Nature" (August 1913), 427–28. "The Story of a Vision" has been recently republished in *The Singing Spirit: Early Short Stories by North American Indians*, ed. Bernd C. Peyer (Tucson: University of Arizona Press, 1989), 69–73; it is, in form and style, a kind of ethnographic sketch like "The Song of Flying Crow," but it lacks the persistent self-consciousness.

that he was also interested in adapting literary forms and strategies to the task of "writing culture."

In this, of course, he was in league with a persistent "literary" impulse in American ethnographic and anthropological writing, aimed at supplementing the social science methodology of Boasian anthropology with the techniques of the personal essay, the autobiography, and the novel. Adolf Bandelier's ethnographic novel of Pueblo life, *The Delight Makers* (1890), is a memorable early expression of this impulse, which, late in LaFlesche's own career, produced a remarkable collection of ethnographic short stories written by distinguished scholars of Indian culture, most of whom were trained by Boas: *American Indian Life (by Several of Its Students)*, edited by Elsie Clews Parsons (1922). The avowedly fictive cast of these narratives can be appreciated in the title and opening lines of one of them, T. T. Waterman's "All Is Trouble along the Klamath (a Yurok Idyll)": "(Mrs. Oregon Jim, from the house Erkiger'i or 'Hair Ties', in the town of Pe'kwan, speaking): 'You want to know why old Louisa and I never notice each other? Well, I'll tell you why. I wouldn't speak to that old woman to save her life. There is a quarrel between her and me, and between her people and mine.'"[6]

In his introduction to the volume, A. L. Kroeber observes approvingly that "[the] fictional form of presentation devised by the editor has definite merit. It allows freedom in depicting or suggesting the thoughts and feelings of the Indians, such as is not possible in a formal, scientific report. In fact, it incites to active psychological treatment, else the tale would lag. . . . The method is that of the historical novel, with emphasis on the history rather than the romance."[7]

Putting aside judgment of its strictly literary merits, *American Indian Life* is a fascinating, adventuresome, but oddly neglected experiment. As Kroeber's comments suggest, the central aim of its contributors' dalliance with the art of fiction seems to have been to transcend some of the felt limits of scientific ethnography—to try to register the individual subjectivities (Kroeber speaks of "psychological treatment") of native subjects. Against the too often faceless, lifeless generalizations of conventional ethnography, individual subjects' diverse and conflicted lives reduced to static formulae of collective cultural identity, Parsons and her contributors (who included Kroeber and Boas himself) were seeking to evoke their sense of their sub-

6. Elsie Clews Parsons, ed., *American Indian Life* (New York: B. W. Huebsch Inc., 1922), 289.
7. See the introduction to *American Indian Life*, by A. L. Kroeber, 13.

jects' lives as ongoing "stories" unfolding within the vague but pervasive "plot" of a given culture. If they persisted here, as in their conventional scholarship, in neglecting questions about their own subjectivities as social scientists, at least they were attempting to find ways to bring "character" and "conflict" and "narrative" into play in the arenas of cultural study. Their experiments point at least symbolically toward the modern "ethnographic novel," of which Chinua Achebe's *Things Fall Apart*, Laura Bohannon's *Return to Laughter*, Jorge Amado's *Tent of Miracles*, James Welch's *Fools Crow*, and Ursula LeGuin's *Always Coming Home* are notable specimens.

Apparently Francis LaFlesche was not invited to contribute something to *American Indian Life* (a pity all around), but early on in his career he followed his literary inclinations in seeking for more sensitive and evocative ways of writing about the phenomena of culture than what current scientific modes allowed. In particular, as a Native American scholar, a staff member of the Indian Office and later of the Bureau of American Ethnology, and the son of an Omaha chief, Iron Eye (Joseph LaFlesche), as someone who had participated as a boy in the last of the great Central Plains buffalo hunts, he clearly felt a strong need to legitimatize in writing his own subjective, *imaginative* identification with Omaha culture and, concomitantly, his awareness of belonging to two worlds, Indian and Anglo, even of existing uncertainly *between* them. His first nonscholarly publication of note, *The Middle Five*,[8] is a richly textured memoir of his boyhood years in a Presbyterian mission school at home on the reservation in Nebraska. Most of the unpublished pieces in the Smithsonian Archives are literarily self-conscious explorations in forms of autobiographical discourse, with persistent emphasis on figures such as the author himself, moving equivocally between native and Anglo cultures.

One of the shorter compositions in the file, a brief memoir of a summertime return to the Omaha reservation entitled "The Song of Flying Crow," especially stands out. I don't know of a more subtle and resonant evocation of the intercultural predicament than this eight-paragraph sketch,

---

8. Francis LaFlesche, *The Middle Five* (1900; reprint, Madison: University of Wisconsin Press, 1963). LaFlesche had "ethnographic" troubles with prospective publishers, who objected that the book did not conform to Anglo stereotypes of "wild" Indian children! LaFlesche's pancultural aspiration is asserted in the dedication: "To the Universal Boy." Evidently, he also considered publishing his short stories and sketches (possibly including the present text) in a collection for general readers but, again, ran afoul of publishers: "One requested that the stories be told with humor on the order of Uncle Remus" (see Green, *Iron Eye's Family*, 189).

which seems to me to be a small gem of its kind, a kind of poem of ethnographic experience, if you will. In what follows after the text itself, printed here for the first time, I try to contextualize "The Song of Flying Crow" and then to explicate its form and content, whose unifying principle seems to be the author's deeply felt need to *mediate* between his new life as a government-sponsored ethnologist and his old, but persisting, life as a member of the Omaha tribe.

The manuscript of "The Song of Flying Crow" is undated, but it may have been written as early as 1895, after the first summer in which LaFlesche is known to have used a graphophone (an Edison-type recording phonograph) in his ongoing effort to record and preserve Omaha music. By 1895, he had already collaborated with Alice Fletcher and the musicologist J. C. Fillmore on *A Study of Omaha Indian Music* (1893), and his continued work in this vein would eventually inform several chapters in *The Omaha Tribe*.[9] The exact date of the singing of Flying Crow's song is not crucial: What *is* important to notice at the outset is the writer's indication that, once again, he has journeyed home from Washington, D.C. to take up residence on the reservation, indeed in a tipi![10] But what Norma Kidd Green has written about such vacations, that "Frank entered fully into the life of the family and of the reservation, leaving the other half of his life far away,"[11] must have been true only for outward appearances—a much more complex and problematic mental occupation must have been the rule for LaFlesche, judging from this text.

2 "The Song of Flying Crow"

At the risk of being accused of "going back to the tent," as many Indian students returned from eastern schools have been accused of "going back to the blanket," I had erected near my brother's cottage, when at home on my vacation, last summer, a real Indian tent for my comfort and pleasure during my stay. The last days of my real tent life came to an end years ago when I with other Indians traveled one whole winter through western Kansas

9. Alice Fletcher, Francis LaFlesche, and J. C. Fillmore, *A Study of Omaha Indian Music*, in Archaeological and Ethnological Papers of the Peabody Museum, I, 1 (1893), 1–152.

10. In her excellent biography of Alice Fletcher, *A Stranger in Her Native Land* (Lincoln: University of Nebraska Press, 1988), Joan Mark notes the pattern: "Francis had a month's vacation at the Indian Bureau, and he usually went to visit his family on the Omaha Reservation" (252).

11. Green, *Iron Eye's Family*, 192–93.

in search of buffalo. At that time my proud possessions were a saddle, a bridle, a lariat, and a gun. In singular contrast to those things, I had with me in my temporary "return to the tent" a number of books, magazines, a leather case, and a graphophone. The great herds that my people and I followed over the plains in the days of my youth have gone the same way that my forefathers have gone, never to return. The songs that expressed the emotions of my people, the songs of war, of peace, and of love that used to ring through the wooded hills of my birth were also passing away, and it was to catch as much as possible the dying echoes that I made my visit home armed with a speech and song catching instrument. The tent was a bit of sentiment, the indulgence of which the civilized people will forgive.

It was late in the afternoon when I took possession of my tent. A gentle rain drummed on the heavy canvas and my thoughts traveled back to the days which my life among the white people has since taught me to look upon as wild. The sound of approaching footsteps brought me back to the present and a familiar voice commenting on the weather warned me of a coming visitor. We exchanged the usual greetings and then began to talk of the various things in which we had a common interest. Then other friends came one by one until the tent was full of people all eager to learn and to teach. My well starched collar and cuffs and polished shoes made not the slightest difference in the intimate friendship that we enjoyed before I left the reservation years ago to dwell in the city of the Nation's Capitol.

When we had all enjoyed the supper that my brother and I had provided and were feeling very good, we filled a huge pipe which we passed around and smoked. A fire was lighted so that we could see each other's faces, and being in a reminiscent mood we began tales of our own adventures and those of other men in other days. Then when the stories of adventures and misadventures, of pathos and of humor began to flag and somebody yawned I said, "Uncle, start for us a song and we will sing, just as we used to do before I went away," addressing a little old man. "Yes," said a friend who sat near me, "let's sing some of the old songs that used to stir the warlike feelings of the men who lived and died long ago."

In a clear and musical voice the little old man gave the first bar of a song familiar to us all and we took it up and made the hills around echo with the sounds of song. Of the thousands of songs in the tribe I knew a few, some five or six hundred, so I did my part of the singing and enjoyed the thrill of the rhythm. Many other songs were sung and the story of each repeated just as I had heard it years ago. The little old man complimented my memory for songs, then said, "Let us see if you know this one." He started it and all sang with a precision that denoted thorough knowledge of the song. I knew the class to which it belonged, from the vocables used and the terminating notes, but I could not follow, for the song was new to me. "It must be an old one just recalled by some old man." "It is a new song," said the little old man, "made and given to us by your friend Flying Crow just before he died not very long ago."

"How did he come to make the song?" I asked. "He knew he was near death," replied the little old man, "and before he died he wanted to say to his friends some words that would not be forgotten the moment he spoke them, so he made the song to hold the words. He lay in his tent one day, all silent, but thinking of the many, many people who came into this life, endured its hardships, and enjoyed its pleasures for a little space of time, then passed to the land of mystery, the land of spirits. Then he thought of the countless numbers that are to open their eyes to the light of the sun and pass on in the same way. He thought of the lives of the birds, the animals, and the little creatures that crawl and burrow in the earth, how their time, as well as that of men, was measured out long before they were brought to the earth. He had no fear of death but he thought of these things as being full of mystery. Struck with the realization that the duration of life at the longest was but brief he desired his friends to strive to make each other happy so that they may enter the next world without fear and with a joyous spirit. Although the words in the song are few they at once bring to our minds all these thoughts—and the memory of our friend."

"Let's sing it again," I said. "I like it and I must learn it."

We sang it again and again and now it is so fixed in my memory that I shall never forget it even if I should live to be a hundred years old.

It was past the hour of midnight when my friends took leave of me to go to their homes among the hills. I could hear their voices in the still night until they gradually died away in the distance, then I took to thinking of the song I had just learned and its maker, Flying Crow. We were boys together and went to the same school that was maintained by the missionaries on our reservation for the education of Indian youth. I remember he used to run away quite often and finally he stayed away altogether. He inherited the beliefs of his fathers who for generations had been the keepers of the sacred rites of the tribe. He learned very little of the instructions given in the schoolroom and much less of those given in the chapel which meant nothing to his untutored mind. Born a pagan he died a pagan, with the song of a pagan upon his lips.

3

From the first sentence on, the author's predicament and something of his sensitivity to it are manifested. He has "come home" again, but can he really claim to *be* home, given his present affiliations and the loss of the Omaha ways of his boyhood: the use of tipis and the great buffalo hunts? To be sure, he has set himself up in a tipi (apparently on his younger brother Carey's farm[12]), but if the tent is "real" (albeit canvas), he knows that his occupation of it is not, and at the very outset of the sketch he wonders jokingly if his Anglo readers will accuse him of atavistic behavior in his whim of going back to the tent, if not, as the saying has it, "to the blanket." The defensive self-mockery of the circumstances of his return in effect brackets and conditions his identification of its *purpose*—to record, against inevitable loss, the traditional songs of the Omaha. Can this purpose itself be just as sentimental and self-indulgent as "going back to the tent"? And is his own position as both returned native son and government researcher tenable?

Already, LaFlesche has situated his discourse in a cluster of interlocking bipolar oppositions: not just Omaha Indian versus Anglo but, more broadly, "civilized" versus "wild" ("the days which my life among the white people has since taught me to look upon as wild"), past versus present (specifically *his* past and present but also that of his people), cultural loss versus the possibility of recovery and preservation. Thus, he reflects on the material possessions of his buffalo hunting days, "a saddle, a bridle, a lariat, and a gun" in contrast to what he brought with him for his scholarly work: books, magazines, a briefcase, and a graphophone. His juxtapositioning of vanished buffalo and vanishing songs, and the instruments for "catching" them—guns and graphophone, respectively—is especially expressive of his predicament: there is nothing much heroic about recording songs with a spring-loaded contraption, he seems to be saying to himself, and if the way of the buffalo is truly gone for the Omaha, "never to return," then is there really any vital value in transcribing some surviving songs from that lost world?

As an ethnologist and cultural historian of his own tribe, LaFlesche had had to struggle in his work with the bleakly pragmatic philosophy of

---

12. LaFlesche eventually retired to Carey's farm, near Macy, Nebraska, and died there on 5 September 1932.

many tribal elders, who, when they recognized that the buffalo were gone, decided that the ceremonies and songs sacred to the buffalo cult should die with them and not be uselessly left to posterity. As Norma Kidd Green puts it, the elders "would not teach the sacred words to any young man; these things could never be a part of the young men's lives."[13] Against such opposition, LaFlesche seems to have felt, in Margot Liberty's words, "a sense of almost unbearable urgency" to record the Omaha legacy;[14] but at what point does one's ethnological advantage of being a tribal member become the basis of exploitation? At what point does the effort to "translate" Omaha culture into ethnographical discourse become a kind of betrayal— *traddutore, tradditore*?

In a few sentences, by way of setting the scene, even before beginning to narrate the events attending the singing of Flying Crow's song, the author establishes a distinctive pattern of emotional and imaginative movement between the polarities of his experience: a kind of dialectic, whose overall purpose seems to be the mediation of these polarities of race, culture, identity, and temporality. I am using "mediation" here as Lévi-Strauss uses it in discussing myth and, in particular, the function of Trickster-figures—to mean a sort of mental dance between opposites, not effecting their resolution or even reduction but rather providing a useful way of holding conflicted and conflicting experience all in mind, rather as Yeats claimed that his ad hoc all-mediating cosmology allowed him to "hold in a single thought reality and justice."[15]

In these terms, LaFlesche's sketch really does have the density and unity (and the pervasive irony!) of a baroque or modernist poem: Nearly every sentence unit makes its own nervous move between opposites and thereby contributes to what seems to me to be the overall effect of the text, one of a bitter and knowing balancing, as if the author were making in words an image of himself not *en abyme* but *en equilibre*, constantly shifting and adjusting to the conflicting claims on his identity as they come to mind, and in the process endeavoring to register a center of gravity for himself.

In the second paragraph, the author's attention fixes on the immediate social concerns of a native son who has returned home to meet his old friends: Will they accept him? Will they let him "come home" without ironic

---

13. Green, *Iron Eye's Family*, 188.
14. Liberty, "Francis LaFlesche," 54.
15. William Butler Yeats, *A Vision* (London: Macmillan, 1965), 25.

difference, despite all that now divides him from them? Far from "going back to the blanket," LaFlesche notes that he is ostentatiously dressed to meet his friends in "well starched collar and cuffs and polished shoes," as if forcing the issue of Anglo acculturation, as if deliberately seeking to put off his Omaha guests. But for a wonder, nothing, he claims, seems to interfere with the cordiality of his homecoming. At least for now, all differences between now and then, here and there, *him and them*, seem to fade away, or so the author gratefully believes.

He and his brother have, in effect, prepared an old-style Omaha social, presumably conducted in the Omaha language, with a meal, followed by a campfire, the passing of a pipe (the most sacred of all Omaha ritual articles),[16] and then the traditional mutual entertainment of storytelling and singing. All goes well, and, at length, after the storytelling has begun to slow (apparently the stories are not *hi'gon*, myths, which would require a more formal setting, but rather personal tales), LaFlesche hearkens to his professional business on the reservation and proposes a session of singing, personalizing the request a little self-consciously: "just as we used to do before I went away." The fact that his guest list happens to include an elderly singing-master further indicates that LaFlesche is aiming to combine scholarly business and nostalgic pleasure here—although there is no mention of the graphophone being brought into action.

What ensues in the singing appears to be doubly affirmative and reassuring, although typically he is reticent about his feelings. First, against LaFlesche's earlier assertions that his people's music is "passing away" (as the buffalo did), he finds that this particular group of Omaha men—presumably of his own generation for the most part—are able to perform the old songs with confidence and pleasure and to recover "the story of each," meaning, apparently, their origins and local meanings. For the moment, at least, the hills are made to resound with something more substantial and vital than the "dying echoes" of a fading culture.

Second, he proves to himself and to his tribal friends that he is still authoritatively conversant with the Omaha repertory of traditional songs, and not just as a scholar armed with a graphophone but as a performer: "I did my part of the singing," he reports with no small self-satisfaction, the personal implication being that if he knows only a "few" Omaha songs

---

16. The ritual and symbolic significance of the pipe is described at length in *The Omaha Tribe*.

(some five or six hundred out of thousands!), he has confirmed that he knows them both *etically* and *emically*, both as a scholarly outsider and as a functioning insider.

At this emotional high point in the narrative, with the author indicating that he is feeling quite at home, maybe even a little smug, he deftly introduces the first of two dramatic reversals in his story. No sooner has the old singing-master complimented LaFlesche for his "memory of songs" than he pointedly challenges that knowledge by introducing yet another song. It is a tense moment, with poignant consequences. I conjecture that the old man has a point to make to his host, one that sharply qualifies the author's earlier assurance that his urban costume and Anglo big-city life and career are inconsequential back on the reservation and that there is not "the slightest difference" between him and his old friends. The old man deliberately chooses a song that everybody in the tipi knows—except for the visitor from Washington; for the first time in this Omaha sing-along, LaFlesche is left incapable of performing—with all eyes on him, no doubt.

Without yet knowing *whose* song it is, LaFlesche somewhat defensively succeeds in classifying it according to "the vocables used and the terminating notes," thinking now like the scholarly informant who has been collaborating with Alice Fletcher and the musicologist Fillmore in a systematic study of Omaha music. In the schema of that study, what he has heard would fall under the general heading of "Individual Songs"—sung either as solos or by companies of persons who are about to engage in a common action"—and, more specifically, under the subheading of "Mystery Songs" ("songs of mystery which directly appeal to the unseen forces which surround man"), but, under the circumstances, such taxonomic knowledge is a painfully inadequate substitute for the simple *emic* knowing of the song, as manifested in his friends' performance of it.[17] No wonder that the author responds with some asperity to the singing-master's challenge to his musical competency: "It must be an old one just recalled by some old man." The reply—as if the final element of a stern lesson—is, in context, unlooked for

17. Fletcher, LaFlesche, and Fillmore, *A Study of Omaha Indian Music*, 18, 43ff. About "mystery songs," the authors note that "songs belonging to this subdivision are potent to secure general benefits" (43)—a quality that seems to tally with Flying Crow's hopes for his song's beneficent effect on his friends. In the Omaha musical scheme, Flying Crow's composition appears to be the mirror opposite in intention to the Omaha Funeral Song, which "is for the spirit of the dead; it is to cheer him as he goes from his dear ones left behind on the earth; so as he hears the voices of his friends, their glad tones help him to go forward on his inevitable journey" (Fletcher and LaFlesche, *The Omaha Tribe*, 593).

and devastating: "It is a new song . . . made and given to us by your friend Flying Crow just before he died not very long ago."

What has happened? Characteristically, LaFlesche does not directly reveal his emotions here, but given the circumstances as reported, he must be experiencing a pang of conflicting feelings. In the embarrassment and irritation of not knowing a tribal song well known to everyone else, he learns that it was, in fact, recently composed by his boyhood friend and schoolmate Flying Crow, just before his death, about which, presumably, LaFlesche has not heard until now! Further evidence, then, that, in truth, he is deeply out of touch, "other" to his people—and the old man's phrasing of the facts seems to be notably disjunctive: "made and given to *us* by *your friend*" (my emphasis).

On the other hand, to the extent that the author is still thinking about the survival of Omaha culture and, failing that, the scholarly preservation of its remaining traditions and artifacts by workers such as himself, there must be something heartening in the recognition that one of his contemporaries has knowledgeably used one of those traditional forms in composing an authentic Omaha mystery song for himself and his friends, thus demonstrating the continuing vitality of the form.[18] But would not LaFlesche also ask himself, reacting further and more personally to what he has just learned, "If Flying Crow was capable of composing such work, what could I, LaFlesche, compose in my turn?" What he has been brought to—more exactly, what he has brought to us, by means of some very skillful writing—is a moment of dramatized ethnological truth, the personal and the tribal, the experiential and the scholarly, the emic and the etic, all interpenetrating one another.

Who was Flying Crow historically? Although LaFlesche explicitly identifies him as one of his schoolmates at the Presbyterian mission school on the Omaha reservation in the 1860s, he does not, in fact, figure in the author's memoir of those schooldays, *The Middle Five* (probably written not long after this sketch, and in a sense narrating early deculturative causes whose adult effects "The Song of Flying Crow" describes), nor is Flying Crow listed in the extensive allotment rolls of the Omaha tribe, as prepared in 1883–1884 by LaFlesche's mentor and collaborator Alice Fletcher.[19] Nor does the name appear in the Omaha scholarly literature,

18. I discuss the validation of traditional forms by the new talents and purposes of modern Indian writers in *Reading the Fire: Essays in the Traditional Indian Literatures of the Far West* (Lincoln: University of Nebraska Press, 1983), 181–94.
19. Fletcher and LaFlesche, *The Omaha Tribe*, 643–54.

from James Dorsey's work in the 1880s on, with one tantalizing exception: In their exhaustive inventory in *The Omaha Tribe* of personal names in relation to clans, Fletcher and LaFlesche note under the *Hon'gan* clan the name *Kaxe'giun* 'Flying Crow'—adding, gnomically, "two of this name"![20]

No doubt as a schoolboy, Flying Crow was arbitrarily given an Anglo name: In *The Middle Five*, not only are the schoolchildren forbidden to use the Omaha language, but upon their admission the teachers gleefully replace their native personal names with the names of Anglo notables, even of Indian fighters such as Phil Sheridan. (In a rare direct censure of such deculturative practices, LaFlesche remarks that the new names were "no less heathenish" than the Indian names they replaced, but he adds that "we learned to call each other by our English names and continued to do so even after we left school and had grown to manhood.")[21] Whatever "Flying Crow" became in this mean-spirited policy of substitution is apparently lost, so that the only distinctive evidence of his life and death we, as readers, have is his friend's account of hearing his last song.

Can it be that Flying Crow is, in fact, *invented*, a fictive composite of tribesmen that LaFlesche knew and left behind as his career led him out of Omaha life and into the world of those he calls in the first paragraph "civilized people"? Certainly there are plentiful ethnographic and anthropological instances of such inventions: Most of the protagonists in the tribal fictions in *American Indian Life*, for example, are, in one way or another, composite figures. Raising such a question about the historicity of Flying Crow inevitably raises a larger question: Can it be that the whole sketch is, however realistic, fictional, made-up, not an ethnographic personal sketch but a tale in earnest?

I know of no way, short of finding extrinsic documentary evidence, to settle either question definitively. But do they really matter, much, as leading questions? As I hope I have already demonstrated, it suffices to recognize that "The Song of Flying Crow" is very much, self-consciously point-for-point, *about* the life and circumstances and intercultural predicaments of Francis LaFlesche. And whether there really, documentably, was a Flying Crow (I am inclined to think that there *was*), the author's presentation of

20. Fletcher and LaFlesche, *The Omaha Tribe*, 156. The crow seems to have been important symbolically to the Omaha because its presence in the sky often served to indicate that buffalo herds were nearby (300).
21. LaFlesche, *The Middle Five*, xvii–xviii.

him here is expressly, personally symbolic. Rediscovered too late for actual resumption of friendship, he emerges in words and indirectly in music as a haunting symbol of the traditional Omaha life that LaFlesche has long since departed from, an alter ego figuring what the author has given up or put aside in the course of his career off the reservation.

Indeed, in his resolutely *pagan* condition (to use the author's own heavily emphasized term), un-Christianized, unschooled (at least in Anglo ways), and unnamed in Anglo terms, Flying Crow may well represent in the author's imagination the programmatic opposite of acculturative processes going back at least two generations in Omaha history, to the years in the middle of the nineteenth century when Francis's half-French father, Joseph/ Iron Eye, was seeking controversial accommodations with the Anglo way, and, in particular, was founding his "progressive" Anglo-oriented community on the reservation, which his traditionalist opponents in the tribe scornfully labeled "The Village of the Make-believe White Men." [22] Against such long-standing acculturative processes, there is clearly nothing make-believe about Flying Crow's Indianness.

First and last, however, his significance is personal and immediate to LaFlesche. To a scholarly recorder of tribal music and an aspiring writer, Flying Crow appears abruptly, out of the forgotten past, *as a song*, as a work of literary and musical creation, distinctively personal in content, traditional in form. Just as all of the preceding pieces in the songfest were given their "stories" of origin and personal meaning, so the little old man reveals—specifically to LaFlesche—why and how Flying Crow composed his mystery song. His motives were, it appears, universal, a kind of Omaha *ars poetica*, in fact. In the face of death, apprehending with the acuity of the dying the mysteries of life, in particular its mysterious combinations of experiential richness and preordained brevity, and the mortal commonality of humans with all living creatures generation after generation, and wanting to express his affirmative feelings about life to his friends in a form that would give them permanence after his death ("the song to hold the words"), he composed the composition now bearing his name.[23]

22. See R. H. Barnes, *Two Crows Denies It: A History of Controversy in Omaha Sociology* (Lincoln: University of Nebraska Press, 1984), 25.
23. The Omaha religion heavily emphasized the concept of "a common and interrelated life, a living form that permeates, and is continuous in, all forms and appearances" (Fletcher and LaFlesche, *The Omaha Tribe*, 588). Hence the trend of Flying Crow's medi-

LaFlesche's response to this account is expressively terse: "Let's sing it again. I like it and I must learn it." If we have an explicit account of Flying Crow's motives for composing his song, we are left to infer what the author's reasons are for wanting so urgently to possess it. What seems to happen is that the dialectic movement of the sketch, its incessant nervous dance between the polarities of the author's self-awareness, now stops; an unexpected balance point has been reached. For the author to say "I like it and I must learn it" is to assert in one breath two heretofore conflicting kinds of claims on his friend's composition: as yet another Omaha song, a late survival of tradition; *and* as the final artistic testament of his lost boyhood friend and tribal alter ego. He perforce likes it and must learn it for equally compelling and (for the moment, at least) nonconflicting reasons.

Perhaps it is not considering the moment too curiously to find in LaFlesche's dramatization of it an auspicious analogy of purpose linking him and his "pagan" tribesman together, despite their radical differences. That is, as Flying Crow's motive has been to preserve in traditional song, against oblivion, something of his identity and his understanding of life's mystery, so, as he tells us at the outset, LaFlesche has aimed at preserving, against cultural oblivion, a record of Omaha culture. The latter effort, in effect, is validated, analogically, by the former.

If, however, Flying Crow's lyrical record was composed for his Omaha friends (now, at last, including LaFlesche), for whom does our author perform his conserving work of transcription and interpretation? For Alice Fletcher back in Washington, D.C.? For the the Indian Office and the Bureau of American Ethnology? For the academic or institutional people who have loaned him his graphophone? For all the "civilized people" who have shaped his career? *Yes, of course*—although those allegiances are attended with ironies and complications, as we have seen. In the reader's eternal pause at the end of LaFlesche's text, as his words run out quietly in renewed rapport with his dead friend, he makes, in effect, a very different answer to the question, "for whom." It is, simply, that *he does not give us the song of Flying Crow!* Not here, in this unpublished manuscript, despite the promise of its title; not in any of his subsequent publications over a long and prolific ethnographic career. "Now," he tells us, "it is so fixed in my memory that I shall never forget it even if I should live to be a hundred years

---

tation, linking the mutability of human lives with those of all creatures, would be, according to Fletcher and LaFlesche, very typical of Omaha thinking.

old." In this fashion, then, it is recorded in memory, preserved alive, carried on in the old oral way, cherished, but not published, not offered to us as an artifact.

So, the story reaches the second of its two reversals. In the first, the song the author does not know turns out to be by a deceased boyhood friend—in tribal terms, his adult opposite; now, in this second reversal, having learned the song, he deliberately and without comment withholds it from this writing and, in fact, from all subsequent publications! If it is a tacit denial of *our* expectation as readers to learn something else about the Omaha, it is also an act of self-fashioning refusal, and it stands as a deeply moving affirmation, I want to suggest, of the wholeness of what LaFlesche knows about himself.[24] Flying Crow's "pagan" song has, against all the intercultural odds, come home to the author, there to stay. Ethnography has stopped short of betrayal.

4

Searching in vain through the extensive Omaha literature for the text of Flying Crow's song (and more and more hoping, I must admit, that I would not find it, thereby tending to prove that what appears to be the author's deliberate withholding of it is just that), I came upon the following text in Dorothy Clarke Wilson's biography of LaFlesche's celebrated half-sister, Susette. Wilson gives it as an "Omaha Death Song," as heard by Susette's mother, Mary Gale, in her girlhood in the 1840s; hence, it cannot be attributed to Flying Crow. Regrettably, Wilson does not give her source for the song, but it appears to be authentic, a fine specimen of Native American traditional lyric in translation; and whatever its provenience, it seems to catch better than I can the poignantly self-reflexive burden of Francis LaFlesche's homage to Flying Crow and his mysterious song:

24. The term *self-fashioning* and the idea behind it were suggested by Stephen Greenblatt's *Renaissance Self-Fashioning: From More to Shakespeare* (Chicago: University of Chicago Press, 1980), and by James Clifford's *The Predicament of Culture: Twentieth-Century Ethnography, Literature, and Art* (Cambridge: Harvard University Press, 1988), especially his essay "On Ethnographic Self-Fashioning: Conrad and Malinowski" (92–113). Clifford's examinations of the "ethnographics" of our literature and art are invariably stimulating and often illuminating. It is odd that he has not taken up the richly problematic writings of native ethnographers such as Francis LaFlesche, William Jones, Archie Phinney, Ella DeLoria, and others.

Where can I go
That I might live forever?
The old fathers have gone to the spirit-land.
Where can I go
That we might live together?[25]

25. Dorothy Clarke Wilson, *Bright Eyes: The Story of Susette LaFlesche, an Omaha Indian* (New York: McGraw-Hill, 1974), 11, 373. The song's currency among the Omaha is also indicated by Francis LaFlesche's brother-in-law, the journalist and politician Thomas Henry Tibbles, who quotes from "An Indian Death Song" as follows: "Where shall I go to live forever? / Where shall I go to live forever?" (see *Buckskin and Blanket Days* [1900; reprint, Garden City: Doubleday, 1957], 243).

If LaFlesche wrote his memoir of the mission school days he shared with Flying Crow *after* writing this piece, why does he omit all reference in *The Middle Five* to his runaway friend? Perhaps because he resolved to focus on instances of acculturation like his own and his tragic friend Rush; perhaps because he had written all he intended to write about Flying Crow.

Europe's Indian, America's Jew:
Modiano and Vizenor

Jonathan Boyarin

For Greg Sarris and Menahem Prywes

The title of this piece could easily be taken to imply a playful inversion of a straightforward analogy. I once thought of using that analogy as my title, writing it as a question in logic: "Europe : Jew :: America : Indian?" The question mark is not coy. Are the relations really that closely comparable— between two empires, on one hand, and two peoples within those empires, both repressed to the point of genocide, on the other hand—that they could be reduced to such a neat, schematic rendering? To do so would cancel out (as we used to say in math class) the specifics of each term in both matched pairs on either side of the double colon. I will not be offering a direct answer to one question implied by the title, which can be articulated thus: To what extent have Jews fulfilled the same function for the imagination of Europe as Indians have in the invention of America? The juxtaposition that constitutes my title, then, is not at all meant to *equate* Europe with America, Indians with Jews. We will not gain any more insight by squeezing disparate yet comparable responses to disparate yet comparable situations into a simplistic prefabricated schema of domination and resistance.

I approach the four terms in my title indirectly, along three major lines of argument. The first is a feature of nation and empire building that Europe does share with America: the tendency to monumental representations. The second is the tendency each exhibits, but at different times and under very different pressures and circumstances, to create fascinated images of and to eulogize the other's victim. One effect of this displaced eulogization is to encourage amnesia about domination closer to home. Third, and most important, I will juxtapose "native" voices inside the respective empires as a way of resisting such amnesia and displacement.

Our tendency to think of relations as analogies—a Greek legacy, of course—is so powerful that I must list some fundamental ways in which this particular "analogy" is contaminated by any number of discrepancies. The American empire is to a large degree an extension of Europe, and so America's Indians are also to a large degree Europe's Indians. The peculiarities of American history are such that American identity is not nearly so thoroughly grounded in the tension between Christian triumphalism and Jewish survival as is European identity. Unlike Native Americans, Jews exist and express themselves as Jewish subjects in both Europe and America. Whereas the latter stages of Indian genocide were accomplished by "Americans" who identified with a relatively unified and monolingual culture, the Europe that Jews have survived in remained murderously fractious and culturally divided at least until the middle of this century. Unlike Native Americans in the United States, many Jews had acquired a relatively central position in European society before the Jewish genocide, which was both much more concentrated and single-minded and also more recent than that suffered by the pre-Columbian residents of the Americas.

These discrepancies should be borne in mind throughout this piece, as I contrast fictions by Patrick Modiano and Gerald Vizenor. It is not enough to say that both are the voices of survivors, written after genocide, on the soil of genocide. Some of the difference between Modiano's cosmic cynicism and Vizenor's fantasy redemption may have to do with when the two books were written. When Modiano published his book in 1968, French Jewry might well have seemed doomed to a literary existence at best. Vizenor's, on the other hand, was published in 1988, in the midst of a Native American renewal that has seen a threefold increase in the number of self-identified Native Americans in recent decades.

Above all, Modiano's and Vizenor's brilliant voices successfully resist any effort to treat them as representatives of self-contained "cultures," to turn them into grist for the homogenizing mill of liberal anthropology. For anthropology, too, has its topoi: cultures and cultural motifs that serve as standard points of reference, enabling those in the "field" to recognize and recruit each other. Working beyond the common places of ethnography challenges disciplinary power and constitutes a bid for new powers. Thus Michael Herzfeld employs a classic rhetorical gesture to authorize his critical ethnography of the dialectic of modern Greek and European identities:

> Greece may be unique in the degree to which the country as a whole has been forced to play the contrasted roles of *Ur-Europa* and humiliated oriental vassal at the same time. These two roles might seem mutually incompatible, were it not for the fact that both imply inferiority to the "true" European of today.[1]

With one keystroke Herzfeld makes a double move, both mocking and mirroring the double move of European romantic nationalism that he is analyzing in these sentences. He points out—and demonstrates painstakingly throughout his text—the double bind of people cast as degenerate descendants of the glorious common ancestors they share with those who now enjoy the power to define them as Other. At the same time he makes an implicit argument that, because they have suffered the implication of inferiority, modern Greeks deserve the sympathetic ethnographic attention that he devotes to them. He grounds his writing not directly within the subordination of modern Greeks, but in counterpoint to the dichotomizing European discourse that he criticizes. His critical ethnography is written not only in the margins of Europe (as his subtitle proclaims), but in the margins of the text called Europe as well. Though Herzfeld's book is nothing if not sober, scholarly, and expensive, still he appears as a kind of anthropological trickster, undermining the certainties of European identity from what the production of that identity calls "within."

In this respect at least, contemporary Jews and Native Americans are in the same situation as contemporary Greeks. They are simultaneously seen as noble cultural ancestors of the groups that dominate them (Christian Europeans and white Americans, respectively) and denigrated as marginal and backward relics. For Native Americans, one symptom of this

---

1. Michael Herzfeld, *Anthropology through the Looking-Glass: Critical Ethnography in the Margins of Europe* (New York: Cambridge University Press, 1987), 19–20.

peculiar addition of insult to injury is that they are present in American consciousness more as totems of commodities (Pontiac cars) and geographic boundaries of power (Manhattan, Massachusetts) than as "our" contemporaries. For Jews, the irony of this double attitude in its most seemingly benevolent form was expressed when the Bishop of Rome, in an unprecedented visit to the synagogue there, embraced the rabbi and referred to the Jews as "our older brothers." I found this rather moving, but on reflection—being a younger brother myself and having read the Jewish Bible—I was reminded of the power of sibling rivalry.

Fortunately, neither European Jews nor Native Americans rely solely on ethnographers to carry out the task of exposing the power illogic within which they are repeatedly placed. Nor do they always fall into the trap of performing a meliorative reinforcement of this illogic by presuming "finally" to offer a picture of what "their people" are really like,[2] a function that the best of humanistic ethnography seems ideally suited to perform.[3]

Modiano's La Place de l'étoile and Vizenor's The Trickster of Liberty avoid that ethnographic trap. In their own ways, both take care not to permit themselves to be taken as pure representatives of Indians or Jews. Vizenor insists, both in his own biography within the book and in the descriptions of his characters, on the uncompromised validity of "mixedblood" Indian identity. Indeed, the mixed heritage is drawn on as a resource in his and his characters' creative efforts to change without losing themselves. Whereas Modiano stays much more outside of his text, his hero, Schlemilovitch, has visions of revenge or redemption through entry into French literature, and thus might almost be taken as a double of his author. Yet Schlemilovitch, as we will see, tries desperately to "become French," but always with a cynical awareness of history that defeats his efforts either to root himself in "la France profonde" or to escape by becoming a normative Israeli. Modiano knows his hero's efforts are doomed from the start and thus marks his authorial distance. What both Vizenor and Modiano do, rather than fit in or declare an illusory solidarity of the oppressed, is instead to try cutting straight through the double bind of domination. Both of these short, picaresque, comic novels question the spatial symbolism of

2. At this point the choice of which words to place in quotation marks becomes almost completely arbitrary, symptomatic of a rare degenerative condition in which the patient is ultimately unable to sustain any pretense at critical writing.

3. Including, of course, my own. See Jonathan Boyarin, Polish Jews in Paris: The Ethnography of Memory (Bloomington: Indiana University Press, 1991).

domination. Both authors proclaim that goal in their very titles. I hope to accomplish three things in these pages: first, to suggest the parallels and contrasts between Modiano's and Vizenor's respective scenes of writing; second, to show some of the contrasting techniques they use to achieve similar rhetorical goals; and third, to develop a bit their implicit critique of monuments.

Modiano's title refers simultaneously to the location of France's glory, the Arc de Triomphe, and to the topos of France's shame, the breast of the Jew on which the yellow star was worn. We know this from the cover of his book. The front shows a young man in a respectable raincoat, with a yellow star bearing the word *Juif* in place of the head, thus warning us in advance that this book will not repeat the pathetic attempt to establish the real person behind the stereotype. The back tells the story from which the title is drawn:

> In the month of June 1942, a German officer approaches a young man and says to him:
> "Pardon, monsieur, where is the Place de l'Etoile?"
> The young man indicates the left side of his chest.

There is no mystery about Modiano's title, then, and he doesn't even claim credit for it (although on the cover the yellow star is displaced from the chest to the head). The same few sentences are reprinted inside, at the beginning of the book, and there identified as "histoire juive." The attribution ironically inscribes Modiano's book within . . . not a Jewish "folklore" tradition, but a Jewish "history," which is inseparable from "story," tricksterlike, necessarily self-inventing and self-deconstructing as the condition of its own existence. This is a revealing contrast to the Arc de Triomphe, which anchors the tourist guide's Place de l'Etoile—"a sort of altar of French patriotism" that "remains as a majestic witness to our national destiny."[4] Such a stone edifice (placed, in a sense, at the center of the world, a sun with boulevards radiating outward) works to hold together the weakening link among French nationalism, progress, Revolution, and Empire. It also guards the phantasm of a unitary and unstoppable national destiny. Fortunately France also has room for voices like Modiano's, which question that phantasm and that link.

Vizenor's title refers to a scale model of the Statue of Liberty renamed and removed to a reservation in Minnesota. The cover of *his* book, rather than commenting on the title, seems more abstractly designed to in-

---

4. *Dictionnaire*, 1964, page 198.

scribe the text within the University of Minnesota Press series on "emergent literatures" within which it has found a home. This rubric is puzzling. "Emergent literatures" certainly seems to fall into the same category as cultural "diversification"—a principle clearly consistent with a wide range of liberatory discourses. Yet the need to find ways to market such works creates a situation where their critical sting can too easily be made painless by creating a new category, a sort of *cordon sanitaire*, within which they can all be managed. There are several questions to be asked when works as different as *The Trickster of Liberty* and Clarice Lispector's Brazilian *écriture feminine* fall under the same rubric: "What are they emerging into? Are they merely being made available, archived, or do they *change* that into which they emerge? Can they emerge without abandoning that from which they emerge?"[5]

Underscoring the subversive effect of the phrase "the trickster of liberty" by placing it against the obvious pun indicated by Modiano's cover helps guard against such sanitary management. Unlike the Place de l'Etoile, which existed before Modiano wrote his book, the Trickster of Liberty is erected only toward the end of Vizenor's book and finds its historical correlative only in 1989, after the book was published—about which more later. But while Vizenor's book was in press, the Statue of Liberty itself was the focus of a massive campaign of material and ideological rehabilitation. Vizenor's erasure of the statue and substitution of a trickster performs the same service as Modiano's story about the "other" star. It helps to dislodge the unquestioned, monumental place the edifice has occupied in our imaginations. To imagine Liberty as tricksterlike helps free us from the trance of our "national destiny" and awaken us to all the chances that dance around us in the present and in the past.

Both Modiano's and Vizenor's disruptions of the monumental metonymies of empire should be read as effective threats to the laborious work of instilling monumental respect. That the inculcation of monumental respect is indeed the project of disciplined work rather than magic is documented in a National Park Service directive regarding the St. Louis Gateway Arch:

> Because the Gateway Arch is a National Memorial equal in dignity and grandeur to other great memorials and is becoming a symbol of St. Louis, it should be utilized in advertising, displays, cartoons,

5. Wlad Godzich, "Emergent Literature and the Field of Comparative Literature," in *The Comparative Approach to Literature: Approaches to Theory and Practice*, ed. Clayton Koelb and Susan Noakes (Ithaca: Cornell University Press, 1988), 18–36.

etc., with restraint. In making use of the arch, one should ask, "Is the proposed use frivolous or ostentatious? . . . Is the Gateway Arch displayed in its proportionate scale to other structures?"[6]

I suppose the mixedblood Chippewa Gerald Vizenor, looking at the Gateway Arch, wouldn't have to be reminded of Walter Benjamin's thesis that "there is no document of civilization which is not at the same time a document of barbarism."[7] Dissenting middle-class intellectuals, on the other hand, usually treat artifacts like the Gateway Arch as nothing more than banal efforts at boosterism, symbols of the overriding American drive for money. Modiano's revelation of the dark side of the "star," however, helps us to see that in America, too, the monuments at the gateways of empire shut some out and others in. The Gateway Arch and the Statue of Liberty, as symbols of redemption, are for the primary use of those descended from European immigrants, those who entered through the Golden Door of the Golden Land. I imagine Miss Liberty is less thrilling to those whose ancestors came in chains, or through Pacific ports, or up from south of the border . . . or to those whose ancestors were here long before Columbus came.

The Statue of Liberty, then, stands for the levelizing inclusion of a certain set of internally differentiated immigrations. Native Americans are especially shut out because they are not included among the immigrants and because (as the Gateway Arch makes clearer) they are an embarrassing reminder that liberty will have its victims. The Arc de Triomphe, of course, makes the latter point much more clearly: it is a symbol of the carnivorous conquest of various nations in the name of *liberté, egalité, fraternité*. The Napoleonic link between the French Empire and the Republican doctrine enunciated in the Declaration of the Rights of Man that "sovereignty resides essentially in the nation" may seem ironic,[8] but it is hardly

6. Quoted in Yi-Fu Tuan, *Topophilia* (Englewood Cliffs, N.J.: Prentice-Hall, 1974), 200. Further, on the link between empire building and monument building, see Henry Nash Smith's quote from a speech by Nathaniel Ames of Harvard in 1758: "Shall not . . . those vast quarries . . . that teem with mechanic Stone—those for Structure be piled into great Cities—and those for Sculpture into Statues to perpetuate the honor of renowned Heroes" (in *Virgin Land* [1950; reprint, Cambridge: Harvard University Press, 1970], 124).
7. Walter Benjamin, "Theses on the Philosophy of History," in *Illuminations*, trans. Harry Zohn, ed. Hannah Arendt (New York: Schocken, 1969), 256.
8. James Der Derian, "The Boundaries of Knowledge and Power in International Relations," in *International/Intertextual Relations: Postmodern Readings of World Politics*, ed. James Der Derian and Michael Shapiro (Lexington, Mass.: Heath, 1989), 3.

the first time in "Western" history that people have been violently set free, whether they liked it or not.[9]

Related to the meliorative "realism" I referred to earlier is the tendency, in the respective imperial contexts of America and Europe, to valorize the other empire's vanquished Other. Within Europe, the point is best made by shifting the focus a bit from the Place de l'Etoile to the focus of anti-Jewish genocide—to Germany, where, long before World War II, the exalted image of the Indian took hold as nowhere else in Europe:

> The German reader single[d] out the Indian as the one exotic race with which he was and still seems ready to sympathize, and even to identify himself. That the Germans should have this special relationship, stronger than that of the French or English, is traceable, most likely, to the fact that Germany was a latecomer to colonialism, and never encountered the Indian as opposing colonization; that her contact with the Red Man was "only literature."[10]

The reader may supply her own critical reflections on the engendering of the German reader as male, of Germany as female, and of Native Americans as the Red Man. I want to insist a bit on the suggestion that, unlike direct colonial encounters where the colonizer's image of the native initially veers between noble and ignoble savagery and eventually coalesces into a stereotype of irredeemable barbarism,[11] an empire that has no direct conflict with a certain set of "natives" can continue to draw on that group as a cultural model or as an exemplary victim of someone else's excesses.

In the German case, the most spectacular example of this is Karl May, who began publishing his novels about the American West in 1892 and is still a best-selling author a century later.[12] May's most successful novel is named after its Indian hero, *Winnetou*. In a preface to the first volume of that novel, May mourns the unjust passing of the Indian:

9. Specifically on the relation between egotism and egalitarianism, see Bruce Kapferer, *Legends of People, Myths of State: Violence, Intolerance, and Political Culture in Sri Lanka and Australia* (Washington, D.C.: Smithsonian Institution Press, 1988), 15, 207.

10. Alfred Vagts, "The Germans and the Red Man," *American-German Review* 24 (1957): 17.

11. Roy Harvey Pearce, *Savagism and Civilization: The Indian and the American Mind* (1953; reprint, Berkeley: University of California Press, 1988).

12. At least part of one of May's books was translated into Yiddish in Warsaw in 1926, under the title *Der geheymer shlos*.

Many questions arise, and this one in particular: What could this race have achieved, had it been given the opportunity? What characteristic cultural forms will forever be lost to mankind with the annihilation of this people? The dying Indian could not be integrated into the white world, because of his unique character. Was that reason enough to kill him? Could he not have been saved?

But what use are such questions in the face of certain death? What good are reproaches where help is no longer possible? I can only lament, but change nothing; only grieve, but not bring a single dead back to life.[13]

Presumably the words are intended not so much as those of May, but rather as those of his impossibly idealized German pioneer hero, Old Shatterhand; the distinction is not important. That both author and hero were wrong about the fate of the Indians is cause for hope, but not the main point here. Apparently his esthetic *required* that the noble Red Man be doomed. In a critical essay, Peter Uwe Hohendahl suggests why this may be so. May's anticapitalism is expressed in his negative portrayals of "Yankee traders."[14] His vision of human solidarity is expressed on one hand by the ideal group discipline and precise unity of his favorite tribe, the Apaches, and on the other by the depiction of fraternal relations between true pioneer "men of the West"—honest, self-reliant, and tough—and individual Indian men bearing the same qualities. Hence May dreamed of a new order of human solidarity against individual greed and the profit motive.[15] But if this vision were to come about through bloodless revolution, as May insisted, it could perhaps only be sustained by an appeal to the inevitability of progress. And progress means the Indian, with all his potential virtues, must pass on for the sake of greater human good. Once again the compatibility of the elegiac mode with the smooth history of genocide is reconfirmed.

A slightly different facet of the notion of the Red Man—here not so much his virility as his mobility, something that the writer can only express as unabashed fantasy longing—is contained in Kafka's fragment called "The Wish To Be a Red Indian":

13. Karl May, *Winnetou*, trans. Michael Shaw (New York: Seabury, 1979), xiv.
14. Peter Uwe Hohendahl, "Von der Rothaut Zum Edelmenschen: Karl Mays Amerikaromane," in *Karl Mays Winnetou: Studien zu einem Mythos*, ed. Dieter Sudhoff and Hartmut Vollmer (Frankfurt am Main: Suhrkamp, 1989), 219.
15. May, *Winnetou*, 230–31.

If one were only an Indian, instantly alert, and on a racing horse, leaning against the wind, kept on quivering jerkily over the quivering ground, until one shed one's spurs, for there needed no spurs, threw away the reins, for there needed no reins, and hardly saw that the land before one was smoothly shorn heath when horse's head and neck would be already gone.[16]

On one hand Kafka seems here to enlist himself as a participant in the German romanticization of the Indian. In contrast, say, to the infinite sorrow of "The Bucket Rider," where the narrator denied coal is carried off "into the regions of the ice mountains and . . . lost for ever,"[17] there seems at first nothing original about the image of the Indian. Its pathos is inseparable from its banality. But at a closer look we see that there is in fact no image of "the Indian" contained here, except for that which the history of the word itself evokes. And there is no static entity here, but rather an experience of free motion. The reader is placed on that racing horse, and there is no room for stereotype, only sensation.

At least one more level is discernible within this *mise-en-abîme* of othering, brought forward into the present: the German admiration and concern for the bitter fate of the "Red Man" is available, post-Holocaust, as a target of contemporary American sarcasm. Thus, in the course of a travelogue of the Great Plains, Ian Frazier quotes without comment a remark by a young German hitchhiker, who explains that he is a graduate student in anthropology:

> He looked at the landscape and said, "Ach! Zo vlat. . . . Za vite people haff destroyed zo many uff za Indians' sacred places."
> I looked at him. "What is your name?" I asked.
> "Gerhard Stadler," he said.
> I asked him to spell it. He did, and then shut up.[18]

Frazier represents himself putting the presumptuous young German in his place. The "eye dialect" reserved for the foreigner and the taking down of his name properly spelled are acts of journalistic policing, doubtless enough to convey to an American reader the smug suggestion that any German is hardly in a position to talk about genocide.[19]

16. Franz Kafka, *The Basic Kafka* (New York: Simon and Schuster, 1979), 242.
17. Franz Kafka, *The Great Wall of China* (New York: Schocken, 1970), 187.
18. Ian Frazier, *Great Plains* (New York: Farrar, Straus & Giroux, 1989), 36.
19. Of course German literature did not simply invent a Red Man in order to avoid ac-

But if this linguistic suggestion by Frazier isn't enough to reinforce the comforting illusion that the historical burden of genocide is someone else's problem, we can rely on yet another monument—the U.S. Holocaust Museum currently being erected in Washington, D.C. A liberal interpretation of the motives for establishing this institution would be that the museum will stand as a moral lesson about intolerance. I suspect it will function more effectively as a bastion of the message that America saved the Jews and is saving Israel now. More important—since remembering the Holocaust is hardly a central project to all American Jews, let alone the majority of U.S. citizens—by advertising that America has the space in its heart and in its capital to commemorate genocide committed elsewhere, the genocidal origins of the United States will be further occluded. How, then, could or should Native Americans react to the fact that there is a U.S. Holocaust Museum but no U.S. Memorial to the Slaughtered Native Americans—especially if they want to avoid offending Jews in the process of expressing any opinion whatsoever?

The strategic response is certainly neither to become caught up in a competition for priority in recognition of genocide nor to assert the sameness of all empires and all genocides. There might be more to be learned through a careful tracing, along back paths not already guarded by the intellectual patrols of neoimperialism, of the borderlines where comparative experiences of imperial victimization and resistance meet and separate.[20] These paths and borders, of course, are not to be found on any Cartesian plane, nor will they stay in the same place as we change our relation to them. As a provisional critical starting point from the Jewish "side," I might indicate that, so long as Jews were useful to Christian Europe as an object lesson in the degradation of the unredeemed soul, some level of Jewish existence was tolerated even when Jews were murdered wholesale; but when the legitimating notion of universal individual redemption gave way to the territorial, this-earthly dream of collective progress through the defined

---

knowledging the social exclusion of its Jew or to suppress the memory of the Jewish genocide, which came long after the Red Man was invented. Such invented Others are always multifunctional. I suspect, nevertheless, that the link between the German identification with an idealized Red Man (pure, strong, living in a natural *Gemeinschaft*) and the anti-Semitic stereotype of the Jew (degenerate, weak, overly urbanized) could be articulated through research.

20. This image is inspired by stories of the *intifada* about Israelis and Palestinians evading Israeli army roadblocks to meet and express their shared desire for peace and independence.

nation-state, there was eventually no room for the Jews at all. On the Native American side, it should be possible to discern the beginnings of a critical trajectory from three linked points: first, the connection in North American settler ideology between collective expansion and individual sedentarism[21]; second, the presumption that all Indians were alike, and thus could be indefinitely shifted further toward the "underused" West without harm to themselves or each other; and third, the idea that the only hope for Native Americans to survive was as individual Christians.[22]

Meanwhile, reading can help us to locate, beyond the shadow cast by these monuments, spaces for European Jewish life after World War II or for Native American life on the North American continent. It would seem that the primary space for European Jews today is within the book[23]; Native Americans have, as well, their poor and struggling reservations. Modiano's text, in any case, resolutely refuses allegiance to any place outside the book, and, as I will describe, his antihero is punished for his one slip, his one attempt to claim such an exterior allegiance. Vizenor's numerous protagonists hang onto their "wild baronage," but neither their identities nor their collective exploits are contained within it.

Caveat Lector: First Variation

My comparison of *The Trickster of Liberty* and *La Place de l'étoile* is grounded neither in oeuvre nor in author's biography. Both Modiano and Vizenor have published several books,[24] but I am writing about two fictions that came to me relatively accidentally. Although I can hardly pretend to erase all traces of an "ethnic writing" effect from my own rhetoric, it is not the enabling situation of the two authors that primarily concerns me but, as David Lloyd puts it, "those processes of [their] writing which sustain a

---

21. Compare Paul Carter, *The Road to Botany Bay* (Chicago: University of Chicago Press, 1989), especially chap. 5.

22. Robert F. Berkhofer, *The White Man's Indian* (New York: Knopf, 1979), 138, 152, 151.

23. I can't leave this assertion seemless, because there is also, remarkably, a growing Jewish voice and presence, especially in France, that is neither limited to intellectual circles nor inevitably obsessed with its image in non-Jewish circles (for a first approach to that phenomenon, see Judith Friedlander, *Vilna on the Seine* [New Haven: Yale University Press, 1990]).

24. Several of Vizenor's books have recently been reprinted by the University of Minnesota Press. Modiano's novels have won various French literary prizes; they are discussed in an essay by Gerald Prince, "Re-membering Modiano; or, Something Happened," *Sub-Stance* 49 (1986): 35–43.

minorness resistant to the proprieties of representation."[25] Far be it from me to explain, to pin down, to fix. For as Lloyd also makes clear, deterritorialization—a refusal to lock identity in place—is critical to this minorness. Thus Modiano's protagonist derides the French fetishism of the soil of native regions. Vizenor's oralizing, landscapizing tricksters explicitly signal the ambiguity of location, as when one of them, homeless, declares his allegiance to a portable fatherland whose creation is attributed to a Jewish name: "Sylvan Goldman invented the nest [shopping] cart, and I declared the tandem a sovereign state on low wheels."[26]

Caveat Lector: Second Variation

La Place de l'étoile is not long, but it contains such a variety of literary and historical references that I cannot possibly know all of them. I don't even know in some cases whether a reference is historical or literary; sometimes I'm not sure whether the reference is borrowed or appears for the first time in Modiano's book. We American readers in general might wish for a skeleton key to *La Place de l'étoile*, because we are not so well acquainted with the history of European venality. My claim in any case is that virtually all of these names are dropped, poured on, farcically; we need not value them the way the antihero Schlemilovitch does in order to catch the savage humor in their deployment.

Anyway, a skeleton key might prove to be more than a macabre metaphor. Anthropologists have traded real skeletons for so long, creating such resentment in the process, that Vizenor comes to fantasize the remains of anthropologists as a sideshow at an international tribal exposition (*TL*, 98).[27] The native's skeleton, so dear to physical anthropologists, is also a perfect trope for the anthropological fetish of a bloodless, fleshless "social structure." Elsewhere Vizenor has helped to explain this fetish by writing of liberal social science as a variation on tragedy, which seals off in silence and

25. David Lloyd, "Genet's Genealogy: European Minorities and the Ends of the Canon," *Cultural Critique* 6 (1987): 175.

26. Gerald Vizenor, *The Trickster of Liberty: Tribal Heirs to a Wild Baronage* (Minneapolis: University of Minnesota Press, 1988), 67. Subsequent references to this text will be cited as *TL*.

27. The horror of our decades is such that viewing skeletons can sometimes be a relief. This was my reaction to viewing Dusan Makevejev's *Sweet Movie*, which interspersed documentary footage of the exhumation of the Polish officer corps at the Katyn Forest with fictional scenes of transgressive body rituals and the slaughter of children.

isolation the comic voice of the trickster.[28] A similar tendency, criticized by the great historian Salo Baron as "the lachrymose conception in Jewish history,"[29] long prevailed in Jewish secular scholarship. That Jewish secular scholarship—originating in Germany as *Wissenschaft des Judentums*— openly saw traditional Jewish communal life as doomed, and set itself the goal of providing Judaism with a decent burial. Fortunately, neither anthropology nor *Wissenschaft des Judentums* was quite right: there are still walking, talking Jews and Indians.[30]

The Other, dead or alive, is an almost inexhaustible symbolic resource. Jews and Indians are invented by those who Other them as good or bad according to the needs of circumstances.[31] Under some circumstances, where the dilemmas of the dominant, collectively imagined self do not call forth genocidal responses, this interaction offers the minority group a space to survive through the symbolic and material goods it provides. Thus Vizenor discusses complex negotiations for the export of "wild" ginseng from the White Earth reservation in Minnesota to East Asia, where it is highly valued. Thus Jews survived in Central and Eastern Europe for centuries as a middleman minority, plying alcohol concessions, trading in textiles, and sometimes making up out of whole cloth news of the wide world when it was demanded of them.[32]

28. Gerald Vizenor, "A Postmodern Introduction," in *Narrative Chance: Postmodern Discourse on Native American Indian Literatures*, ed. Gerald Vizenor (Albuquerque: University of New Mexico Press, 1989), 3–16.

29. Salo Baron, *History and Jewish Historians: Essays and Addresses*, ed. Arthur Hertzberg and Leon A. Feldman (Philadelphia: Jewish Publication Society, 1964).

30. Nor is it the case that what is buried and dead is no longer potent. Past relations of violence produce skeletal aftereffects of particular force. Detouring for a moment to Argentina, we find links between the mystical, malevolent power projected onto Jews by the Argentine junta (see Michael Taussig, "Culture of Terror, Space of Death: Roger Casement's Putumayo Report and the Explanation of Torture," *Comparative Studies in Society and History* 26 [1984]: 487) and the demonized, mystical "Indian" produced by colonizing society in general in the process of brutal subjugation.

31. See Berkhofer, *The White Man's Indian*, 28, 110–11; Pearce, *Savagism and Civilization*; and the introduction to Sander Gilman, *Pathology and Difference* (Ithaca: Cornell University Press, 1985).

32. Jack Kugelmass, "Native Aliens: The Jews of Poland as a Middleman Minority," (Ph.D. diss., New School for Social Research, 1980). See also Jack Kugelmass and Jonathan Boyarin, *From a Ruined Garden: The Memorial Books of Polish Jewry* (New York: Schocken, 1983), 15.

Thus, in contemporary Latin America a complex symbolic economy involves "lowland shamans as mythic objects to fulfill the colonially inspired mythology that grants the

How do I avoid at least a blind fall into the trap of that exploitative fallacy? The mere assertion of my Jewishness, far from enabling me to leap over the trap, would more likely propel me into it. It may be that a degree of autocannibalism (self-absorption?) is inevitable for an academic writing about the problematics of "his own" collective identity. Let the reader (who, of course, tomorrow will be me) beware—and revise wherever necessary and possible.

Caveat Lector: Third Variation

I have an ulterior motive. In some measure at least, my engagement of an elite Native American text in this essay is intended to help prepare me for my work in and about Israel and Palestine. I participate in America, though I rarely think of myself as an American. I am implicated in the history of Israel, though I am hardly an Israeli. I want to acknowledge some of the ways in which as an American (an identity I usually explicitly deny) I benefit from a prior obliteration of the Native American Other. This tangential engagement of a legacy of domination in which I share might help prevent me from following the common tendency to identify some originary source of oppression (Zionism, patriarchy, Christianity, European imperial nationalism), from which I could safely dissociate myself.[33]

But given this explicitly historicizing and political project, I must stress

---

pagan power" of the upland shamans who cure "whites," mestizos, and other Indians (see Michael Taussig, *Shamanism, Colonialism, and the Wild Man: A Study in Terror and Healing* [Chicago: University of Chicago Press, 1987], 153). I imagine the examples could be multiplied with sources from around the world.

33. In his book *Beyond Geography* (New Brunswick, N.J.: Rutgers University Press, 1980), Frederick W. Turner attempts to locate that originary source in the Jewish Bible. But Turner's brave attempt at a comprehensive account of the interactions among history, myth, nature, and empire suffers from a powerful anti-Jewish bias. Turner overwhelmingly valorizes myth (without distinguishing between state-empire myth and autonomous, non-class-group myth) and denigrates history (without distinguishing between the histories of dominating and dominated peoples). There is no notion of collective memory in Turner's book, although since he cites Jung so often, he probably does believe in a collective unconscious. There is also no room in his account for the annual Jewish reenactments of founding historical events such as the Exodus. For Turner, the shift away from myth, polytheism, women-centered worship, harmony with nature, and ethnic tolerance toward history, monotheism, patriarchy, alienation from nature, and genocidal impulses is epitomized and encapsulated in the Hebrew Bible, conveyed (like the infectious diseases he makes much of) into the decaying Roman Empire, and thence onward and upward into modern imperial history. Turner's causal explanations as well as his categories are often

that I am not writing of "the Indians" or of "the Jews." I am referring rather to the stereotyped currency of identity. The stereotypes have an interesting and contingent life of their own. Thus, for example, both authors play with the idea of Jews and Indians as in some way regarded as Orientals. Vizenor, without announcing himself, retraces the hypothesized original trek across the frozen Bering Strait when several of his tricksters make their careers in China. And Modiano's Schlemilovitch, in his misogynist adventure as a white slaver, balks at the prospect of kidnapping a young French noblewoman for sale to an Arab noble: "Transform Eleanor of Aquitaine into an inmate of a bordello! The idea revolted him. One can bear the name Schlemilovitch and still have a bit of compunction at the bottom of one's heart. . . . He would never deliver this princess, this fairy, this saint to the Saracens."[34] Here Modiano presents us the Jew as Crusader. Even with a Jewish name, Schlemilovitch declares, one can remain civilized enough to side with Christian Europe against the Orient.

• • • •

It's almost time to have done with my own critical compunctions, but before I do, let me discuss the scenes of torture in both books. Schlemilovitch's tormentors are Nazis and agents of the Israeli secret service (by the end of *Place de l'étoile*, there is no distinction between the two). In *Liberty*, the torturers are animal researchers, but the two dogs White Lies and

---

anachronistic. Thus, for example, "Christianity's turn from myth toward history may have an interior historical explanation, for its first converts were Jews, as were its first authors" (62). But when "its" first converts were Jews, "it" was not yet Christianity. So in effect, Turner validates an imaginary (I'm tempted to write "mythical") original "Christianity" corrupted both by its tainted connection to the Jews and then by its ideological service of the Roman Empire. No wonder, then, that Turner describes the book as "an essay in spiritual history . . . founded on that surest of realities: the human spirit and its dark necessity to realize itself through body and place" (7), (whatever that means).

While I, too, am concerned about the connections among history, myth, nature, and empire, Turner's book seems so tendentious as to make me almost want to defend Christianity and argue for the common liberating strands of the putative "Judaeo-Christian tradition." Ironically, for someone so obsessed with the need to unmask the link between history and mastery, Turner squeezes the past 5,000 years of Western experience into a monovocal, predetermined schema. His plea for the natives is logocentric in the extreme, dangerous, and needing of closer critical attention than I have the stomach or the stamina to give it here.

34. Patrick Modiano, *La Place de l'étoile* (Paris: Gallimard, 1968), 126–27. Subsequent references to this text will be cited as *LP*.

Chickenlips have by that point in the book become such animated tricksters that the reader joins in anger at "those assholes in life sciences." And hasn't much of anthropology long aspired to be one of the "life sciences?"

Vizenor will do anything to get anthropologists to stop being so damned serious; he even has one of the dogs "hobble[] into the library . . . and mount[] the anthropologist at the kitchen table" (*TL*, xii). Modiano, too, comments on anthropology, when his hero travels to a pristine Alpine village in Haute-Savoie to kidnap a woman for white slavery: "Above all, avoid arousing their suspicion. Stifle my ethnological curiosity, like Lévi-Strauss. The Savoyards are more clever than the Indians of Parana. Don't look at their daughters like a pimp would, or they'll guess my Oriental ancestry" (*LP*, 100). The clutch of associations here is consistent with Schlemilovitch's fanatic embrace of anti-Semitic stereotypes. Lévi-Strauss's Jewishness is revealed (and his "stifling" pretense of ahistorical, structural objectivism lampooned), while the "white" Europeans are simultaneously exoticized and exposed as potential victims of Semitic ethnopimping.

But training, if not blood, will out, and at some point I, too, start thinking like an anthropologist, wondering whether the contrast between Modiano's comic rage and Vizenor's comic tease (whose mascot is White Lies, the dog that reappears in every doggie generation) is connected solely to the relative pace and intensity of the two genocides, or whether there are "cultural" reasons involved as well. Are there Jewish sources of Modiano's energy, Native American sources for Vizenor's playfulness?

Jewish messianism is obviously out of the question for Modiano. There's no hope of redemption at *La Place de l'étoile*; there are only the ruins of the hopes of the past. Modiano's antilogic is inscribed within a "space of death."[35] This space of death would seem to have no room for the trickster; Schlemilovitch is closer to a pantheon of pariahs, like "Franz Kafka, the older brother of Charlie Chaplin" (*LP*, 42).[36] The pariah, as outsider and arriviste, effectively disrupts the fetishism of territory, as when Schlemilovitch reveals that imitation is the sincerest form of mockery:

> I only knew the French provinces through the mediation of the Michelin guide, and of certain authors such as François Mauriac. One text by this native of the Landes moved me especially: *Bordeaux, or Adolescence*. I recall Mauriac's surprise when I passionately recited to

35. See Taussig, "Culture of Terror."
36. On "The Jew as Pariah," see Hannah Arendt, *The Jew as Pariah: Jewish Identity and Politics in the Modern Age* (New York: Grove, 1978).

him his beautiful prose: "The city where we were born, where we were a child, an adolescent, is the only one we are forbidden to judge. She is part of us, she is ourselves, we bear her in ourselves. The history of Bordeaux is the history of my body and my soul." (*LP*, 56–57)

But Modiano refuses (or is not yet ready) to counterpose to this territorial fetishism a "Jewish" insistence on the possibilities of fulfillment in time. In fact, the only temporal power granted to Schlemilovitch and to his employer/ accomplice, Charles Lévy-Vendôme, is a negative disruption of "pagan," cyclical time. The latter, Orientalized in a red turban, declares "they need me at Constantinople to perform the gradual cessation of the cycle. The seasons will change bit by bit, first spring, then summer" (*LP*, 143). No, decidedly, Schlemilovitch is not in the business of recuperating the ancient resources of Jewish tradition to help mend the world. In *Place de l'étoile* the only effect a Jew can have on the course of time is by assuming the position of the Oriental and thereby slowing time down.

For Vizenor, on the other hand, Trickster remains as a genuine source not only of unpredictability but also of renewal. Vizenor's tricksters are able to "relume" (Vizenor's word) and upset the flow of domination in both time and space. One of his tricksters "carried a holster to shoot time, dead time on the clock" (*TL*, 40). But this desire to stop the tyrannical rule of clock time is hardly a feature of Native American culture as opposed to Jewish culture. Perhaps it is something that both share with revolutionary culture, as documented by Walter Benjamin's quotation of a French revolutionary poem about "new Joshuas" shooting at the clock towers.[37]

With regard to space, Vizenor both documents and undermines the territorial fixing of a subaltern people. His "mixedblood" Chippewas seize the opportunity to retain a scrap of land and declare themselves "tribal heirs to a wild baronage." The whites see it as poor land; that's why they leave it to the natives. In the utilitarian valuation of the settler Americans, the idea of a wild baronage appears oxymoronic, as Tocqueville wrote: "The wonders of inanimate nature leave [Americans] cold. . . . This magnificent vision. . . . is always flitting before [their] mind[s]."[38] But these native "barons" are not duped: they know better than to turn White Lies and Chickenlips into their serfs.

37. Benjamin, "Theses on the Philosophy of History," 262.
38. Cited in Lee Clark Mitchell, *Witnesses to a Vanishing America: The Nineteenth-Century Response* (Princeton: Princeton University Press, 1987), 1.

There are anti-Cartesian chronotopic conflations in both books, but here again Modiano leans toward comic despair, Vizenor toward a mocking fantasy redemption. Toward the end of *La Place de l'étoile*, Schlemilovitch decides to set sail for Israel. In a conversation with the Israeli Admiral Levy, in which the latter expresses his admiration for the liberal traditions of France and the sweetness of its countryside, Schlemilovitch reaches— just this one time—for a positive identity, an identification with the Israeli authority figure: "I'm not altogether French, admiral, I'm a French JEW. French JEW" (*LP*, 178). Schlemilovitch is immediately arrested on an implicit charge of diasporic degeneracy and thrown into the hold. When he is taken out, he finds himself in the Paris of the Nazi Occupation, where the rest (almost) of the action will take place. This fade without transition from the sea near Israel to occupied Paris belies the general assumption that the Occupation is in the past, that the establishment of Israel has put all that behind us. The return to that seeming past is the nightmare complement of Benjamin's revolutionary suspension of temporality. There has in fact been neither revolution nor liberal progress. The last sections of this book, which was published in 1968, might be taken as a cri de coeur against the very resumption of bourgeois society after the disaster of World War II.

Vizenor's most striking bending of time, place, and genre boundaries pictures Tune Brown, one of his tricksters, getting an honorary degree at Berkeley, in the notable presence of the famous ethnographer Alfred L. Kroeber. The scene is reminiscent of Woody Allen's Zelig. But there is no Zelig here; when Vizenor's tricksters change guise, they don't experience Zelig's vertigo. The absence of that anxiety leaves room for Vizenor to perform an anamnestic recovery of Ishi, last member of a California Indian tribe, famous in the history of anthropology for being put on museum display as a living relic. Vizenor mixes the three genres of historiographic reconstruction, scholarly citation, and invented oration in a single sentence:

> "[Roy] Wagner [in *The Invention of Culture*] tells how Ishi, the last survivor of the Yahi tribe in California, 'brought the world into the museum,' where he lived and worked after our capture," Tune confessed as he threw his shirt and the ribbons from his braids to the audience. (*TL*, 47)

It would be self-defeating to ask us to revisit Ishi as a tragic figure. The only way Ishi[39] can be rescued is through a comic celebration, bringing

---

39. Although I happen not to share the belief of Frederick the Great that Hebrew is the original language, I can't resist remarking that *Ishi* means *my man* in Hebrew.

dead anthropologists and Indians together with living scholars and invented Indians onto the same page. Fortunately, the page is willing.

Schlemilovitch is more of an iconoclast than a trickster, even though his method of breaking the idols is tricksterlike: he places himself inside them, and they burst because they cannot contain him. It may be plausible to relate this to the irredeemable, rapacious misogyny of Schlemilovitch's iconoclasm. While in the first part of La Place de l'étoile he aims to subvert the sanctity of French letters and patriotism, he subsequently abandons scholasticism for a concentrated assault on the purity of French Catholic womanhood. Certainly Modiano intends this as a characteristically transgressive assertion of the stereotype of the Jew as white slaver—a stereotype that once again reared its ugly head in the city of the Maid of Orleans just about the time La Place de l'étoile was published.[40] I imagine that for most readers, when the book was first published, these passages were taken as an attack not on women, but on the institutions of the church and nobility. They can no longer be given that charitable reading. I have no choice but to recoil and renounce my affiliation with the author of La Place de l'étoile on reading the passage where Schlemilovitch describes his "idyllic week" with a debauched countess, who collaborates with his fantasies of raping "the duchess of Berry . . . Bossuet, Saint Louis . . . Joan of Arc, the count of Toulouse and General Boulanger" (LP, 135). Unlike the dominating discourse of anti-Semitism, this sexual violence is never turned against Schlemilovitch. The homosocial compact of literature,[41] even between "the (male) Jews" and their victimizers, remains intact.

The discourse of gender in Vizenor's text, written twenty years later, seems indeed to indicate a measure of progress. His critico-fictional prologue focuses on the androgyny of Trickster, who is embodied in a female trickster storyteller named Sergeant Alex. The tragically fixated Euro-anal anthropologist Eastman Shicer insists on pinning her down as a specimen: "Alexina, why did you disown your given name? . . . Worried about being identified as a woman?" (TL, xii).[42] Another member of the Browne

40. Edgar Morin, Rumour in Orleans (New York: Pantheon, 1971). For a social history of the phenomenon, which demonstrates among other things that the victims of Jewish pimps were themselves Jews, see Edward J. Bristow, Prostitution and Prejudice: The Jewish Fight against White Slavery, 1870–1939 (New York: Schocken, 1983).

41. Eve Kosofsky Sedgwick, Between Men: English Literature and Male Homosocial Desire (New York: Columbia University Press, 1985).

42. The allusion here is to Herculine Barbin, a nineteenth-century French hermaphrodite who was known as Alex/Alexina. See Michel Foucault, Herculine Barbin: Being the Recently Discovered Memoirs of a Nineteenth-Century French Hermaphrodite, trans.

family of tricksters becomes a priest named Father Mother. Vizenor also presents a mixedblood male professor with the ambiguous name of Terrocious Pan-Anna and empathetically describes trickster Tulip Browne's recoil from Pan-Anna's sexually predatory efforts to capture her via a presumed racial connection. On the other hand, Vizenor engages in a good bit of lesbian-feminist bashing of his own (*TL*, 80 ff.).

Beyond the gap in time and place between Modiano's writing and Vizenor's, the contrast in their use of gender leads toward the European psychoanalytic question of male ego formation. Vizenor's tricksters are multiple, although all members of the same clan; Modiano's text is ferociously monological, his narrator voraciously egotistical. Vizenor creates his resilient tricksters through the resources of a rich orality and kin ideology, which, if not intact, remain reinventable. Schlemilovitch, Zeliglike, obsessed with figures of the colonizing Other irredeemably inside him, can't even make up his mind on a literary model for his own death: "Nerval or Kafka? Suicide or the sanatorium?" (*LP*, 169).

But Schlemilovitch's musings are not in the nature of a serious philosophical reflection on the postgenocidal Jewish condition. Nor do his references have anything to do, except perhaps by way of yet another parody, with the idea that Jews are "people of the book." Insofar as it is grounded at all, the ground is intertextual, a bitter critique of Sartre's thesis that the Jew is a reflection of the non-Jewish gaze. The Jew portrayed in Modiano's book struggles through bitter satire with and against the one-dimensional existence he is granted by Sartre—whereas Vizenor's characters struggle with and against the richer, but still reified and stereotyped, way they are represented in ethnography. Through his critique, Schlemilovitch finds a point of reconciliation and solidarity with his father, presented as a gauche wholesaler from New York dressed in a mauve suit and Kentucky green shirt:

> I wanted a policeman to stop us. I would have explained it to the French once and for all: I would have repeated that for twenty years we'd been perverted by one of their own, an Alsatian. He had affirmed that the Jews would not exist if the *goys* didn't deign to pay attention to them. Thus we have to attract their attention by means of motley clothes. For us Jews, it's a question of life and death. (*LP*, 68) [43]

Richard McDougall (New York: Pantheon, 1980).
43. Modiano's satire anticipates in significant ways Alain Finkielkraut's exploration of the theme of "the imaginary Jew" (see *Le Juif imaginaire* [Paris: Le Seuil, 1980]).

This moment of ironic solidarity is enabled by a contest of textualizations. Schlemilovitch endlessly complicates his young author's bid to gain admittance into the sphere of elite French literate culture by an original satire of that culture. Above and beyond all the disguises from French and Jewish literature and history that he adopts, Schlemilovitch is a negative image, a parodic extension and breathless summary of "Marcel"/Proust:[44] "I remember that Des Essarts compared our friendship to that which united Robert de Saint-Loup and the narrator of *Remembrance of Things Past*" (*LP*, 21). Thus *La Place de l'étoile* is also a retrospective evaluation, *après Holocauste*, of the assimilationist pretensions of the French "Israelites."

If Schlemilovitch remains more of a self-conscious cynic than a clownlike trickster, it is not because Jews are inexperienced at surviving by changing. It may be rather that in his author Modiano's view, culture is over; creative transformation is no longer possible, and the only hope for breathing space is in parody. Certainly we are given no clue that there are available internal Jewish resources that might serve such transformation. Indeed, Schlemilovitch/Modiano holds in abeyance the question whether there are "real Jews" existing outside of the reactive Sartrian dialectic. There is no midrashic textual heterodoxy in Schlemilovitch's narrative, unless it is reflected in the general tactic of guerrilla semantics, the forceful reappropriation of meaning for survival. In the decomposed European modernist tradition within which Modiano is still writing, heterodoxy can only take this relentlessly negative form.

Does this mean, in fact, that Trickster never lived or has died in Europe, that there is nothing at all of Trickster in the figure of Schlemilovitch? If the "hero"-victim dichotomy of European high culture is the proper antithesis of Trickster's ambiguity, this should not blind us to figures very much like Trickster in Jewish and other "Western" folklores—characters who survive by changing themselves as they point out and work through the frozen forms of their cultural surroundings. These stories are popular everywhere because they help living people negotiate the need for boundaries and the resistance to boundaries. We can grant these figures their due without denying the unique genius and central elaboration of the trickster motif in a range of Native American worlds.

44. Albert Sonnenfeld, speaking on the theme of noses in Proust, has pointed out how, toward the end of *Temps*, "Marcel"/Proust mocks the idea of his own nobility (see "Swann's Nose," [Lecture delivered at the Modern Language Association, Washington, D.C., 1989]).

Like the cynical pariah Schlemilovitch, then, Vizenor's tricksters are like him in that they also subvert their creator's authority, invading and deconstructing the university that constitutes Vizenor's base of operations. His prologue pays passing and ambivalent tribute to a contemporary pioneer of "Native American literature": "Momaday, of course, the most quoted and least read" (*TL*, xiii).[45] Against what he identifies as Momaday's tragic view, however, Vizenor embraces impurity, as when Terrocious Pan-Anna explains that his father took the last name from the Pan-American Exposition of 1901, in which the father had been an exhibit. Vizenor insists that the real Indians are the mixedbloods (*TL*, 118). Transgressing his own renunciation of the anthropological tragic mode, he enlists the support of the authorization of traditional orality in the criticism of dissident folklorists such as Dell Hymes and Dennis Tedlock, at the same time contentiously authorizing his own *book*: "If you don't believe what tribal people say in my stories, then I don't believe what whites have said in those stories printed in your law books" (*TL*, 145–46).

• • • •

Both books seem to end arbitrarily; neither has a teleological plot. In his "last" chronotopic shift, Schlemilovitch finds himself on Sigmund Freud's couch but resolutely refuses psychoanalysis. For Schlemilovitch, history is a nightmare from which there is no hope of awakening, because he is relentlessly *in* it, always being spatially confined, fatally and literally so when he attempts a sentimental voyage to the land of his ancestors (*LP*, 188).[46] For Vizenor's tricksters, there is no fundamental, unchanging nightmare. Not only do they retain a problematic sovereignty over their wild baronage, at the end their solution to material survival is to become, in a sense, Jews, active in tricksterlike hustling commerce, like Schlemilovitch's father the kaleidoscope king.

For Schlemilovitch, America exists only insofar as his father is a failing businessman in New York. Is this because America is, here again, seen as a blank slate, which does not offer even the inverted potential for identity contained in *Anti-Semite and Jew*? Central to the idea of "America" is the

45. Arnold Krupat sharply criticizes Momaday's monologism, which seems consistent with being more quoted than read (see *The Voice in the Margin: Native American Literature and the Canon* [Berkeley: University of California Press, 1989]).
46. Remember Sartre's play *No Exit*? The predominant French literary mood in 1968, of course, is still existentialism.

assertion that history is not merely ineffectual but ideally absent altogether, that a direct correspondence between human society and natural law is possible in the New World.[47] Indeed, the greater invisibility of genocide in America may be related to the general devaluation of history here compared to Europe.

Here we return to the problematics pointed to by Herzfeld with which I began: the incorporation of the Other as both mythic ancestor and allegory of degradation. Native Americans would seem to be even more problematic as "ancestors" for European Christian settlers than Jews for European Christian civilization. The relatively recent appellation "Native Americans" doubtless represents a liberal attempt at incorporating the Other. Yet the term masks one of the basic causes of the European settlers' genocide: the unbearable presence of human beings who contradicted the "virgin land" ideology of the American incarnation.[48] Thus the sculpture by Horatio Greenough titled *Rescue Group*, showing a giant, godlike European stopping a naked Indian clad in a phallic sort of loincloth from slaughtering a European woman and child, is aptly used as the frontispiece to Roy Harvey Pearce's *Savagism and Civilization*. First by being here, then by resisting encroachment, and finally by their failure to be readily assimilable, the Indians were inevitably trapped in the symbolically linked roles of threat to white womanhood and illegitimate dweller in the land. Like the Statue of Liberty, the Gateway Arch, and the U.S. Holocaust Museum, the ideology of the pure and virgin land had no place for "Native Americans."

Can a similar analysis be made concerning the Jews? Certainly the Jews were an awkward reminder that the very same people who were around during the life of Jesus had rejected his message. But they were also a persistent challenge, a reminder that the missionary task of Christianity had not yet been completed—and, insofar as their conversion was linked to the Second Coming, Jewish souls were prize game for Christian hunters. It would seem, as I suggested earlier, that only when this dominant rationale for the irritating fact of continued distinctive Jewish existence became inadequate did an essentializing suspicion of the Jews harden into the conviction that they constituted the fly in the ointment of European solidarity and progress.

The question of how "minorities" are exploited and excluded in the

47. Myra Jehlen, *American Incarnation: The Individual, the Nation, and the Continent* (Cambridge: Harvard University Press, 1986), 3.
48. Smith, *Virgin Land*.

reproduction of domination is inseparable from the various conceptions they and the dominant group form of their integrability into the state. Both Modiano's and Vizenor's works are problematic as inscriptions of ethnicity in the legitimating culture of the dominant group. Modiano, of course, writes in French, not a Jewish language. Vizenor writes in English, and the destabilizing potential of *The Trickster of Liberty* is tamed by the suggestion that it belongs in the affirmative action category of emergent literatures. I say this not to suggest that their dissident claims need to be demystified, and not only because even resistant literatures often have their origin in imperial narrative,[49] but also because demystifying critiques often fail "to address some of the crucial ways in which myth and history achieve their emotional potency, for the critics of whatever kind adopt a mode of reasoning which is not that of the myths."[50]

Rather, I want to conclude by pointing to the elements in both books, growing out of the authors' choices to criticize society through pariah iconoclasm and tricksterism, which have proven ironically prophetic. At one point after his arrest by the Israelis, Schlemilovitch finds himself in a concentration camp for recalcitrant Diaspora Jews. There are indeed concentration camps in Israel now,[51] not for entire Jewish families and communities, but for thousands of Palestinian men who, like the Zionists once did, are struggling to secure a homeland for themselves and for their people in Diaspora. And Vizenor's story of a Chinese deal to build a Trickster of Liberty statue on the White Earth reservation has found its heroic, hence tragic, realization in the defiant symbolism and martyrdom of Tiananmen Square.[52] These

49. See Rolena Adorno, *Guaman Poma: Writing and Resistance in Colonial Peru* (Austin: University of Texas Press, 1986), 8–9. See also Roberto González-Echevarria, "The Law of the Letter: Garcilaso's *Commentaries* and the Origins of the Latin American Narrative," *Yale Journal of Criticism* 1, no. 1 (1987): 128.

50. Kapferer, *Legends of People, Myths of State*, 40.

51. As is well known and well documented (but generally ignored by such organs as the *New York Times*), the so-called Ansar III or Ketziot prison in the Negev desert contains thousands of Palestinian men living in tents. Many of them are never formally charged, but are held without recourse under so-called administrative detention. The legalistic rationale for their confinement dates back to the British emergency regulations imposed during the chaotic end of the British mandate after World War II.

52. These two examples of fiction preceding history cast a revealing light on Linda Hutcheon's discussion of "historiographic metafiction" as a characteristic mode of postmodernism (see *A Poetics of Postmodernism: History, Theory, Fiction* [New York: Routledge, 1988]), suggesting that the phrase *metafictive history* would be just as applicable. They might also be relevant to the predicament of Salman Rushdie—clearly a case of history bites fiction.

connections suggest once again the relevance of reading and writing to the interrelated possibilities of Statues of Liberty and restriction to reservations, of concentration camps and Arcs de Triomphe. This essay could hardly serve as an adequate response to that suggestion, but I hope at least to have underscored the urgency of our collaborating on a comparative study of Otherings in the consolidation of the dominant collective self.

Manifest Manners: The Long Gaze of Christopher Columbus

Gerald Vizenor

Christopher Columbus was denied beatification because of his avarice, baseness, and malevolent discoveries. He landed much lower in tribal stories and remembrance than he has in foundational histories and representations of colonialism; nonetheless, several centuries later his mistaken missions were uncovered anew and commemorated as entitlements in a constitutional democracy.

Columbus has been envied in a chemical civilization that remembers him more than the old monarchs and presidents. The dubious nerve of his adventures would be heard more than the ecstasies of the shamans or even the stories of the saints; alas, he has been honored over the tribal cultures that were enslaved and terminated in his name.

The 1893 Columbian Exposition in Chicago, for instance, celebrated his discoveries as an enviable beat in the heart of the nation. Antonín Dvořák composed his occasional symphony *From the New World*. Frederick Jackson Turner presented his epoch thesis, "The Significance of the Frontier in American History," that same summer to his colleagues at the American Historical Association. At the same time, the federal government issued a memorial coin on the quadricentennial with a stamped impression of Columbus on one side and "the *Santa Maria* on the reverse." A similar commemorative coin has been struck for the quincentenary, and a "certificate of authenticity" is issued with the purchase of each coin.

President Ronald Reagan announced, when he signed a proclamation designating October 12 a federal holiday, that Christopher Columbus was a "dreamer, a man of vision and courage, a man filled with hope for the future." In other words, the adventurer must be the simulation of manifest manners, the countenance of neocolonial racialism. "Put it all together and you might say that Columbus was the inventor of the American Dream."

Columbus wrote at the very end of his first journal, "I hope to Our Lord that it will be the greatest honor for Christianity, although it has been accomplished with such ease." He has become the invariable conservative candidate in the constitutional democracy that has honored his names with such ease.

"The Spaniards were unable to exterminate the Indian race by those unparalleled atrocities which brand them with indelible shame, nor did they even succeed in wholly depriving it of its rights," wrote Alexis de Tocqueville in *Democracy in America*, "but the Americans of the United States have accomplished this twofold purpose with singular felicity; tranquilly, legally, philanthropically, without shedding blood, and without violating a single great principle of morality in the eyes of the world. It is impossible to destroy men with more respect for the laws of humanity."

Ishi and Literal Banishment

The outset of manifest manners, that felicitous vernacular of political names and sentimental neocolonial destinies, was the certain denial of tragic wisdom and transvaluation of tribal consciousness; the tribal stories that were once heard and envisioned were abused, revised, dickered for a mere sign of discoveries, and then were construed as mere catecheses.

Tribal nicknames were translated as surnames and, without their stories, were a literal banishment; the ironies and natural metaphors of bent and chance were burdened with denatured reason, romantic nominations, and incumbent names.

The metaphors turned over here are about the representations of a consumer culture and the political power of common names in histories, the images, names, and gazes that would represent historical significance. Tribal nicknames, in this and other senses, were seldom heard in the vernacular of manifest manners. Consider the communal humor of nicknames, the clever humor that honors the contradictions and preeminent experiences heard in tribal stories, the natural and uncertain shimmer of metonymies that would overturn the "long gaze" of neocolonial assurance.

Ishi, for instance, was a new nickname, a tribal word that means "one of the people" in the language of Yana, but that was not the name he heard in his own tribal stories. Alfred Kroeber, the anthropologist, decided that would be his name at the museum. Ishi was esteemed by those who discovered him as the last of his tribe, an awesome representation of survivance in a new nickname; this natural mountain man had evaded the barbarians and then endured with humor the museums of a lonesome civilization.

"Long gaze" Columbus, on the other hand, could become one of the most common surnames discovered and discounted in this quincentenary; indeed, "long gaze" could become an ironic nickname for those who recount manifest manners and the mistaken colonial discoveries.

Christopher Columbus is an untrue concoction, the ruse of his own representation. He is the overstated adventurer, to be sure, and the lead signalment of colonial discoveries on this continent; at the same time, he is the master cause of neocolonial celebrations in a constitutional democracy. The obverse of his dubious missions is manifest manners, and the reverse is censure.

Columbus must be the slaver, the one who sailed on the inquisitions, and landed on a commemorative coin at a national exposition, and heard a new symphony in his name. The "long gaze" of his names has reached from colonial monarchies to the *Santa Maria* and on to the White House in Washington.

"Representation is miraculous because it deceives us into thinking it is realistic," wrote David Freedberg in *The Power of Images*, "but it is only miraculous because it is something other than what it represents."

Columbus is the "miraculous" representation of the long colonial gaze, that striven mannish stare with no salvation. Indeed, the quincentenary is a double entendre: the "long gaze" celebration of colonial civilization in his names, and the discoveries of his names in a constitutional democracy. The want of humor must cause a vague nostalgia for lost monarchies and must simulate once more the grievous tragic ironies of colonialism.

The Dominican Republic, for instance, commissioned an enormous and expensive quincentenary monument to celebrate the "long gaze" of

Columbus. The *El Faro a Colón* "is equipped with lights that can project the shape of a cross high into the clouds" over the slums of Santo Domingo, reported the *Sunday Times* of London.

"Despite criticism that such extravagance is incompatible with the country's grim economic predicament," the blind, octogenarian president, Joanquin Balaguer, said, "the people need shoes but they also need a tie." Columbus is a commemorative curse not a communal tie; his names are the same as disease and death in the memories of the tribes on the island.

The Spaniards first landed on Hispaniola, wrote Bartolomé de Las Casas in *The Devastation of the Indies*. "Here those Christians perpetrated their first ravages and oppressions against the native peoples. This was the first land in the New World to be destroyed and depopulated by the Christians, and here they began their subjection of the women and children, taking them away from the Indians to use them and ill-use them, eating the food they provided with their sweat and toil." The long colonial gaze is now a cross in the clouds, a remembrancer of cruelties and abandoned death.

The Government of the Bahamas has issued a one-dollar note that commemorates the unmeant ironies of colonial cruelties in the name of Christopher Columbus. The narrow gaze simulation of the adventurer on the souvenir note is based on a portrait by the Florentine painter Ridolfo Ghirlandaio.

"The long gaze fetishizes," continued David Freedberg, "and so too, unequivocally, does the handling of the object that signifies. All lingering over what is not the body itself, or plain understanding, is the attempt to eroticize that which is not replete with meaning."

Columbus is the national fetish of discoveries.

Ishi is the representation of survivance.

Tribal nicknames are metonymies, neither surname simulations nor a mannish western gaze; tribal nicknames bear a personal remembrance in communal stories and are not mere veneration, cultural separations, or the long gaze fetishism of discoveries in a lonesome civilization.

Professor Alfred Kroeber, for instance, an eminent academic humanist, is seldom remembered for his nicknames. Mister Ishi, on the other hand, remembered the anthropologist as his "Big Chiep," which was his common pronunciation of *chief*. Ishi used the tribal word *saltu*, or white man, a word that could be used as a nominal nickname commensurate with his own: Mister Ishi and Mister Saltu.

Now, consider my proposal to change the name Kroeber Hall at the University of California, Berkeley, to Big Chiep Hall to celebrate a nickname, rather than the reverence of a surname, and to honor the stories of his close association with a noble tribal survivor. The anthropology department would be located in Big Chiep Hall. Ishi Hall and Big Chiep Hall, or even Saltu Hall, would be located on the same campus; the stories of two men and their nicknames would be an honorable encounter with an erotic shimmer of trickster humor.

Ishi told a tribal interpreter, "I will live like the white people from now on." The Bureau of Indian Affairs had promised him protection, but he would remain with his new friends in a public institution. "I want to stay where I am, I will grow old here, and die in this house." Tuberculosis ended his life five years later.

Kroeber wrote that "he never swerved from his declaration." Ishi lived and worked in the museum at the University of California in San Francisco. "His one great dread, which he overcame but slowly, was of crowds." Ishi said *"hansi saltu"* when he was taken to the ocean and saw the crowded beach for the first time. The words were translated as 'many white people.'

Ishi is the representation of tribal survivance; nevertheless his name and stories must be rescued from manifest manners. He told stories that were to be heard, and he told his stories with a natural humor, a sense of presence that was communal and that unnerved the want of salvation. His tribal touch has been revised and simulated, but his humor must never end in a museum.

Nicknames in the Quincentenary

Native American Studies is located in Dwinelle Hall, near Sproul Plaza, at the University of California, Berkeley. In the past two decades, this new course of undergraduate studies has grown stronger in tribal histories, literatures, and film studies, and it now includes a doctorate program in the Ethnic Studies Department.

"Gerald Vizenor, a visiting professor in the Ethnic Studies Department, has made an official proposal," reported the *Daily Californian* on 15 October 1985, "to rename the north part of Dwinelle Hall as Ishi Hall." The student senate unanimously supported the name change.

My first proposal landed in a common space committee, and there a faculty member, concerned with manifest manners, said the name could be misunderstood as a slang variation of the word *icky*. The proposed naming ceremony, to be held on 16 May 1986, seventy years after the death of Ishi, never recovered from literal banishment in a committee dominated by manifest manners and the "long gaze" of Christopher Columbus.

Chancellor Chang-Lin Tien received my second proposal six years later "to change the north part of Dwinelle Hall to Ishi Hall in honor of the first Native American Indian who served with distinction the University of California."

Christopher Columbus and the quincentenary of his dubious missions should not overshadow the recognition and survivance of Native American Indians. The chancellor must have read that his would be an unmistakable moment for historical emendation, and the precedence of a tribal name on a campus building would be sincere and honorable.

My proposal is both moral and practical at the same time because nothing would be taken from the honor of the existing name, and a new tribal name for the north section of the building would resolve a serious problem of identification between the two wings.

Dwinelle and Ishi would name sections of the same structure; their names would reverse the racial surnames and entitlements in a state that once hounded the tribes to death and, at the same time, honored those who stole the land and resources and wrote the histories of institutions. One of the most eminent universities in the world was founded on the receipt of stolen land.

John Whipple Dwinelle was born 7 September 1816 in Cazenovia, New York. He studied the origin of words and practiced law when he moved to San Francisco in 1849. Dwinelle was elected to the state legislature and wrote the charter that established the University of California. The bill was passed on 21 March 1868, about six years after the estimated birth of Ishi in the mountains of Northern California.

Dwinelle served as a member of the first Board of Regents at the University of California. He died on 28 January 1881. The *Daily Californian* reported that "he fell into the Straits of Carquinez from a transfer ferry and was drowned." Dwinelle Hall was dedicated in his honor in September 1952.

"The process of naming, or renaming, a campus building involves review at several levels on the campus and at the Office of the President," wrote Chancellor Tien. "Your proposal must" pass through the Dwinelle Hall Space Subcommittee, "the Provost of the College of Letters and Science, the Naming of Buildings Subcommittee, and the Space Assignments and Capital Improvements Committee. Following positive review of these parties, if I concur, I would forward the proposal to the President for consideration and final approval by the Regents."

The Dwinelle Hall Space Subcommittee twice denied the proposal to honor the name of Ishi. The historians resisted the name, as if the ironies of institutional histories would sour with new communal narratives. *Dwinelle* was circumstantiated at the university; *Ishi* and other tribal names have been renounced in the histories of the state.

Ishi lived five years in the museum; his name endures with honor, but he would never survive the denatured reason of modern governance, the bureaucratic evasions, and the incredulous responses of the university administration. Once more, my proposal has been terminated in a common space committee, as were tribal nicknames and histories in the past; the other reviews are the neocolonial sanctions of manifest manners.

The sheriff secured a "pathetic figure crouched upon the floor," the *Oroville Register* reported on 29 August 1911, thirty years after the death of Dwinelle. "The canvas from which his outer shirt was made had been roughly sewed together. His undershirt had evidently been stolen in a raid upon some cabin. His feet were almost as wide as they were long, showing plainly that he had never worn either moccasins or shoes. In his ears were rings made of buckskin thongs."

Alfred Kroeber confirmed the newspaper report and contacted the sheriff who "had put the Indian in jail not knowing what else to do with him since no one around town could understand his speech or he theirs," wrote Theodora Kroeber in *Alfred Kroeber: A Personal Configuration*. "Within a few days the Department of Indian Affairs authorized the sheriff to release the wild man to the custody of Kroeber and the museum staff." Ishi was housed in rooms furnished by Phoebe Apperson Hearst. She had created the Department and Museum of Anthropology at the University of California.

Ishi served with distinction the cultural and academic interests of the University of California. Alfred Kroeber, who has been honored by a building in his name, dedicated in March 1960, pointed out that Ishi "has perceptive powers far keener than those of highly educated white men. He reasons well, grasps an idea quickly, has a keen sense of humor, is gentle, thoughtful, and courteous and has a higher type of mentality than most Indians."

Saxton Pope, a surgeon at the medical school near the museum, said he took Ishi to Buffalo Bill's Wild West Show. "He always enjoyed the circus, horseback feats, clowns, and similar performances," he wrote in "The Medical History of Ishi":

[A] warrior, bedecked in all his paint and feathers, approached us. The two Indians looked at each other in absolute silence for several minutes. The Sioux then spoke in perfect English, saying: "What tribe of Indian is this?" I answered, "Yana, from Northern California."

The Sioux then gently picked up a bit of Ishi's hair, rolled it between his fingers, looked critically into his face, and said, "He is a very high grade of Indian." As we left, I asked Ishi what he thought of the Sioux. Ishi said, "Him's big chiep."

Thomas Waterman, the linguist at the museum, administered various psychological tests at the time and concluded in a newspaper interview that "this wild man has a better head on him than a good many college men."

Some of these college men, however, had unearthed a tribal survivor and then invented an outsider, a wild man as the "other," the last one to hear the stories of his mountain tribe, with their considerable academic power and institutional influence over language, manners, and names. These were not cruelties or insensitivities at the time, but these scholars and museum men, to be sure, would contribute to the cold and measured simulations of savagism and civilization. That tribal survivance would become a mere simulation in a museum, and three generations later an observance in a common academic space committee, is both miraculous and absurd in the best postcolonial histories. Miraculous, because the name is neither the representation nor simulation of the real, and absurd, because the felicities of manifest manners are so common in academic discourse and governance.

Ishi is one of the most discoverable tribal names in the world; even so, he has seldom been heard as a real person. The quincentenary of colonial discoveries and manifest manners is not too late to honor this tribal man with a building in his name, a nickname bestowed with admiration by Alfred Kroeber.

Ishi "looked upon us as sophisticated children," wrote Saxton Pope. "We knew many things, and much that is false. He knew nature, which is always true. . . . His soul was that of a child, his mind that of a philosopher."

Theodora Kroeber wrote in *Alfred Kroeber: A Personal Configuration* that "Ishi was living for the summer with the Waterman family where Edward Sapir, the linguist, would be coming in a few weeks to work with him, recording Ishi's Yahi dialect of the Yana language. . . . They noticed that he was eating very little and appeared listless and tired. Interrupting the work with Sapir, they brought Ishi to the hospital where Pope found what he and Kroeber had most dreaded, a rampant tuberculosis."

Ishi died at noon on 25 March 1916. Kroeber was in New York at the time and wrote to Edward Gifford, a curator at the University Museum, "As to disposal of the body, I must ask you as my personal representative to yield nothing at all under any circumstances. If there is any talk about the interests of science, say for me that science can go to hell. We propose to stand by our friends. . . . We have hundreds of Indian skeletons that nobody ever comes near to study. The prime interest in this case would be of a morbid romantic nature."

Four days later, the *San Mateo Labor Index* reported that the "body of Ishi, last of the [Yahi] tribe of Indians, was cremated Monday at Mount Olivet cemetery. It was according to the custom of his tribe and there was no ceremony." Saxton Pope created a death mask, "a very beautiful one." The pottery jar that held the ashes of Ishi was placed in a rock cairn.

The Deranged Humors of Civilization

President Ronald Reagan told students in Moscow, "Maybe we made a mistake in trying to maintain Indian cultures. Maybe we should not have humored them in wanting to stay in that kind of primitive lifestyle."

Reagan is a master of felicities and manifest manners, but he must have been talking about simulated Indians in the movies. Many of his friends played Indians on screen. Maybe *he* made a mistake in trying to maintain the movies as a real culture; he should not have humored so many of his friends to play Indian in western films. Reagan embodies the simulacra of the mannish western movies.

"Long gaze" Reagan might have been thinking about his many *sooner* friends at the University of Oklahoma. He honored the mannish manifest manners of the frontier more than he would even remember the beleaguered tribes that lost their land to thousands of neocolonial *sooners*.

H. L. Mencken wrote in *The American Language* that the *sooners* were those "people who insist upon crossing bridges before they come to them," the people who "sneaked across the border before the land was thrown open to white settlement." These were the "long gaze" *sooners* who stole tribal land in the name of manifest manners.

Richard Van Horn, president of the University of Oklahoma at Norman, was concerned about a "better learning environment" and asked students to be more friendly toward minorities, according to a letter and a report in the *Daily Oklahoman*. "Saying hello to minority students on campus . . . will help to create a better living and learning environment for all."

Van Horn's manner is simple enough, his statements are generous over brunch, even romantic overseas, but he does not seem to understand the nature of institutional racism. Such academic salutations, the measures of manifest manners, would burden minority students with even more blithe, simpering, and ironic atonements; the *sooners* maintain their "long gaze" of racialism and neocolonial domination. How would students be taught to recognize the minorities on campus so that they might please the president by saying hello? Would recognition be made by color, class, manners, humor, gestures, the *sooner* "long gaze," or by being the obvious "other," the outsider?

"Long gaze" Columbus says "hello" to Ishi.

"Hello, hello, hello at last," said an eager white fraternity student to a crossblood Native American Indian. That casual interjection is not an invitation to a discourse on tribal histories, miseries, or even the weather on campus; the gesture is a trivial cue to turn the other cheek to a western gaze and manifest manners. Moreover, racial salutations and other public relations snobberies serve those who dominate minority students rather than those who liberate the human spirit from institutional racism.

"Go out on the campus and say hello to our tribal neighbors," sounds too much like the basic instructions given to missionaries. Never mind, it would seem to the president, that treaties were violated, tribal lands were stolen, and that the crimes continue to be celebrated in state histories as a beat in *sooner* civilization.

The University of Oklahoma and other state institutions were founded on stolen tribal land; such moral crimes are not revised with salutations and manifest manners. The University of California was founded on the receipt of stolen tribal land.

Native American Indian scholars hired to teach in various academic departments on the campus would create a better "learning environment" than a new order of pale sycophants saying hello to minorities. "Long gaze" Reagan and Van Horn must have learned their manifest manners with other presidents at the western movies.

Rennard Strickland, the lawyer and historian, wrote in *The Indians in Oklahoma* that the "process by which the Indian became landless is part of the dark chapter in white Oklahoma's relations with its Indian citizens. Millions of acres and other accumulated resources were wrested from the Indians. Of the thirty million allotted acres more than twenty-seven million passed from Indians to whites" by fraudulent deeds, embezzlement, and murder. "The Oklahoma Indian was asked to sacrifice many of the best parts of his culture for most of the worst parts of the white culture."

Chitto Harjo, the traditional tribal leader who resisted the allotment of tribal land at the turn of the last century, said that "when we had these troubles it was to take my country away from me. I had no other troubles.

I could live in peace with all else, but they wanted my country and I was in trouble defending it."

"Long gaze" Van Horn would be better heard and remembered if he learned how to say the words "tribal reparations" more often than common interjections. Reparations are wiser invitations to an education on campus than mere racial salutations and manifest manners.

"Yet, despite all the sorrows and emotion-laden events in the Indian's history in Oklahoma," wrote H. Wayne and Anne Morgan in *Oklahoma*, a standard history of the state, "he gave the new state a unique heritage. Many of his attitudes persisted amid the burgeoning white civilization. His image and customs were more than quaint, as much a heritage of America's frontier civilization as those of the whites who displaced him. . . . Oklahoma's past remains vivid, exciting, and unique. She will not abandon it lightly, nor should she. The question is, can she learn from it?" Such rhetorical poses are misrepresentations that bear no historical burdens for the sins of the *sooner* state.

"Say Hello, OU President Urges" was the headline on the front page of the *Daily Oklahoman* in Oklahoma City. Once more, manifest manners seemed to be one of the most important stories of the day. The same conservative newspaper published an unsigned editorial the following day: "Some have chuckled at OU President Richard Van Horn's modest suggestion for students to 'Say hello to minority students' on campus. That's a gesture, but he's on track. Respect. Diversity. Dialogue. These create an environment in which learning can occur. The words describe values which are not black, white, Hispanic, or Asian, but American." One blithe gesture in the *sooner* "long gaze" begets another, but the unnamed editorial writer never mentioned Native American Indians.

The Oklahoma Tourism and Recreation Department, on the other hand, has published a folded calendar map that celebrates the "Year of the Indian." Thirty-seven tribes, forty-three galleries and gift shops, and thirty bingo halls are named on a state map. "Oklahoma is Indian country," the calendar announces. "A place where time-honored American Indian traditions, cultural experiences and artistic expression are components of everyday life. Oklahoma currently leads the nation in total Indian population and offers a wealth of Indian-related museums, art galleries, festivals and powwows."

President Van Horn, in the "Year of the Indian," must create at least fifty new faculty positions in the next decade for Native American Indians. The presence of tribal scholars in various departments, and their new

courses on tribal histories, literatures, economics, legal studies, comparative cultures, and religion, would be more than manifest manners. Real reparations would overturn the mannish western gaze at the campus movies;
reparations for colonial domination, institutional racism, and manifest manners are measures of how a state and a civilization would endure in popular
tribal memories.

The University of Oklahoma and the University of California owe
more to tribal cultures than any other universities in the nation, and they
must learn how to practice reparations for the moral and civil crimes that
have been perpetrated against tribal cultures. At least a hundred or more
new and permanent faculty positions for Native American Indians at these
universities in the next decade would be an honorable gesture of reparations for stolen land, the fetish misrepresentations of tribal cultures, and the
cold mannish gaze of manifest manners.

"'Long gaze' Presidents Say 'Hello' to Ishi."

"Now that's a real *sooner* headline," said Griever de Hocus, the nov-
elist and crossblood chair of postmodern manifest manners. "Columbus
and Reagan said the same thing, you know, but even so none of them could
ever be more than a Little Chiep."

The University of California and the University of Oklahoma have
natural reasons and moral warrants to lead the nation in Native American
Indian scholarship, and these universities must demonstrate to the world
that the tribes are neither the eternal victims of racial simulations nor the
fetish cultures of the long gaze of Christopher Columbus.

President Van Horn could encourage the students to say "no, no, no
to hello, no more western gaze, no long gaze, overturn manifest manners,
and sustain tribal reparations." Chancellor Tien must do more than hold a
pose over the remains of tribal cultures and the receipts of stolen land.

Ishi said "evelybody hoppy" in Little Chiep Hall.

Columbus, Reagan, Tien, Van Horn, and other mannish adventurers,
presidents, chancellors, saints, curators, and discoverers, tried to be heard
over the trickster stories on campus, but no one listened to them that year
in Little Chiep Hall.

Pierre Clastres wrote in *Society Against the State* that a tribal chief
must "prove his command over words. Speech is an imperative obligation for the chief." The leader "must submit to the obligation to speak, the
people he addresses, on the other hand, are obligated only to appear not
to hear him."

Tricksters are heard as traces in tribal stories: the erotic shimmer and beat on a bear walk, the beat that liberates the mind with no separations as cruel as those in a chemical civilization. There are no last words in tribal stories, no terminal creeds, no closures. Tricksters are nicknames near an end that is never heard. Ishi heard trickster stories; he was not a chief, and he never set his new watch to western time.

Christopher Columbus and the other discoverable men of manifest manners are the "long gaze" chiefs on a tribal coin struck to commemorate the lonesome heroes in a chemical civilization; with each coin the tribe will issue a certificate of authenticity.

If Texts Are Prayers, What Do Wintu Want?

Linda Ainsworth

As early as 1939, Kenneth Burke criticized Freud and psychoanalytic theory for its too-static model of literary interpretation.[1] According to Burke, psychoanalysis overlooked the fact that a text can be a "prayer," not just the manifestation of wish-fulfillment (229). As "prayers," texts constitute rhetorical gestures that take at least part of their meaning from the ends they wish to bring about. These ends may be purely affective ones, requiring something as seemingly innocuous as an emotional response, or they may require some action on the part of the audience. In either case, the purpose of the text is to bring about some change in the way the audience acts or feels about some issue or issues. What bothered Burke most about the Freudian psychoanalytic model was that it was too eager to accept the text as a manifestation of the *fulfilled* desires of the speaker and the audience, no matter how well mediated the symbolic language.

We might well argue that Freud never intended nor would have endorsed such a reductionist application of psychoanalytic theory. Nevertheless, such thinking prevails in much psychoanalytic interpretation of texts,

1. "Freud—and the Analysis of Poetry." Reprinted in *The Philosophy of Literary Form: Studies in Symbolic Action*, rev. ed. (New York: Random House, 1961).

especially those from so-called alien or exotic cultures. It abounds, for example, in functionalist interpretations of traditional narrative art. Many of these interpretations suggest that texts dealing with subjects such as incest exist to reinforce taboos about incest; that is, texts exist to augment prevailing cultural practices.

More recent readings of Freud, as well as the resurgence of interest in object relations theories, have led to the introduction of new psychoanalytic models that allow for much richer interpretations of literary texts, even ones we are least familiar (and least comfortable) with, including those from the oral Native American tradition. One such model, derived primarily from object relations theory, focuses our attention on the rhetorical features of the text and demands that we consider not only what the text seems to represent but also why such a representation is necessary at all if cultural consensus prevails regarding a particular practice. It also asks us to consider the quality and nature of the text's appeal and to whom it might appeal.[2] It is a model, in other words, that allows for an examination of the culture-making processes that go into the creation of certain texts and not just the itemization of the cultural practices manifest in a text.

Object relations theory retreats from Freudian theory in its emphasis on pre-oedipal stages of development. It centers on the relationship between infant and mother, not oedipal child and father, and argues that the primary object of concern in character formation is the breast and not the phallus. Both Melanie Klein and Donald Winnicott stress the importance of the weaning stages to the attachments infants form to "transitional objects," objects essential to the development and maintenance of the cultural symbols that, through their contiguity with other cultural practices, form the boundaries between cultures. Klein argues, in the words of Peter Brooks, that "the mother's body, especially the breast, provides the original object of symbolization, and then the field of exploration" for what Brooks terms the "epistemophilic impulse," or the urge to know.[3] Part of what the child wants to know, according to Klein, is where she stands in relation to the

---

2. The object relations theorists I have in mind are Melanie Klein, especially her "Criminal Tendencies in Normal Children" (1927), "Love, Guilt and Reparation" (1937), "On the Theory of Anxiety and Guilt" (1948), and "Envy and Gratitude" (1957), and Donald Winnicott, most especially his *Playing and Reality* (New York: Routledge, 1989), hereafter cited as *PR*. Klein's essays are reprinted in *The Writings of Melanie Klein*, the first two in vol. 1 and the other in vol. 2 (both New York: Free Press, 1975), 170–85, 306–43, 25–42, and 176–235.
3. Peter Brooks, *Body Works: Objects of Desire in Modern Narrative* (Boston: Harvard University Press, 1993), 7. Brooks paraphrases Klein's argument, found variously in her

absence of the primary object and the introduction of secondary objects. What is made manifest throughout the weaning process is that the child engages in sadistic fantasies designed to transform her anger and anxiety at the loss of the breast into a rejection of the breast and a preference for substitute objects.

Winnicott turns his attention to the importance of transitional objects in the development of play (*PR*, 11–15). He argues that "the place where cultural experience is located is in the potential space between the individual and the environment (originally the object [i.e., the breast]). The same can be said of playing. Cultural experience begins with creative living first manifested in play" (100). All creative life results from the accommodations the child makes in relation to the once present, then absent, breast and the objects she adapts to forestall feelings of loss. Winnicott stresses the term *potential space*, because it is in all instances a hypothetical space full of paradoxes. It exists as space to be repudiated and filled with transitional objects. Though symbolically nullified as soon as manifest, its presence is essential to the development of the cultural life of the child, and the transitional objects that succeed in diverting attention away from the primary object form the basis for the symbolic ideation that "feeds" the cultural experience. The exact contours and qualities of this potential space cannot be known in generalized terms, but only through close examination of the relationship between any one baby and its mother. Generalizing statements about its contour or quality must be stated in the idiom of the culture itself and at best can be only proximate.

Both Klein and Winnicott emphasize what is lost in the culture-making process all individuals engage in. Burke, too, in his insistence on the text as "prayer," focuses our attention on what the text attempts to bring into existence, that something which is absent in the culture as it stands. No matter how fervently we defend cultural practice and no matter how eloquently we articulate its many subtleties, we must nevertheless recognize that the symbols that encode cultural practice are but flimsy substitutes for the objects we, even in maturity, still long for. What seems most important is the way in which texts, when considered as elaborate and sophisticated transitional objects, mediate to fill the space between what we have and what we have not. In other words, texts are very much about consolation prizes, about accommodations we make in lieu of having what we want.

The recognition of such is essential to understanding the complexity

---

writings but well articulated in "Early Stages of the Oedipus Conflict," in *Contributions to Psycho-Analysis, 1921–1945* (London: Hogarth Press, 1950), 202–26.

and richness of the cultural symbols found in such a story as "Talimlɛluhɛrɛs and Rolling Head Loon Woman."[4] In this tale, cultural taboos related to the onset of menses and the expression of inappropriate incestuous feelings fail to defend a family against the all-consuming oral aggressiveness of a young daughter. Giving rein to such feelings, no matter how innocently she does so, the pubescent girl brings about the destruction of the family.

Talimlɛluhɛrɛs and Rolling Head Loon Woman

Long ago there came into being some people who had four children, two boys and two girls, and who owned a big earth lodge. The adolescent boy stayed in the earth lodge always. In the meantime his younger sister reached adolescence. So they left her in the menstrual hut for some nights. Now his younger sister loved him who was in the earth lodge, Talimlɛluhɛrɛs. So she went to him, got into bed with him, tickled him and sat all over him. However her elder brother said, "What is the matter with you, younger sister?" and she left. So she came to him, sometimes in the evening, sometimes in the early morning, and she bothered him as before, tickling him. And as before he said, "What is the matter with you, younger sister?" So at last her elder brother told his sister, "Elder sister, here to me, all the time to me, comes to me my younger sister," he said. And his sister went to her younger sister and asked, "Why do you always bother my younger brother?" And the other said, "I never bother him." Then the other said, "Younger sister, go get maple. Make yourself a front apron." So she went to get it, climbed around on the maple trees and peeled, kept on peeling, and cut her finger. And for a while she stood there with blood dripping to the ground. Then she sucked the blood. She did not know what to do, so she sucked it in and spat it out, and as she did so the blood tasted sweet to her, so now, first because she wanted to swallow blood and then because she wanted to eat her flesh, she devoured her flesh and turned into a Rolling Head (K'opk'opmas). All around the world she went, devouring people. She left for herself only her elder sister, her younger brother, and her elder brother.

Now they were afraid and started to climb up above. They heard her below going about wildly everywhere asking everything, the rock

---

4. This story and variants are published in Cora DuBois and Dorothy Demetracoupolou, "Wintu Myths," *University of California Publications in American Archaeology and Ethnology* 28 (1931): 355–64.

beings, the tree beings, asking all. And they said, "We don't know." They added, "You grew into something else and yet you know nothing." So she asked some ancient faeces and they said, "You grew into something else and yet you know nothing. Look up above." So she looked up and saw them going halfway up. So she jumped up, and grabbed, and pulled down, and then lay on her back, and spread her legs. He who was going above, her elder brother, fell between her thighs. She was very excited.

And the rest went above empty-handed. "Oh, dear, our own child has orphaned us," said the old man. They cried. And the older daughter said, "However long it may take, I'll find my younger brother." So they went up above.

Now her elder brother would have nothing to do with her, and turned on his side. So, in one lick as it were, she devoured him, his heart alone she hung around her neck and went toward the north drainage, alighted with it on a big lake, swam about with it, stayed there with it. Every evening at sunset she came, skimming the water, to a large sandy beach on the east shore, south, south to the sandy beach, on the south she alighted and stayed.

The people wanted to catch her but did not know how. Humming-Bird said, "Let me go," he said, "let me watch." The people said, "Yes," and he said to the elder sister, "Make a good cooking basket," he said. "Then have on hand white rocks, good ones which will hold heat," he said. He did not come, and did not come, and then finally he arrived. He arrived and told them, "I saw her," he said. "She has a heart hung around her neck. At sunset she alights on the sand on the south beach. From the north she comes." And the people said, "Let's go and watch," they said. Then they said to the little boy, "You go and watch," they said. They gave him a good sharp untipped arrow. "When you see her, pierce her, and when you pierce her she'll go south, she'll get out and make a bee-line, and go south to the sand beach." To the woman they said, "You go and sit on the south bank, on the sandy beach. Have the cooking basket half full of water and heat the white rocks well and drop them in. And when he pierces her go quickly, get her, grab her, and slip the heart off over her head. Put it into the cooking basket and cover it up quickly."

At sunset they were there. And the elder sister sat on the south bank on the beach, as she had already been directed. She went there and watched. As she watched at sunset the water was heard roaring in the north. She did not come, and then, at last, she saw her come and get out on the south bank, and behold, she had been pierced by the untipped arrow. She went quickly and slipped off the heart and put it into the cooking basket. Then she took it home. "This is my younger brother's heart," she said. So they steamed it, and while they were steaming it, it came to life, but though he was a person he did not look right. He did not live very long.

Even a cursory reading of this story reveals a number of universal clichés about the female body and the threat to social integrity posed by expressions of female sexual desire. Moreover, it cannot be doubted that the story serves to reinforce taboos surrounding menstruating women and incest. I do wonder, however, whether this story derives its power from its articulation of the familiar and accepted notions and practices of Wintu culture.[5] On the contrary, I would say, the story speaks more eloquently about the fears that give rise to cultural taboos than it does about the taboos themselves. In its representation of the perversions of oral longings, it speaks more insistently of desires that cannot be satisfied than it does of cultural resolutions of age-old problems. Indeed, the story seems to suggest that the cultural taboos surrounding female sexuality are as destructive to the culture as the desires they are designed to repress since they depend in large measure upon the female's conspiratorial acceptance of the need to conceal female sexuality and, thereby, a fundamental ingredient in female identity.

Incest taboos similar to those of the Wintu can be found in many cultures. This is not to say that all cultures enforce incest taboos in like fashion; it means simply that we recognize something fundamentally human in any effort to repress incestuous desires. More important than our recognition of similarity, however, is our recognition of the ubiquity of human failure. We can locate in all structures designed to conceal such longings the inadequacy of doing so, since the very existence of these structures offers poignant reminders of the needs they are designed to mask.[6]

The Wintu address the issue of incest in culturally idiosyncratic ways that provide the basis for cross-cultural dialogue, but it is a dialogue that

5. Cora DuBois documents practices surrounding the onset of menses in *Wintu Ethnography. University of California Publications in American Archaeology and Ethnology* 36 (1935).
6. According to Gregorio Kohon, "*What makes sexuality in human beings specifically human is repression*, that is to say, sexuality owes its existence to our unconscious inces-

suggests resolutions that may be at best only latent in many Western cultures. The vagina dentata motif prevalent in much pictorial art of the twentieth century offers a case in point. We are more likely to recognize castration anxiety as the motive for representations of orally aggressive females than we are the projection of an entire culture's desire to consume the female body. Our Wintu story, on the other hand, suggests that, for the Wintu, pre-oedipal longings sit much nearer the surface than they do for modern Western culture. Western culture has, in a sense, allowed its substitution, the orally aggressive female, to function as if it were the thing itself, the desire to incorporate the female body at the earliest stages of development.

Unlike depictions of monstrous women who are compelled to castrate as they devour, the Wintu Rolling Head Loon Woman is not introduced as a gaping-mouthed, shark-toothed female. The story begins with a sister who loves her brother and who wishes to play with him as, we might imagine, she has done many times before. The onset of adolescence, however, brings about a recoding of behavior so that what was once play can no longer be viewed as such. The behavior associated with play has become a "bother" to the elder brother. Lying in his bed, tickling him, sitting on him— all these are indications that something is wrong with the younger sister.

That there is lack of consensus over what constitutes "bother" is clear when the elder sister asks the younger, "Why do you always bother my younger brother?" and she replies, "I never bother him." Unless we are meant to divine that the younger sister lies about her behavior—and I see no reason why we should—we are left to construe that behavior in and of itself does not constitute "bother"; rather, bother is dependent upon context. As a matter of fact, the narrative does not impute to the younger sister any malevolent wishes toward the brother or the rest of her family. What she does, she does because it is pleasurable. Her sole motive is to enjoy these pleasures, not to cause harm to others. This is true even to the point of devouring herself. She devours her own body because her "blood tasted good" and because "she wanted to eat her flesh."

---

tuous fantasies. Desire, in human sexuality, is always transgression; and being something that is never completely fulfilled, its object cannot ever offer full satisfaction." See "Reflections on Dora: The Case of Hysteria," in *The British School of Psychoanalysis: The Independent Tradition*, ed. Gregorio Kohon (New Haven: Yale University Press, 1986), 371. The italics are Kohon's. I take Kohon to mean that because we must repress the desires associated with the mother's breast and transfer desire onto a substitute object, recognition of sexuality always carries with it a sense of loss.

The parallels between the blood that drips from the young girl's cut finger and the bloodlike discharge of the menstruating female cannot be overlooked, in part because of the great pleasure she takes in tasting her own blood and in part because of the association that is made in the story between onanism and cannibalism. On one hand, the satisfaction she experiences when tasting her own blood suggests satisfaction with her emerging female sexual identity. She takes pleasure in the new body awareness that accompanies the onset of puberty. On the other hand, the conjunction of onanism and cannibalism suggests some of the uncertainties associated with the pre-oedipal longings on which Klein and Winnicott dwell. The desire the child has to incorporate the breast stems from confusion about the boundaries between child and mother. From the child's point of view, the oral gratifications supplied by the breast are an extension of the body's need, or hunger. The breast satisfies the needs of the body and the child experiences pleasure. It is only when the breast is withdrawn during the weaning process that the child recognizes a need or desire to cannibalize the breast in order to ensure that it is ever-present. A certain degree of sadistic pleasure accrues, as well, since by cannibalizing the mother, the child can exact some revenge on her for having withdrawn the source of oral and bodily pleasure.

The conflicting needs satisfied by the conjunction of onanism and cannibalism manifest themselves in other ways as well. Because the young girl's experience of pleasure depends so much upon the disappearance of her body, her actions seem too easily to suit the needs of the community at large. The young girl herself experiences no shame and sees no need to conceal her maturing body. Her parents, elder brother, and elder sister, however, compel her to hide her body, first in the menstrual hut and then behind the menstrual apron. The pleasure she takes in devouring her body suggests a willing complicity on her part to incorporate the wish of the family that her body disappear. The fact that the elder sister conveys the family's wishes to her sister suggests a willing complicity on the part of all the women in satisfying the needs of the larger group. The narrative itself satisfies the culture's need to conceal its own anxiety regarding female sexuality behind a grotesque representation of the young girl's delight in her own body.

Paradoxically, it is the conflation of the young girl's pleasure with the wishes of the community that problematizes her status as a monster. We might judge that it is her own insatiable oral needs that transform her into Rolling Head Woman, but we might equally judge that it is the desire of the community to suppress female sexuality that unleashes the oral aggression of the young girl, in which case her aggression serves as a reasonable defense against the culture's wish to deny an essential part of her identity.

I believe, however, that we need not choose between these two possibilities. The young girl is Rolling Head Woman because she has insatiable needs *and* because she wishes to defend herself against the desires of the community. In order to make this point clear, we must remember that the nursing child has no gender identity that could be differentiated from the mother's. The mother functions as an extension of the child. As a consequence, from the point of view of the child, the mother and child form an undifferentiated whole. In her role as adolescent in the story, the young girl represents all undifferentiated children entering the stage of differentiation. Her oral longings symbolize those of each member of the culture. Her isolation at the onset of adolescence represents that experienced by all members of the group. Moreover, her aggression constitutes a defense against separation and isolation similar to that experienced by each Wintu somewhere in a less verbally articulate past. She wishes to be joined to the group, and she satisfies this need by devouring the group. Culture, however, dictates that she join the group in a less anarchic fashion. Conforming to cultural practice, in this case accepting the taboos regarding menstruation and incest, offers each member of the group a symbolic mode of incorporation. The story suggests that the Wintu have not resolved for themselves the inevitable tension and resulting confusion about identity that distinguishes swallowing the group and being swallowed by the group.

Clues to why the narrative places the young girl in the position of transmitting this psycho-sociological information may be found in this story as well. Among the many striking features of the story is the number of siblings in this Wintu family: two boys and two girls. They function as units in the story, the women being called upon to shift alliances from gender to birth order as the needs of the story dictate. The elder boy and girl speak in a single voice in their condemnation of the younger sister's seemingly inappropriate advances to the elder brother. On the other hand, the sisters form a unit when gender-specific cultural practices are foregrounded. Such restructuring of alliances suggests that women can be asked to endorse behaviors that undermine same-gender alliances for the sake of preserving cultural identity. Women are called upon to condemn female behavior that undermines the integrity of the culture. This is not a demand placed upon the men in the story. Though they form alliances with women, they never do so at the risk of sacrificing their identities as members of the group made up of Wintu males.

The actions of the father and younger brother help illustrate this point. The father's voice is distinguished from that of the choral "they" only once in the story. This occurs after we are told that the family "went above empty-handed," and the father says, "Oh, dear, our own child has orphaned us." The empty hands of the family refer, no doubt in part, to the loss of material possessions that coincides with their hasty retreat from the monstrous daughter. Nevertheless, empty hands are also associated with the loss of the elder son, and the patriarchal voice draws attention to this fact. The loss of the valued son brings much more grief to the family than the loss of the (undervalued?) daughter. Her loss, which is represented in a number of different ways in the story—through her exile from the earth lodge, through the concealment of her female sexuality, and only finally through her transformation into Rolling Head Woman—occurs without comment on the part of the family members. The elder sister vows to find her younger brother but not to redeem the younger sister.

In addition, the family—and the natural world at large—solicits the younger brother's help in the rebirth of the elder brother. I may be guilty of a too-formulaic reading if I say that the cultural impulse toward regeneration and renewal is evident in the introduction of the incidents associated with the lake. A symbolic womb, as it were, provides the setting for the regeneration of the elder brother and is the site, moreover, of the clandestine plotting of the elder sister and younger brother. The rebirth of the elder brother depends upon the younger son's piercing Rolling Head Loon Woman and the elder sister's cooking of the heart, clearly activities deemed gender-appropriate by the Wintu. We can only speculate as to whether or not these activities also refer to intercourse and gestation, because we have too little information about Wintu language itself. If they do, they offer clear evidence of the sublimated incestuous desires of the other siblings in the story.

At every juncture of the story, we are given invaluable information about Wintu culture, and the story inevitably functions as a carrier of this information. The narrative itself, however, serves other, more important ends as well. Narrative configures cultural information in such a way as to recreate the needs and desires that give rise to cultural practices.[7] In doing

---

7. Karl Kroeber makes a similar point in his reading of the Nez Perce story "Red Willow." Kroeber observes that "like all good works of literature, the story does not merely illustrate a conventionalized attitude toward a particular phenomenon nor simply restate a familiar taboo, but, instead, explores and dramatizes the tensions out of which arise cultural attitudes, beliefs, presuppositions and restrictions" ("An Introduction to the Art of Traditional American Indian Narration," in *Traditional American Indian Literatures: Texts and Interpretations* [Lincoln: University of Nebraska Press, 1981], 20).

so, narratives demonstrate the anxieties surrounding any culture's answers to its most pressing questions. Even though cultural practices may prevail and have the consent of a majority of a culture's members, they may at the same time be viewed as only contingent solutions to a cultural dilemma or problem. They constitute solutions to problems, but they are solutions that members of the community recognize as being conditional or even flawed.

The cultural practices associated with incest and menstruation cannot control the desires they attempt to contain. They offer, at best, partial solutions that work ineffectively, and sometimes not at all. Were this not clear in other ways, it certainly is clear from the contamination that infects the cultural hero (a representation of the culture itself). The Wintu inability to defend itself against the threat from within results in a culture aware that it might not "live very long."

It is the unmanageability of certain taboos and the feared disintegration of culture itself that the Wintu examine every time they tell or listen to this story. In other words, the story functions not only to indoctrinate boys and girls in the ways of Wintu culture. It serves as an acceptable outlet for criticism of the indoctrination (and culture-making) process itself. The Wintu understand, if only unconsciously, that cultural practices alone do not guarantee the survival of Wintu culture: there are some longings that cannot be reasoned away, no matter how rhetorically successful the argument against them.

December 1890–1990

Wendy Rose

It was a thing to melt
the heart of man,
if it was of stone,
to see those little children,
with their bodies shot to pieces,
thrown naked into the pit.
—observer of the mass burial
at Wounded Knee, December, 1890

O
how I wish
your heart would
melt

      Do you see?
      It was that way
      we had
      to become
      the stones
      that have bruised

your feet
on the plain

so that every step
must remind you
of the babies in the snow,
wind and blood, ice
and the sky, the aching
of the marsh for geese,
     or the ground to tremble
     and start its seeds . . .
     we became
     stones
cradled in the dry wash,
hiding from the gold
and the men who wrestle
the ghosts in the mines.

Retrieving Osceola's Head
Okemah, Oklahoma
June 1985

Wendy Rose

> *Dr. Weedon was an unusual man . . .*
> *He used to hang the head of Osceola*
> *on the bedstead where his three*
> *little boys slept and leave it there*
> *all night as a punishment.*
> *—Weedon's granddaughter,*
> *quoted by Peter Mathiessen*
> *in* Indian Country

Hotter than the comet that skims the earth,
wilder than the wild winds of earth that blow into our lungs,
we burn, burn, sweeping clean the holy ground with spring
bobbing on the flood that rises within, submerging and breaking
into sunlight with glittering eyes. We remember something
inevitable as biting insects and tricky as the black swamp.
        We have learned
        to keep our heads.
        Just use the umbilical string
        uprooted from the ashes,

stretch it as far as you can
and hold it with one hand.
Wipe from your back and nipples
the sand, turn around, speak
directly to the perpetrator
or risk becoming him.
We are the dust that settles on the heart.
We are the twin deer drinking in the temple.
We are the whirlpool of blood stealing the books.
We are the apricots dancing and bursting in summer.
We are her and we are him.
We are all of the murders returning.

Own

Katharine Pearce

I hear your voices,   on the wind,
faint in the exile   my ancestors gave;
I glimpse the fires   of your hearths and homes
in the trodden land   my people stole.
I hear your stories   in words my family caught
or see your words   on a scattered page.
I feel your songs   inside my soul—
but rest content   with my heritage.
A daughter of pillagers, don't let me steal
that last life from you: the dignity
to sing your songs   in your voices, your words.

Index

Contributors

Linda Ainsworth is a former associate editor of *Studies in American Indian Literatures* and has taught at Columbia University and Johannes Gutenberg Universität, Mainz. She currently teaches at Barnard College.

Jonathan Boyarin, an independent scholar, is affiliated with the New School for Social Research. His most recent books are *Polish Jews in Paris: The Ethnography of Memory* (1991) and *Storm from Paradise: The Politics of Jewish Memory* (1992). He is also the editor of a collection of essays entitled *The Ethnography of Reading*, to be published by the University of California Press, 1993.

Raymond J. DeMallie teaches anthropology and is director of the American Indian Studies Research Institute at Indiana University. He is the editor of *The Sixth Grandfather: Black Elk's Teachings Given to John G. Neihardt* (1984) and other works on the Sioux Indians. He is currently completing the translation and editing of the George Sword collection of Lakota texts.

Elaine A. Jahner is professor of English at Dartmouth College. In addition to the books presenting James R. Walker's manuscripts, she has published many articles on cross-cultural literary criticism and on contemporary American Indian literature. She is completing two books on cross-cultural literary criticism.

Karl Kroeber is Mellon Professor in the Humanities at Columbia University. His most recent book, *Retelling/Rereading*, deals with narrative theory and makes substantial use of traditional Native American stories. He is editor emeritus of *Studies in American Indian Literatures* and is preparing for publication a collection of essays on American Indian storytelling.

William Overstreet, a former managing editor and associate editor of *boundary 2*, is a professional writer. After completing M.F.A. and Ph.D. degrees in English, he went on to coauthor half a dozen reference works in political science and international economics. A free-lance writer and editor for the past six years, he moved in July 1990 to Fort Defiance, Arizona, where his wife is a physician in the Indian Health

260 American Indian Persistence and Resurgence

Service. Among his fiction publications, he has a short story, "This Is a Place Where a Door Might Be," in *Writers' Forum* 18.

Douglas R. Parks teaches anthropological linguistics and is associate director of the American Indian Studies Research Institute at Indiana University. He is the editor of *Ceremonies of the Pawnee*, by James R. Murie (1981, new ed. 1989), and translator and editor of *Traditional Narratives of the Arikara Indians* (4 vols., 1991). He is currently completing the translation and editing of the Roaming Scout collection of Pawnee texts.

Katharine Pearce is a writer and works as a literary editor in New York.

Jarold Ramsey is professor of English at the University of Rochester. His publications on Native American literatures include *Coyote Was Going There: Indian Literature from the Oregon Country* and *Reading the Fire: Essays in the Traditional Indian Literatures of the Far West*. His fourth book of poems, *Hand-Shadows*, was a QRL International Poetry prizewinner for 1989.

Wendy Rose currently teaches in Fresno, California, and is one of the best-known contemporary Native American poets. Among her volumes of poetry are *Lost Copper* (1980), *What Happened When the Hope Hit New York* (1982), and *The Halfbreed Chronicles and Other Poems* (1985).

Jack Salzman is director of the Center for American Culture Studies and faculty adviser to the Program in American Studies, both at Columbia University. He is the editor of *Prospects: An Annual Journal of American Cultural Studies*. His most recent books include *New Essays on "The Catcher in the Rye"* and *Bridges and Boundaries: African Americans and American Jews*. He is currently completing a five-volume work, *Encyclopedia of African American Culture and History*, to be published in 1993.

Edward H. Spicer (1906–1983) was professor of anthropology at the University of Arizona for almost forty years. *Cycles of Conquest: The Impact of Spain, Mexico, and the United States on the Indians of the Southwest, 1533–1960* (1962) and *The Yaquis: A Cultural History* (1980) are two of a long list of books and articles. He was also editor of the *American Anthropologist* and president of the American Anthropological Association. Since his death, his widow, Rosamond B. Spicer, has prepared several of his unpublished studies for publication in various journals.

Gerald Vizenor teaches Native American Indian literature at the University of California, Berkeley. He is a member of the Minnesota Chippewa tribe. His most recent books are *The Heirs of Columbus*, a novel, and *Landfill Meditation*, a collection of stories. *Griever: An American Monkey King in China* won the Fiction Collective Prize and the American Book Award. *Dead Voices: Natural Agonies in the New World*, his fifth novel, was published this year.

Priscilla Wald is assistant professor of English at Columbia University. She writes about United States literature and culture, and her previous publications include essays on Melville, Hurston, and Stein. *Constituting Americans: Cultural Anxiety and Narrative Form*, from which the essay that appears here is partly excerpted, will be published in 1994.